www.wadsworth.com

wadsworth.com is the World Wide Web site for Wadsworth and is your direct source to dozens of online resources.

At *wadsworth.com* you can find out about supplements, demonstration software, and student resources. You can also send e-mail to many of our authors and preview new publications and exciting new technologies.

wadsworth.com
Changing the way the world learns®

ETHICS ON THE JOB:
CASES AND STRATEGIES

Third Edition

Raymond S. Pfeiffer
Delta College

Ralph P. Forsberg
Delta College

THOMSON ™

WADSWORTH

Australia • Canada • Mexico • Singapore • Spain
United Kingdom • United States

THOMSON

™

WADSWORTH

Philosophy Editor: Steve Wainwright
Assistant Editors: Lee McCracken, Anna Lustig
Editorial Assistant: Barbara Hillaker
Technology Project Manager: Julie Aguilar
Marketing Manager: Worth Hawes
Marketing Assistant: Annabelle Yang
Advertising Project Manager: Bryan Vann
Print/Media Buyer: Emma Claydon

Permissions Editor: Sommy Ko
Production Service: The Cooper Company
Copy Editor: Peggy Tropp
Cover Designer: Yvo Riezebos
Cover Image: Jean B. Tate
Text and Cover Printer: Webcom
Compositor: International Typesetting
and Composition

For more information about our products, contact us at:
Thomson Learning Academic Resource Center
1-800-423-0563

For permission to use material from this text or
product, submit a request online at
www.thomsonrights.com.

Library of Congress Control Number: 2003117016

ISBN 0-534-61981-9

Wadsworth/Thomson Learning
10 Davis Drive
Belmont, CA 94002-3098
USA

Asia
Thomson Learning
5 Shenton Way #01-01
UIC Building
Singapore 068808

Australia/New Zealand
Thomson Learning
102 Dodds Street
Southbank, Victoria 3006
Australia

Canada
Nelson
1120 Birchmount Road
Toronto, Ontario M1K 5G4
Canada

Europe/Middle East/Africa
Thomson Learning
High Holborn House
50/51 Bedford Row
London WC1R 4LR
United Kingdom

Latin America
Thomson Learning
Seneca, 53
Colonia Polanco
11560 Mexico D.F.
Mexico

Spain/Portugal
Paraninfo
Calle Magallanes, 25
28015 Madrid, Spain

We dedicate this text to our teachers, from whom we learned that wisdom is the basis of a good life.

CONTENTS

GUIDE TO TOPICS IN CASES

Advertising/Marketing: 18, 21
Affirmative Action: 17
Competition: 9, 41, 42, 44
Computer Use: 9, 10, 21, 42
Corporate Responsibility: 8, 13, 17, 18, 19, 21, 23, 24, 32, 35, 36, 41, 45
Discrimination: 1, 3, 12, 13, 14, 15, 16, 17, 18, 20, 26, 33, 34, 39, 45
Diversity/Relations with Other Cultures: 1, 3, 17, 18, 19, 26, 33, 43
Employee Rights: 3, 4, 5, 6, 7, 11, 12, 13, 15, 16, 17, 19, 20, 22, 24, 26, 27,
    30, 31, 34, 37, 38, 39, 40, 43, 45
Employer-Employee Relations: 4, 5, 6, 7, 8, 12, 13, 14, 15, 16, 20, 22, 24,
    26, 28, 29, 30, 31, 34, 40, 43, 45
Environment and Pollution: 35, 41
Finance: 25, 38

PREFACE TO
THE THIRD EDITION

The passage of time, world events, and reactions to them have led to no decline of interest in the importance of ethical decision making. The mild recent resurgence of interest in virtue ethics has not eclipsed the question of just how a good person should best decide what to do in difficult circumstances. The study of this process of thinking is as pressing today in the wake of the Enron and WorldCom scandals as it was in the eras of arbitrage abuse and pyramid schemes. The presence of corruption and weakness testifies to a continuing need to address ethical questions and the methods for answering them.

Allegations that much of an entire generation of M.B.A. graduates is committed to the principle that short-term profit is the supreme value in business raises the question of how educated people could think that way. Yet this primer in ethical decision making does not aim to change people's values or behavior. No book, no academic course of study, and no known teacher has had a high degree of success in such a mission. Our contention is, rather, that the study of ethical decision making can strengthen those who want to do what is right. It can show them that what is best may be difficult but is also worthwhile.

Study of the RESOLVEDD strategy of ethical decision making requires students to understand, apply, and then evaluate the importance of major ethical principles that are fundamental to civilization. To apply the strategy and such values to real-life, practical ethical issues confronted by ordinary people in mid-level jobs in the workplace is to practice the effort to do what is right. For a student to strive to find what is right is to learn some of the value of virtue.

This third edition incorporates numerous refinements, revisions, and additions. It begins with a revision of the leading case in the book. We have incorporated a new section in Chapter 2 that clarifies the concept of professionalism and its ethical roots and implications. There are substantive revisions and additions to sections in Chapter 2 on the principles of lawfulness, do no harm, and fidelity, and the concept of job duties has been added. Chapter 3 incorporates revisions in keeping with the revision of the first case in the book. Chapter 4 includes addition of the concept of situation ethics, and revision of the sections on evaluation and on moral arithmetic. It includes a new section 4.9 offering detailed explanation of the unique nature and need for the evaluation stage in a RESOLVEDD analysis, and a set of exercises to help the student apply that information.

The new cases focus on ethical issues surrounding suspicions of terrorist connections, employee drug testing, selling pornography, discriminatory promotion practices, and questions of the social and moral acceptability of business clients.

The following list identifies unchanged, revised, and new cases:

Unchanged: 2, 5, 6, 7, 8, 10, 11, 12, 14, 15, 16, 18, 19, 20, 22, 24, 25, 26, 29, 30, 31, 32, 33, 34, 35, 36, 38, 40 (case #1 from the second edition), 41, 43

Revised: 4, 9, 13, 21, 28, 42, 44, 45

New: 1, 3, 17, 23, 27, 37, 39

Overall, the book remains largely unchanged from its original basic format. We encourage those who use it to contact us with suggestions for further improvements.

ACKNOWLEDGMENTS

The first two editions of this book were born of the growing awareness among teachers of applied ethics that ethical decision making involves ways of thinking that differ in significant respects from those appropriate to the philosophical study of ethics. The first two editions brought to fruition many ideas and lessons growing out of a long process of reflection, dialogue, and experimentation spurred on by the commitment to improve the value of our teaching for our students. The third edition continues to respond to the same concerns, as well as to incorporate new issues and respond to comments from students about weaknesses in the previous editions.

Raymond Pfeiffer first became aware of the need for a decision-making strategy when teaching bioethics to Delta College nursing students in 1979. He found that ethical theories traditionally studied in courses in philosophical ethics have limited value for making decisions in everyday contexts. Professor Richard A. Wright, a consultant sponsored by the National Endowment for the Humanities, suggested the importance of offering a practical strategy for students to apply when confronting ethical issues on the job. The RESOLVEDD strategy, developed over a period of years and through a number of earlier strategies, is the outcome of this suggestion.

Ralph Forsberg's teaching of applied ethics at Harper College, Ripon College, and Loyola University of Chicago had led him to become aware of the limitations of many of the cases presented by business ethics texts that were geared for those in upper management. He undertook, beginning in the early 1980s, to develop cases that would be more typical of the kinds of employment his students would have during college and in the first few years beyond. The valuable conversations about business and ethics he has had with his special friends, Frank and Kate Flasch, both accomplished business professionals, have been especially enlightening.

When the authors became colleagues at Delta College in 1989, they discovered the complementary nature of their interests, which continues to the present.

The philosophy editor at Wadsworth at the time of our first edition, Ken King, was an important source of encouragement and guidance, as was Peter Adams, editor of our second edition.

Like other textbook authors, we owe a debt to the many thinkers from whom we have learned and adapted many ideas and approaches. Our work has grown from participation in an extended community of teachers, scholars, and philosophers whose integrity and wisdom have inspired and motivated us. It would be impossible to fully credit all of these people, for which we apologize.

CHAPTER 1

ETHICS AND ETHICAL DECISION MAKING

1.1 A PERSONAL ETHICAL PROBLEM: THE CASE OF "THE NOT SO GREAT GATSBY"

The hourly employees at Appleberg Electric Company are protected by a union contract. You, a shift supervisor, have good relations with your workers and treat them as colleagues. Yet Gatsby, 56, a senior worker who is minimally competent, is an exception. He ignores any attempts you make to relate to him or motivate him. He operates a punch press and produces at barely the standard rate, often with more than twice the average number of defective parts. But since he makes the minimum, he is meeting his obligations.

He reacts badly to your discussions and suggestions, insists that his work is not below union standards. Gatsby is nasty, uncooperative, and lacks motivation to change. Your boss knows and detests Gatsby, as do Gatsby's coworkers. He often makes offensive jokes about them, abuses them in public, and many avoid him altogether. But there is no real negative effect on the other workers and no one has ever filed a formal complaint.

Your boss now suggests that you take steps to motivate Gatsby to seek employment elsewhere, by moving him among the least desirable jobs and assigning him to inconvenient swing shifts. This is entirely legal, not a violation of the union contract, though certainly it violates the spirit of the contract and union-management relations. Your actions will surely be noticed and easily documented, should Gatsby or the union wish to file a grievance. It could cause a rift between the workers and management, even though they dislike Gatsby. How should you respond to your boss's demand?

Such a situation presents you with a personal ethical problem. Whatever you do, you must choose. Whether you recognize it or not, ethical values are at stake. If you do nothing, you have decided against taking steps likely to benefit your employer. Your refusal to act appears to indicate that your duty to your employer is less important than other considerations. Your choice has consequences.

If you do carry out your boss's suggestions, you are clearly harming Gatsby, treating him in a less than fully honest, underhanded way. You are sacrificing your duty to be fair, the spirit of the union-management agreement, and perhaps your reputation. You are following your supposed duty to your employer at the expense of

1

your own commitment to honesty and other important personal values. Due to these complexities and conflicts, you face an agonizing decision.

This book's RESOLVEDD strategy will help you think through and respond to such personal ethical problems. A perfect solution would uphold all your personal ethical values, violate none, and yet achieve your most important goals. However, when a perfect solution does not exist, you must settle for the best of those available. The RESOLVEDD strategy shows you how to address various questions that help you find the best available solution.

To make a responsible decision, you should consider the choices available, the outcomes of each, and their likely impacts on people's lives. Also, what ethical values are upheld and violated by the alternatives are essential factors. You must decide which values are important or unimportant, and carefully weigh them all. You should consider, as well, how upholding or violating certain values affects your own sense of integrity and your moral character. Deciding whether your ethical values are more important than your other personal goals presents another challenge.

The authors assume that ethical values are important to each of us, and that we want our decisions to compromise them as little as reasonably possible. The process of evaluating and choosing among our ethical values, our personal goals, and the likely consequences of our actions is far from simple. Following the RESOLVEDD strategy presented in Chapter 3 will help you arrive at a decision that can achieve your most important goals while compromising ethical values as little as reasonably and ethically justifiable.

The RESOLVEDD strategy is designed to help you arrive at decisions that implement an ethical point of view. Consideration of certain basic aspects of this point of view may help you understand the spirit of the strategy. Each of us must weigh such decisions from our own perspective and against the background of our own ethical beliefs. From whatever set of personal values or beliefs you view ethical decisions, the RESOLVEDD strategy can clarify the *process* by which we apply our values. The strategy presupposes no one particular ethical theory or perspective, but is a procedure designed to be helpful regardless of any theory or perspective you hold.

1.2 ETHICS, JUDGMENTS, PRINCIPLES, AND VALUES

Ethics can be viewed as the study of the justification of ethical value judgments. An ethical value judgment is a judgment of right or wrong, good or bad, better or worse, virtue or vice, or what ought or ought not to be done. Justification involves giving reasons or evidence for the truth or falsehood of a given judgment.

Consider the following **value judgment** as it applies to the case of "The Not So Great Gatsby":

I have a duty to do what my superior tells me to do.

To determine the likely truth or falsehood of such a judgment, you would examine the evidence for and against it. To cite and evaluate such evidence is the purpose of applied ethics.

Ethical principles are commonly used to justify ethical judgments. In the effort to justify the value judgment above, you might state:

All employees have a duty to follow the orders of their superiors.

This is an ethical principle. It makes an ethical value judgment about a range of cases, not simply one particular situation. Ethical principles are important because we use them as reasons to evaluate a given decision or more specific value judgment as good or not so good.

People often refer to their ethical principles as ethical values. "It is against my values to treat an employee in such a nasty, sneaky way" might simply mean that treating an employee that way violates some ethical principles you take seriously. The terms *ethical values* and *ethical principles* are used almost interchangeably throughout this text.

People at times disagree about ethical values for a variety of reasons. For example, there may be disagreement over the proper formulation of ethical principles. Thus, you might disagree with the above principle on the grounds that employees do not have a duty to follow orders that are illegal or ethically objectionable. People also disagree over whether or not an ethical principle applies to a specific situation, or how it applies. You might argue that although the principle is true, it does not apply to the case of "The Not So Great Gatsby" because your boss did not give you a direct order to do anything, but merely suggested it to you.

Which ethical principles are most important in a given situation is another source of disagreement. You might believe that the principle stated above is not nearly as important as the principle that people have a duty not to violate the rights of workers. You could argue that this principle pertains directly to the case because moving Gatsby around is a clear violation of his right to fair, open, honest treatment, and to be informed of management's opinion of him.

1.3 AN ETHICAL POINT OF VIEW: THE PRINCIPLE OF EQUAL CONSIDERATION OF INTERESTS

We assume both that you want to improve your ability to make ethical value judgments and that you want to approach personal ethical problems from an ethical point of view. That point of view is expressed by the principle of **Equal Consideration of Interests (ECI)**, which may be summarized as follows:

You should make judgments, decisions and act in ways that treat the interests and well-being of others as no less important than your own.*

ECI does not imply that ethical behavior means treating the interests and well-being of others as more important than your own, nor that you never take your own interests into account. Rather, it implies fairness and impartiality in your dealings with other people. It requires, for example, that you not move Gatsby around as suggested

---

*Peter Singer, *Practical Ethics* (Cambridge, UK: Cambridge University Press, 1979), p. 19.

just because you dislike him. It requires that your own personal likes and dislikes not count as reasons to think something is right or wrong, or ought or ought not be done. It also requires that you count your own interests as equal to the interests of others, neither more nor less important than theirs.

ECI requires that you use your ethical principles as reasons, and that you apply these principles equally to yourself and to others. If you believe it is wrong for a manager to move you around in the manner suggested for Gatsby, then you should oppose moving Gatsby or other workers around in that same manner. Whether you are a manager or a worker like Gatsby, or whether he is a worker or manager, is irrelevant to the ethical reasons why treating him this way may be wrong. An ethical person applies ethical principles impartially, recognizing that all persons have equal moral value.

An ethical decision, then, is a decision that (1) implements an ethical point of view, upholding ethical principles, while not violating ECI; (2) compromises ethical principles as little as reasonably and ethically justifiable; and (3) allows you to achieve your personal goals to as great an extent as is consistent with (1) and (2).

1.4 CONFLICTING GOALS

Our personal goals sometimes conflict with our ethical value judgments. In deciding what to do about Gatsby, you might think that on ethical grounds you should not move him around, but that failing to do so might end up costing you your job. Your failing to act might erode the good will of other workers and the union, weakening your position in the company. Furthermore, the job and personal relationship with your workers may in fact be important to you. This sort of personal conflict must be taken seriously, and can be addressed by several strategies.

First, you should investigate the nature of the possible threat to your personal goals. How real is that threat? Are you protected by a union contract or by any regulations or management policies at Appleberg? Are there policies guaranteeing you due process before being fired? Could you persuade your supervisor of other, more preferable steps? Is there some sort of compromise that can be reached? Could you obtain support from your supervisor or some other person in a position of authority? Will your workers really object to your actions and thus compromise your ability to function as a supervisor? Further investigation might reveal that the risk to your job is minimal.

Second, you should investigate the weight and firmness of your ethical beliefs relevant to the situation. Is the suggested treatment of Gatsby clearly unethical? If so, to what degree?

Third, you should consider the importance of your personal goals in the case. How much ambition do you have for your career at Appleberg? What is worth sacrificing in order to pursue that career? Is it more important than your conscience, your reputation, or maintaining good relationships with those who work for you?

Fourth, you should assess the chances of success in proceeding to act on your ethical convictions. Can you formulate an alternate solution that is clearly preferable to the one suggested? Are you likely to be successful in persuading your boss of your view of the subject? Who else might support you, why, and how might you obtain such support?

Fifth, you will likely benefit by discussing the issues with other people. Such discussions may reveal unnoticed options, new information, different perspectives, or alternate value judgments, and may expand your understanding and grasp of the issues. As a result, you will more likely arrive at a decision in which you can have confidence.

A responsible decision should not ignore your own legitimate or ethically defensible personal goals. To the extent that our goals in life are legitimate, we owe it to ourselves to take them seriously. Ethics does not require us to ignore self-interest or make personal sacrifices for trivial or ill-considered reasons. Again, we must weigh our own interests as equal to those of others, neither ignoring ourselves nor giving extra weight to our own interests.

The RESOLVEDD strategy, fully introduced in Chapter 3, will help you arrive at decisions with which you can live—in the full sense. An ethical decision is one in which you can take pride, and willingly explain to others. The study of ethical decision making can help you maintain your integrity and live with a clear conscience.

1.5 ETHICAL JUSTIFICATION

Decisions about personal ethical problems should be based upon assessment of the evidence for and against the various options. Study of this evidence reveals which option is most justified. Justification thus involves the reasons and evidence for and against a particular judgment. Ethical decision making requires that you judge the significance of the reasons and evidence in order to arrive at the most clearly justified choice given the circumstances.

Two main kinds of reasons can be offered as evidence to justify an ethical deci-sion. You can offer reasons based on the effects of the decision, and reasons based on relevant ethical principles. Responsible ethical decisions emerge from a careful eval-uation of both kinds of reasons for and against all the available options.

In the case of "The Not So Great Gatsby," you might argue that your duty to uphold the right to fair and open treatment of employees requires you to seek some other solution. If so, you are citing the right to fair and open treatment of employees as an important ethical principle to uphold. Because this principle is relevant to the case, it can be offered as a reason not to follow your boss's suggestion. Of course, you would need to state clearly just what that principle is, and might need to check on the considerations that support it.

Another reason not to move Gatsby around as suggested might be that doing so leads to important, undesirable consequences. Gatsby might in time figure out that he is being treated this way by design, and might file a grievance with the union. As the word spreads among his coworkers, they might resent how you are treating him and come to resent you personally. Your effectiveness as a manager could, in turn, be compromised. This would be bad for Appleberg as well as for you.

In making any ethical decision it is important to identify and evaluate both the relevant ethical principles and consequences. In the RESOLVEDD strategy, the con-sequences are to be identified in steps 4 and 5; the principles in step 6. There is no simple procedure for conducting an evaluation of the relevant reasons for and against a given option. However, some reasons are better than others. This difference can be discerned by comparing and contrasting the possible solutions and the principles and consequences that support them. The task of doing this is the seventh step in the RESOLVEDD strategy, explained in Chapters 3 and 4 and illustrated in Chapter 5.

1.6 ETHICAL VALUES: JUSTIFIABLE EXCEPTIONS

Ethical values are principles that assist us in making decisions that implement an ethical point of view. Ethicists largely agree that there are three characteristics that any principle must have in order for it to be an ethical principle for a given person. First, the principle must be important to the person; second, the person must believe that all people should treat it as important; and third, the person must believe that it should be applied in accordance with the principle of Equal Consideration of Interests.

1. To qualify as one of your ethical principles, an ethical principle should be important to you. That is, it should be important enough to override some of your personal preferences. If honesty is one of your ethical principles, then you should be willing to tell others the truth even if it causes you personal inconvenience. Someone willing to lie for a petty gain does not hold honesty to be an important ethical value.

2. For a given principle to be your ethical principle, you should believe that other people should also live in accordance with it. This requirement rules out many uniquely personal preferences. Thus, your preference for Blue Moon–flavored ice cream is probably not an ethical principle for you. As much as you love Blue Moon ice cream, your preference is not one of your ethical values or principles unless you believe that all people have an obligation to prefer it.

On the other hand, people ordinarily believe that their ethical principles are principles that others should follow. Those who value honesty typically believe that other people should value it. They act in accordance with their own ethical principles in the firm belief that the world would generally be a better place if all people acted in accordance with those principles.

3. For a principle to be an ethical principle for you, you must believe that you (and others) should follow it in a way that implements the principle of ECI. If honesty is one of your ethical principles, then you will not be honest merely when convenient, since this treats the interests of others as less important than yours.

These three requirements do not imply that an ethical principle should never be violated. There are situations in which it is impossible not to violate some ethical principles. You might, for example, find yourself in a situation in which every possibility violates either the principle of truth (that you should not deceive people) or the principle of harm (that you should not do things that harm people). If so, you must choose an option that violates one of these principles. To act ethically, you should try to determine which option violates the more significant principle, which upholds the more significant principle, or does so in the most significant manner. Such choices are discussed more in Chapters 3 and 4, and illustrated in Chapter 5.

Although ethical principles are important, you need not assume that they are universally inviolable, or absolute. It is possible, although controversial, to recognize the importance of certain ethical principles, and to implement an ethical point of view, without maintaining that any principles make absolute, unexceptionable, or inviolable demands on your life. An ethical principle may be important even if you recognize justifiable exceptions to it. To recognize such exceptions does not necessarily reduce the importance of that ethical principle. If you recognize exceptions to the principle that one should not kill people (such as capital punishment or euthanasia), you may still object just as strongly to the murder of an innocent, blameless individual. Whether you view capital punishment or euthanasia as ethically justifiable or not is irrelevant to the question of how wrong it is to murder an innocent person.

Whether or not ethical principles are absolute is in one sense irrelevant to ethical decision making. To act ethically, you must have ethical principles, recognize their importance, follow them unless there is clear and strong ethical justification not to do so in a specific case, and apply them consistently, equally, and fairly in all of your relations to others. Whether those principles are peculiar to you or widely held, or whether you believe they are absolute and unexceptionable, need not be decided in order to make responsible ethical decisions in specific cases.

1.7 WHY SHOULD I ACT ETHICALLY?

This is one of the historically important questions of philosophical ethics and has been addressed by many of the great philosophers, beginning with Socrates, Plato, and Aristotle. A full answer is outside the scope of this book. However, it is worth noting briefly one direction such an answer might take.

To act ethically is, at the very least, to strive to act in ways that do not hurt other people, that respect their dignity, individuality, and unique moral value, and that treat others as equally important to oneself. If you believe these are worthwhile goals, then you have reason to strive to act ethically. If you do not believe these are worthwhile goals for human beings to pursue, then you may believe that it is not important to act ethically.

Those who renounce the importance of ethics either renounce these goals completely, or they believe that such goals can just as well be pursued on occasion, when convenient, to maintain appearances, and can just as well be ignored when inconvenient. There are probably very few people who renounce such goals altogether. A lifestyle characterized by complete lack of ethical behavior would be so antisocial that it might well result in imprisonment or social ostracism.

Many people, however, seem to think that they can live their lives in ways that are ethical much of the time, but unethical at other times. Such an intermittently unethical lifestyle has many pitfalls, some of which are worth listing briefly here.

1. Such a lifestyle, when discovered by others, usually leads them to lose trust in the person.

2. Those who discover such behavior sometimes seek to retaliate against the offenders.

3. Living in such ways sometimes leads people to act unethically at the wrong time. We all rely on our habits and inclinations when there is too little time to deliberate.

Unethical behaviors weaken our inclinations to act ethically, and may lead us, in times of stress, to act in ways we later regret. We may, over time, even develop into the kind of person who finds acting unethically completely acceptable, or as Aristotle said, become a vicious person with no regard for our own or others' good. By acting unethically on occasion, we may develop the habit of acting unethically in general.

4. Living in such ways may make us feel guilty if we have been brought up in families and societies that established in us a sense of conscience.

5. Acting ethically only at selected times leads us to lose trust in ourselves. As a result, we may become worried, unsure, and anxiety-filled about the possibility that we may make a mistake and act unethically at the wrong times.

6. Acting unethically, when we choose, leads us to occasional violations of many values that are important to us, such as those presented in the next chapter. It leads us to violate honesty, loyalty, consistency, fairness, and many other important ethical principles.

7. The intermittently unethical lifestyle may violate our religious beliefs.

In summary, an intermittently unethical lifestyle can cause us more misery than an ethical lifestyle. However, this does not prove conclusively that each of us will live better if we strive to act ethically all of the time. Whether that is true is a matter each person must judge as life progresses. In making such choices, we should not ignore our society's cultural, religious, literary, and moral traditions. Our values have emerged from and are deeply enmeshed in these traditions. They often teach important lessons concerning the difficult decisions we face in life.

1.8 THE CONTEXT OF ETHICAL DECISION MAKING IN BUSINESS: ELEMENTS OF A CAPITALIST SYSTEM

In America today, capitalism is the economic system within which business operates. Throughout the world, more and more countries have abandoned other economic models to embrace capitalism. While there still exist countries in which capitalism does not dominate (e.g., Cuba), even those countries must work within the capitalist system when conducting international business. Even for organizations outside business, many capitalist values and principles play a guiding role. In order to address ethical issues in workplaces, it is essential to recognize the main principles and values of capitalism.* Those most relevant to ethics are profit, the institution of private property, competition, and the concept of fairness or justice.

---

*The analysis here owes much to Marshall Missner, *Ethics of the Business System* (Van Nuys, CA: Alfred Publishing Co., Inc., 1980).

Profit

Profit is simply the amount of money earned in excess of the costs of doing business. Once the expenses of raw materials, wages, production, taxes, and other elements necessary to produce a product or deliver a service are covered, profit is the income over and beyond those costs. Within the capitalist framework there are many reasons and justifications for allowing profits to be made. Without the profit motive and the freedom to pursue it, capitalism does not exist.

Recognizing that businesses exist to make a profit is not to say that profit is the only reason they exist. While profit is a major motivator for those owning and operating businesses, society permits businesses to exist because it wants the services and products they provide. The profit motive is an effective means to promote innovation and invention, as well.

The profit motive itself is the desire of business owners and operators for monetary gain over time. Generally, a company is economically successful only to the extent that its profit margin increases. Companies whose profit margins remain level or decline are headed for financial trouble. Investors want to see increases in profit margins, and accept a degree of risk in exchange for that potential increase. In the capitalist system, companies are given the right to make a profit as long as they obey the law. Any economic system that does not allow businesses to make or keep a significant proportion of their profits is not a capitalist system.

The justification of profit-making begins with the argument that those who put forth and thus risk their own resources deserve the benefits once they fulfill their contractual agreements and pay their employees. What remains after payment of these contracts belongs properly to the owners and investors, since if a business enterprise fails, it is the investors who lose their money. Employees might lose their jobs, but can find employment elsewhere. So, because investors back business enterprises explicitly to make a profit, and take considerable risks in doing so, they have a right to the profits.

Other considerations can be cited to justify profit. Corporate profits are measures of a company's success, and are indicators of effectiveness promoting intelligent investments. In most cases, increases in profit require high-quality products and low production costs combined with increasingly satisfied customers. The quest for profit also encourages creativity in the development of new products, production, marketing, and sales. Finally, a profitable company is more likely to reinvest in the economy in ways that create jobs and other benefits for society.

It is important to understand the reasoning that justifies limitations on profit. Governments routinely tax business profits, and for reasons widely thought to be justifiable. Businesses exist at the discretion of government, and for the benefit of society. Tax revenues may be used to benefit society in ways that businesses otherwise would not. These revenues may be used to maintain a business environment that fosters competition and thus promotes socially beneficial business activities. Moreover, socially harmful business practices can, as a result, be regulated, limited, or outlawed. Profit-making is thus justifiably limited by the well-being of society. Within such legal and ethical limits, however, profit-making is an accepted and necessary practice in capitalist economies.

In the capitalist marketplace every participant seeks some sort of financial gain. Consumers gain by shopping for bargains and comparing competitors' prices for equal quality and quantity of products. The workers gain from higher wages, greater benefits, or increased work opportunities without increased working hours or other job responsibilities. An economic system built on the drive for profit can provide benefits of various kinds to all members of society. The freedom to pursue profit is a basic right of the capitalist system. However, considerations of justice may warrant limitations on such gains, as described below.

Private Property

Profit cannot exist without the institution of private property. To profit from a sale you must own or have control over the disposition of the product. Owning private property is the right to have an extensive degree of control over what you have acquired. You must have acquired the object legitimately to own it. Legitimacy is usually defined by the laws and customs of a given society. Within our society, you have the right to ownership only if you have not violated the laws governing ownership and acquisition (including civil law, antitrust laws, tax laws, laws prohibiting insider trading, cheating in various ways, etc.). For further justifications of private property, see the works of philosophers Thomas Hobbes and John Locke.

The degree of freedom to control, use, or sell property varies with the laws of a given society. There are numerous legal constraints on ownership. To own a gun is not to have the legal or moral right to shoot people; to own a car is not to be justified in driving it at full speed on public highways; to own a house in a city is not to be able to drill for oil legally in your backyard. Furthermore, ownership often obligates you to pay taxes. Ownership has, perhaps, never implied an absolute, unqualified right to control.

The question of which legal constraints on ownership are fair or justified continues to be a matter of dispute. Some theorists have argued that ownership justifies the right of management to exercise almost complete and total power over production, employees, and company policies of all kinds within the law. This is reflected in the **employment-at-will principle**, allowing the owner of a company to hire and fire any employee at will, with or without just cause. Another argument is that businesses in one country cannot compete successfully on world markets unless managers have extensive powers ensuring flexibility in business practices. Workers, conversely, have argued that there must be limits on the power of management. They maintain that workers have certain moral rights to safety, privacy, freedom of expression, and due process that justify such limits. Some managers, finally, have maintained that the realities of a free and open job market are a sufficient constraint on management's power. Managers who fail to respect the well-being of employees will lose them to the competition.

Competition

Competition is natural to many aspects of human life, but is an essential defining element of a capitalist economy. Critics of economic competition see it as a scramble for possession of limited commodities, a way of keeping workers alienated from each other and thus more manageable. Worst of all, it is viewed as a perversion of human relationships.

Thomas Hobbes, the seventeenth-century English philosopher, traces competitiveness to the desires found essentially in human nature. For Hobbes, "The desire to acquire what is pleasurable and to avoid what is painful are the governing motivations for all human behavior." Moreover, as life progresses, our natural desires increase and we seek to satisfy them. But even as these desires are satisfied, new ones appear. It is almost impossible to satisfy all of our desires. Competition, says Hobbes, occurs when two or more people want goods or other desirable items that cannot be shared, such as the same plot of land. This can degenerate into a "war of all against all" if no restraints are followed, Hobbes notes.

In a capitalist economy competition produces relationships of supply and demand. As demand for a given product or material increases and stockpiles are depleted, supply may fall. As the supplies of some material or product increase and it becomes more easily obtainable, its price will fall and profit may decline. It is competition for limited materials and products that drives supply and demand, prices, and profits in a market economy. The extent to which such competition is good or bad, the extent to which our present economy follows regularities of supply and demand, and the extent to which supply and demand should be regulated by the government are important questions which cannot be addressed here. It should be clear, however, that an economy that is not heavily regulated by a strong government tends to be governed by regularities of supply and demand.

Capitalist economic systems generally allow every person the right to pursue profit, which in turn sets the stage for competition, which in turn produces efficiency, innovation, and satisfaction of desires. The extent to which any economy lacks incentives to compete economically is the extent to which it will fail to satisfy human desires and thus fail to do what an economy exists to do: produce human wealth and well-being, according to advocates of capitalism.

Competition, however, creates a number of ethical problems. Violence and other questionable conduct such as lying, stealing, or cheating will inevitably occur to some extent in a competitive environment. How to determine what sorts of conduct are acceptable in a complex market system requires evaluation of different kinds of benefits. Like comparing apples and oranges, it may be extremely difficult to determine which of such competing benefits is more desirable. If government prohibits bribery in order to promote genuine competition, enforcement of such a law will be intrusive, meddlesome, and ultimately expensive for businesses. How much enforcement is appropriate? How far should the government go to enforce rules designed to keep competition fair and thus socially constructive and beneficial? Governments in the industrially developed countries have formulated and enforce laws against monopolies in order to maintain an economic climate that promotes competition and thus efficiency and innovation.

Fairness or Justice: The Ethical Component

The question of fairness or justice in business is partly related to questions of worth, taxes, labor-management relations, and the nature of fair competition. Is a professional athlete worth $12 million a year but the President of the United States worth only $250,000? What constitutes just reward? That is, does the winner deserve to win, and has the winner earned the reward? When we ask if someone deserved to win, we are usually asking if all the rules have been followed and the player played well. When we ask whether capitalism, the business system, is fair, however, we are asking whether the rules of business are themselves fair. The concept of fairness in use here is that central to the concept of justice.

Asking if capitalism is fair is to ask whether or not the capitalist system follows the characteristics of distributive justice. Those who maintain a conservative view of distributive justice will tend to advocate the fairness of capitalism more than those who maintain a liberal or more leftist view. Conservatives and those to their right maintain that a society that permits profit-making, private property, and competition will be more distributively just than one that restricts them (there is more concerning justice in Chapter 2).

All major capitalist theorists, such as Adam Smith, Ludwig von Mises, and John Kenneth Galbraith, have recognized the importance of limitations and rules that govern the marketplace. Without such rules, some businesses will become dominant and take over the others, thus gaining control of the market and eliminating real competition. Even Milton Friedman, who argues that profit-making is the sole moral duty of a corporation, maintains that corporations should not violate the law. Adam Smith was well aware that the business climate must ensure fair competition or fail. Laws that cover fraudulent sales practices, insider trading, labor bargaining, bidding, price gouging, and the like are designed to ensure a free and fair marketplace.

There are also laws that govern the interactions of participants in the business system in order to protect their rights. A consumer's right to know, the worker's right to safety, or the seller's right to be paid are all protected by business law. Such protections are justified by many considerations, but all contribute to the establishment of a fair marketplace. They reveal another way in which economic success is not the only standard by which society judges business operations. Such laws are designed to ensure success within the needs of society, not success at any cost gained by any means.

Some economists have argued that one of the main virtues of a capitalistic market is that it will reward producers who correctly read the market, provide good products at a fair price, and best satisfy the customers' needs. Part of the freedom of the market is the freedom to fail, as well as to succeed. Both success and failure can be earned or undeserved. A company that makes bad business decisions, such as producing gas-guzzling cars when there is a gas shortage, may be viewed as deserving to fail. The competing manufacturer who reads the situation correctly and produces economy cars perhaps ought to succeed. The word "ought" here implies an ethical value judgment based on a conception of justice or just desert. It also assumes that neither manufacturer succeeded or failed due to unfair practices or illegal actions.

Some advocates of capitalism maintain that government intervention normally upsets the balance and ultimately the justice of the marketplace. An example of an unfair action that corrupted competition, according to many free market economists, was the government bailout of Chrysler Corporation. Whatever we may feel about Chrysler's recent success and profit or how many people have benefited from it, many economists say the bailout was wrong, an unethical manipulation of the free market. Chrysler had in fact spent itself to the brink of bankruptcy; one might say it had earned the right to fail. However, it was instead rewarded, rather than punished, with a government guarantee of $4 billion in loans which gave it the working capital to compete against GM and Ford, both companies that were not offered any such support. They had operated profitably but were given no rewards for having done so.

Instead, they were faced with new and stiffer competition from Chrysler, which meant that their sales and profits would suffer as a result in the following years. Both GM and Ford were put at a disadvantage that was not of their own doing. Instead of allowing Chrysler to suffer for its weakness, the government rewarded it and by doing so in effect penalized GM and Ford.

Whether we agree or disagree with the above analysis of the Chrysler bailout, the point is that all economists, ethicists, and participants in a capitalistic market maintain that fairness is an essential characteristic of a successful capitalistic environment. Illegal and unethical practices are objectionable because they unfairly upset the balance of economic competition. Any clear demonstration of unfairness in business practices or in the rules can be enough to lead to the passage of new laws or regulations directed to maintain the market in a state of dynamic balance.

Taken together, profit, private property, competition, and fairness are essential to the capitalist system. Inherent in each of these is an ethical element. It might seem easy to scoff at this last idea in view of the many scandals and unethical practices in business that are regularly exposed to public view. But the very outcries against such revelations indicate the gravity of the need to maintain an economic system with clear and effective rules that are designed to promote a dynamic and productive economic system providing broad social benefits. It is important to recognize that businesspeople themselves advocate an economy that provides opportunity and that rewards efficiency and innovation.

Of course, there are many criticisms of capitalism and its practices. Among the most serious are those raised by Karl Marx, especially his theory that capitalism alienates workers from all that makes human life worthwhile, and his claim that the economics of capitalism are self-destructive. Other criticisms have come from socialists and opponents of private property like the French philosopher Proudhon, who said that all private property is theft. Most recently, environmentalists have criticized the excessive materialism and the ensuing destruction of the environment following increased production caused by adherence to the capitalist socioeconomic model. One central question debated by environmentalists and defenders of capitalism is whether or not capitalism is compatible with saving the environment.

There is much informative and provocative writing supporting or renouncing these criticisms. However, it is not our purpose to present the debate between the pro- and anticapitalist positions. Rather, we recommend that students or instructors who wish to explore these more philosophical debates do so—they are well worth the effort. Our purpose here is merely to present the capitalist model and its major features as the currently accepted context for ethical decision making in contemporary workplaces and for business in general. It should be clear that ethical considerations play an important role in any understanding of that context and in the decisions faced by those in it.

CHAPTER 2

ETHICAL PRINCIPLES

2.1 THE IMPORTANCE OF ETHICAL PRINCIPLES

Ethical decision making relies on ethical principles for two main reasons. First, they express our most deeply held convictions. If we want to act ethically, and a given principle expresses one of our ethical convictions, then we are said to have an ethical obligation to uphold that principle. Second, ethical principles play an important role in the effort to arrive at a decision about what is best in a given case. Because of their moral force, solutions that uphold them are ethically preferable. Applying these principles to a given case helps us determine what our ethical convictions demand of us.

When our ethical principles conflict with one another in a given case, we must determine which possible solution upholds the most important of our principles or, at least, sacrifices the least important of them. Although this is sometimes difficult to do, we can often find good reason to think that one solution sacrifices fewer ethical values, or that the values sacrificed are of less importance in this case than others.

A number of ethical principles are shared widely. The following list may be helpful in making decisions when faced with personal ethical conflicts. The list is offered not as definitive nor as a complete ethical system. There are certainly other ethical principles which are important, but not listed here. Furthermore, there are alternative formulations of these principles. The following formulations are offered as coherent statements of some widely and deeply held ethical values. Historically, many ethical systems and theories do accept and apply these principles, although exceptions may exist.

You need not assume that the following ethical principles are absolutes. If they express important ethical values of yours, and you are committed to trying to live by the ethical point of view, then you will find strong reason to follow them or to try not to violate them. However, leading an ethical life does not require that you never violate such principles. It demands that you do so only to uphold some other ethical principle which is more justifiably upheld in the circumstances. Ethically, you must not violate them solely for purposes of self-interest or for ethically trivial reasons. Violating ethical principles must not be done casually, and doing so should have strong justification.

2.2 SOME ETHICAL RULES

Broad ethical principles are sometimes referred to as rules.* Such principles will help you apply the principle of equal consideration of interests to specific situations. Following are some particularly useful principles or rules to use when making ethical decisions.

The Principle of Honesty

This is the principle that you should not deceive other people. There are many ways of deceiving people, and all of them violate this principle. One form of deception is lying, which may be described as stating what you believe is false in order to mislead someone intentionally. A second is stating a half-truth, deliberately omitting information, in order to mislead. Another is the failure to speak at all when you know the truth and know that silence will result in someone's drawing false conclusions. In addition, there are many ways of misleading people while stating the truth: body language, facial expressions, and tone of voice may be used to lead others to false conclusions. Winking and shaking your head can be used as a false signal and thus to mislead.

It is important to note that withholding information does not always violate the principle of honesty. You can withhold information from another person, even one who has a right to it, without deceiving that person. You might frankly and openly refuse to tell the person what you know. If they do not, to your knowledge, draw false conclusions as a result, the principle of honesty may not have been violated. Honestly forgetting to tell someone something that you should have (because, say, you were too busy) is not normally a violation of the principle of honesty.

The principle of honesty is important because it is the source of trust. If we are unable to trust others, communication, cooperation, and other necessary social functions become difficult, if not impossible. This is because people normally expect to be treated honestly and usually want others to believe that they will treat them honestly, too.

The Do No Harm Principle

This principle requires that you avoid doing things that harm other people, or that damage their projects, efforts, or property. We have a strong duty to avoid worsening the lives of others. This duty is essential for social harmony. Unless we respect the well-being of others, we cannot justifiably expect them to respect ours.

It is important to understand the ethical nature of the do no harm principle. If you do something that harms someone, you do not necessarily violate the principle! Your act might have harmed the person accidentally, unpredictably, or unexpectedly. In such cases, ethically, you are not at fault. On the other hand, if you do something that does not harm anyone, you may still have violated the principle of do no harm! Recklessly and unnecessarily risking the well-being of others violates that principle regardless of results! The principle of do no harm counsels careful, responsible

---

*We broadly follow Bernard Gert's approach in *Morality: A New Justification of the Moral Rules* (New York: Oxford University Press, 1988).

action. Those who genuinely strive to live in a thoughtful, considerate manner generally avoid violating the principle of do no harm.

The principle of do no harm does not require us to improve the lot of others. It merely requires us to avoid harming others in direct and indirect ways. It is an idea embodied in the U.S. Constitution, the laws of most countries, and in many codes of professional ethics, such as nursing, medicine, advertising, marketing, and others. The principle of do no harm is essential to the idea of legal rights, and is an important basis for each of the other ethical principles described here.

The Principle of Fidelity

This principle holds that you should fulfill your commitments and act faithfully. It means, first, that you should fulfill the agreements, pledges, contracts, and promises you make. Second, you should fulfill the special obligations of the relationships you maintain.

We make commitments in a variety of ways. Sometimes we sign our names in writing; other times we orally commit ourselves to do certain things. In business and law such agreements usually take the form of a contract, and we are expected to live up to the terms of that contract. We also make commitments by entering into and continuing in certain relationships. When others have expectations of us, if we know what they are, and allow them to continue, then we are responsible for fulfilling them. Such arrangements are sometimes called "implied contracts" and may be taken to be as binding as formal contracts. But whether or not we call such commitments contracts, when we make them others do expect us to keep our word and act accordingly.

Fidelity is an essential value for all human relationships and institutions, and is the core of trust and cooperation. It is the tie that binds, carrying us beyond an isolated individualism, and motivating us to implement the principles of honesty and do no harm. It can be intensely personal in nature, and violations of fidelity are often resented profoundly by others. It is an important basis for trust, and violating it often leads others to distrust us.

The requirements of the principle of fidelity vary widely in different contexts. Within our families, fidelity leads us to respect privacy and provide emotional support. Sometimes referred to as loyalty, fidelity may require trustworthiness and the willingness to put the well-being of others before our own. At work, fidelity requires that we follow standard workplace practices, respect lines of authority and established decision making procedures, and that we fulfill the basic duties of our job. Sometimes referred to as *role duties* or *job duties*, these are the duties that are specified as part of the job, and for which one is paid. It is important not to view these job or role duties too legalistically. Not all role duties are actually listed in job descriptions or employment contracts. Jobs and roles change as time passes. Moreover, no one has an obligation to fulfill assignments that are abusive, illegal, or unethical. But as time passes and you continue to accept payment for your job, this continual acceptance is evidence that you accept whatever changes have been made over time unless you voice a clear objection to those changes.

Fidelity to our subordinates, coworkers, associates, and superiors requires that when we have a problem with their performance, we first tell them the problem, offering them a chance to solve it before we take it to their superiors. It requires, as well, that we treat our subordinates fairly and equally. Beyond this, fidelity implies that we fulfill the duties of our jobs, maintain certain levels of performance, act to support and assist, and provide timely notice when we plan to terminate employment.

There are, of course, limits to the demands of fidelity. Fidelity is not the highest ethical value, and usually does not justify violating the principle of equal consideration of interests, or performing unethical or illegal actions. Promoting your employer's best interest, for example, does not justify violating the law. Concealing pertinent product information from a customer may help make a sale but may violate the customer's right to know, or even harm the customer. Such concealment is generally unethical and exceeds the demands of fidelity to one's employer.

To follow the principle of fidelity is to act in ways that uphold the principle of do no harm toward those with whom we have special relationships. But fidelity requires us to do more than simply avoid harming others. Fidelity encourages us to contribute to the lot of others in various ways appropriate to the relationships we have.

The Principle of Autonomy

An autonomous person has the ability to act in informed, considered, rational ways that are largely free from coercion. Autonomous people are responsible for their deeds, and may be said to deserve praise or blame for them. Having access to information that is available and essential to making a good decision, such people decide on their own what is best in the circumstances. The principle of autonomy is the principle that we have a duty to allow or enable other people to act in informed, considered, rational ways.

There are many ways of violating the principle of autonomy. You might exaggerate, deceive people, omit relevant information, or use threats and other forms of coercion. Most people who violate this principle do so from the desire to ensure that others act as they want. But you can also violate the principle of autonomy by simply acting carelessly, without any particular motive. Any action on your part that somehow compromises another person's ability to obtain and use needed information, reason correctly, or act freely upon an informed choice can be a violation of that person's autonomy.

We take autonomy seriously in our society. We spend more money and energy promoting this principle than perhaps any other. Our entire educational system is directed to help other people develop their autonomy. Laws that forbid deception in business, government, and other areas of life are designed to respect and facilitate autonomous actions. In fact, part of what is meant by a "free market" is that both producers and consumers exercise their autonomy in making, choosing, and purchasing a product. The principle of autonomy is important because violations of it result in severe consequences. People react in extreme ways, become resentful and even strike back with vengeance when they discover their autonomy has been violated. This reaction is due in part to the psychological fact that people's sense of dignity is connected to their belief that they are self-determining, self-directed, independent, and personally free individuals. Vehement reactions to prejudice in society are reactions to denials of autonomy. Indeed, various forms of social oppression involving denials of autonomy are detested by the oppressed, and promote conflict as well as movements for liberation. Discrimination based on race, ethnic origin, sexual orientation, and gender is often a denial of autonomy. Finally, respect for the principle of autonomy is essential for successful functioning of human institutions in a democratic and capitalistic society. Capitalism, as noted in Chapter 1, presupposes a market populated by autonomous producers, sellers, and consumers.

The principle of autonomy is intimately and reciprocally related to other important moral principles. It is part of the basis of the principle of honesty, in that one major reason to treat others honestly is that this helps them to act autonomously. Deceiving people, on the other hand, deprives them of the truth and information that they need to make an informed, rational decision. The principle of autonomy also provides important justification for the principle of do no harm. One major reason not to harm or deceive others is that this goes against their wishes or deprives them of information they need to make a rational, autonomous decision.

Finally, fidelity also requires a respect for the principle of autonomy, and vice versa. An important part of most human relationships is the need for each party to respect the autonomy of the other. This expectation lies at the core of most contracts and agreements. It is other people's autonomy we are protecting by making such formal contracts, thus freeing them to act in expectation of our promise of performance. When in writing, contracts offer tangible (but not necessarily conclusive) evidence that we have not deceived others, deprived them of information necessary to make a rational choice, or otherwise coerced them into a deal they ordinarily would have refused. In most cases, acting in ways that respect autonomy also leads us to show respect for fidelity.

The Principle of Confidentiality

Closely connected to the principles already presented is the principle of confidentiality. Although it is, in a sense, derived from a certain combination of them, it is worth considering separately because of its special relevance to the workplace. Confidentiality may be viewed as a uniquely professional work-related or role-based ethical principle.

The principle of confidentiality asserts that some information should not be shared with people outside of certain circles. These circles or groups may be defined by the roles of the people within them, their duties, responsibilities, need to have access to certain information in order to perform their jobs appropriately, and their right to know the pertinent information. Respecting the principle of confidentiality protects people from being harmed by information falling into the wrong hands. Following it can also prevent violations of the right to privacy.

Whether or not information is confidential in nature can be discerned by considering three factors: (1) the potential effects of releasing the information; (2) the origin of the information; and (3) the intent of those who might be affected by releasing it. If the release of certain information to someone could harm a third party in some significant way, the information is probably best treated as confidential and maintained within the appropriate circles. Considering the origin of information can also indicate whether it is confidential or not. Information obtained from medical records, corporate research plans, personnel files, or private conversations is usually best treated as confidential. If someone has a right to expect that certain information be kept confidential, and would likely intend that it be kept confidential, then there is significant reason to treat it as such. Fulfillment of any one of these three factors provides sufficient reason to say that the information in question is confidential. The principles of harm, honesty, autonomy, lawfulness, and fidelity also offer justification for treating information as confidential.

The Principle of Lawfulness

There are four types of law, based on the source of each. First and most basic are *constitutional* laws, which define the political procedures of the nation, its states, and their subdivisions. Second are *legislative* laws, which are passed by formal votes of the federal and state legislatures and signed into law by the executive branches of governments. Third are *executive* or *administrative* laws, which are interpretations of the first two by the executive branch, which is charged with implementing constitutional and legislative laws. Fourth are laws formed by *judicial decisions*, which interpret and apply to specific cases the constitutional, legislative, and executive laws. The principle of lawfulness prescribes the duty to know these laws, to follow them, to cooperate with those who lawfully implement and enforce them, and to seek to change them only by lawful and ethical means.

Although it is certainly true that not all laws are fair or ethically justifiable, there is still a general, ethically based duty to obey the law, especially in a free and democratic society. In such a society, all citizens have potential influence on the law. Even if they do not find the time to exercise that influence, or choose not to do so, their continued presence in that society can be interpreted as a general agreement to abide by all of its laws. The principle of fidelity is thus one basis for the obligation to abide by a society's laws.

Many laws are justified by their success in fulfilling the principles of do no harm and autonomy. Violating the law might harm others directly or indirectly, or violate their autonomy, and therefore is unjustifiable. Such considerations offer a powerful justification for following many laws, even if not all of them.

If people try to change a law but are unsuccessful, they have the option of leaving the geographical area under the jurisdiction of that law. If they choose to stay and continue to oppose the law at the same time, they are nonetheless bound by the principle of lawfulness to follow it. In so doing, they become a part of what is known as the *loyal opposition*. They are loyal by not violating the law, though at the same time they oppose it and try to change it.

People sometimes resort to *civil disobedience* in opposition to unjust laws, as was done by those in the Civil Rights Movement of the 1950s and 1960s. Civil disobedience includes public violation of the law in order to dramatize the need for change. Whether civil disobedience is ethically justifiable is an old and complicated issue, which need not be addressed here. It should be noted, however, that civil disobedience does not include private violation of the law for the sake of one's own advantage. Citizens who quietly cheat on their income tax because the tax seems too high are not engaged in civil disobedience. This action violates the principle of lawfulness.

Laws are often made in order to protect individual rights. Violations of the law may thus involve violations of individual moral or political rights. Laws often function to ensure that certain duties are carried out, as well. Contract law may enforce performance of an agreement even when one of the parties would rather avoid that duty. I may not wish to pay you for the car you delivered yesterday, but the law may force me to live up to my duty to do so if I have signed a valid contract. Validity here includes, among other things, the free, uncoerced signing of the contract while fully understanding all it implies. The next section considers the nature and importance of rights in general, and some specific rights.

Mere violation of a law does not necessarily constitute violation of the ethical principle of lawfulness. If you act in a way that violates a law, but have no knowledge of the law and no duty to know about it, you may not have violated the principle of lawfulness. If you have a duty to know what the laws are and to follow them, then even an accidental violation counts as a violation of the principle of lawfulness. Since it is a general, known duty that business professionals must find out about the relevant laws, just as taxpayers must, violations by such persons are usually violations of the ethical principle of lawfulness.

2.3 RIGHTS AND DUTIES

A right is a justified claim to something (e.g., a livable environment) or from someone else (e.g., that they not prevent me from speaking freely). That is, if someone is truly making a rights claim, then there is good reason for the claim to be recognized. If you have a legal right, then the legal system supports your exercise of that right. Laws are often statements of legal rights. A moral right, on the other hand, is justified within a moral system that supports your claim to exercise your right.

Rights are options which you may or may not choose to exercise. Even if you do not exercise a right, you still have it. However, a right is not in fact recognized, respected, or realized unless the opportunity to exercise it is a viable option that you can enact without penalty. If you have a right to vote, but are penalized for doing so by your employer, then your right to vote has not been respected by your employer. But your failure to vote in order not to miss your favorite TV program is not a limitation on your right. Missing the program may be a loss, but is not a penalty imposed on you by an external source. Finally, some cases do not fall into a definite classification. Here you must evaluate them according to each situation to determine if you are being denied your rights by an outside source.

If you have an ethical or moral right to something, then you may choose to exercise it without acting unethically. If you have a right to something, then someone else has a duty either to fulfill the right or at least not to interfere with your effort to fulfill it. If you have a right to know an employee's off-duty activities, then the employee should provide the needed information concerning those activities or submit, for example, to drug tests. If you have a right to privacy, on the other hand, your employer probably has a duty to refrain from monitoring your off-duty activities.

Ethical rights differ from legal rights in several ways. The former may or may not be upheld by the law. A legal right, however, is always a right that is guaranteed by the law. Only ethical reasons and principles can justify the belief that you have a given ethical right. The mere presence of a legal right, however, is not by itself proof that the right is ethically justified. Many unjust and immoral laws have existed in every society. However, good ethical reasons and principles can often fully or partially justify a legal right. For example, laws limiting privacy are justified in part by the principle of doing no harm: an employer monitoring someone's private activities may prevent an employee from coming to work while drunk and harming other workers.

Ethical rights may be justified in part by other ethical principles or rules. The principles of do no harm and autonomy offer good reasons to think that government has an ethical right to require corporations to avoid false advertising. If false advertising were allowed, more people would be misled, their autonomy curtailed, and their money wasted.

Moral and ethical rights are interrelated with ethical rules. You may be said to have a right to be treated by others in accordance with the ethical rules described earlier. The justification of those rules offers good reason to think that people ought to be treated accordingly, and that failing to do so is ordinarily wrong. Moreover, ethical rights claims may offer good reasons to think that people should follow certain ethical rules.

People sometimes make very forceful and insistent claims that they have certain ethical rights. Such claims can sound convincing, and even intimidating. But you should not assume from this that they are justifiable. Those making the claims might be upset and overstate their case. It is important not to be persuaded by the authoritative sound of the language of rights. For example, a student might claim that she paid her tuition and therefore has a right to a passing grade regardless of her actual performance in the course. To claim such a right is easily done, but to justify the claim requires considerable supporting evidence. A claim and a justified claim are not the same thing.

One effective way to approach a rights claim is to ask what duties are involved, who has them, and why. Such questions may well lead you to discover that such a statement is unjustified. Although it may at first sound plausible that someone has a certain right, consideration of the nature and justification of the corresponding duty may reveal cause for doubt. Would the teacher of the student in the example above have a duty to pass every student who paid tuition? This seems a very doubtful claim, and honoring the claim would render grading itself meaningless.

Most rights imply limitations on the actions of others; some justify burdens on others. Consider the manager who asserts that she has a right to fire a subordinate. If she means that she has a legal right to do so, consideration of the law and policies of the company should resolve the question. If she means she has an ethical right to do so, consideration of the corresponding duties may help you evaluate the implications and justification of her claim. If the manager has an ethical right to fire the employee, then her superiors have an ethical duty to allow her to do so. If, however, the employee is productive, reliable, respected by his peers, and cooperates with other managers, the manager lacks an ethically justifiable reason or right to fire him. Firing this employee might be unfair to him and do more harm than good for the company. In such a case, upper management might well have no duty to allow him to be fired, and might better transfer him to another division of the company in order to resolve the problem. Thus, examination of the duty associated with a supposed right may help clarify the existence of the right.

2.4 SOME IMPORTANT ETHICAL RIGHTS

The number of nameable rights is very large. Some, however, are particularly useful in evaluating ethical conflicts at the workplace. The following rights and their corresponding duties express important ethical values, but need not be thought of as absolutely inviolable. Like other ethical principles, you may view them as offering strong but not absolute ethical reason to act in certain ways.

The Right to Know

The right to know is closely connected to the duty to inform. People in certain roles and occupations have a right to know certain kinds of information. Others, in certain relationships to them, sometimes have ethical duties and sometimes legal duties to provide them with the information. For example, if a personnel director discovers that the credentials and resume of the Chief Executive Officer's personal assistant were falsified, he has a duty to inform the CEO, who has a right to that information.

However, while one may have a right to know something, there may be circumstances in which another may not have a duty to inform. Rights are options, so that one may have a right to know without choosing to exercise the right and without trying to find the information. Although a customer of a mechanic has a right to know that there are better cars on the market than the one he is now driving, the mechanic does not necessarily have a duty to tell him (unless his present car is unsafe).

It is important to recognize that one can violate the duty to inform without violating the principle of honesty. Consider the personnel director who is having a busy day, frustrated by many interruptions. The director might forget to note on an applicant's file folder that there are reasons to check the resume for accuracy before sending the file to the CEO. Although this violates the duty to provide information to the CEO, the information was not intentionally concealed and there was no deception. Of course, the personnel director may be charged with dereliction of duty or even incompetence, both of which are violations of the principle of fidelity.

The Right to Privacy

This is the right to control information about yourself, or access to it. It is also the right, as defined by one member of the Supreme Court, "to be left alone." To have this right is not necessarily to exercise it. We reveal information about ourselves whenever we appear in public or engage in cooperative work. It is common knowledge that in certain situations, some information about us will normally be made available to other people. We may also act in public ways that reveal aspects of our private life. Although much of this information is not clearly of a private nature, some of it can be. We might give information of a personal nature to our colleagues without clarifying its personal or private nature, just as we might act in ways that open our private lives to others.

Acting in ways that reveal private information to others does not necessarily count as permission to pass it on. A yearly evaluation of an employee's work performance is private information, and should not be passed on by the employer without permission of the employee. The misuse or gathering of information about a person may itself amount to a violation of the right to privacy.

It is possible for someone to violate your right to privacy even if you have given permission to obtain the information. If you gave permission under threat or coercion, whoever gathered the information has violated your right to privacy. Such permission should be given of your own free will. Clearly, the gathering of private information about you, such as downloading your non-job-related, personal email found on your home Internet server, is a violation of your privacy if you have not freely agreed to it.

Someone who has the right to know does not necessarily have the right to use any means available to obtain the information. Your employer has the right to know who is stealing supplies from the stockroom, but does not have the right to invade your privacy in order to catch the thief by searching your car without permission. The right to know does not justify obtaining information however someone chooses.

Your right to privacy can be violated at home or at work. Besides spying on you at home, it is possible to spy on you in questionable ways at work. The fact that your employer owns the workplace and is paying for your labor and time does not by itself justify clandestine gathering of information about you by any means, although this is often given as a justification for such actions. In some cases this is an acceptable justification, but usually there must be other reasons given in support of such invasions of privacy. The courts have, however, upheld the right of employers to monitor your use of a company computer, company email account, and your Web activities during working hours, with or without your permission or knowledge. This applies to both internal and external email, including your Web-surfing and purchases made using the company computer during working hours.

The right to privacy is important for a number of reasons. First, it is often justified by the principle of fidelity. If it is mutually understood that a work evaluation is private, fidelity requires the employer to guard the disclosure of that information. Second, if the invasion of privacy is done against your wishes, it may also violate the principle of autonomy by, in a sense, "forcing" you to reveal personal information without your consent. Third, violations of privacy often violate the principle of do no harm, causing embarrassment, loss of prestige, or even loss of a job. The feeling that you can maintain your own privacy is essential to your attitude toward life. Violations of privacy can be seriously damaging to one's sense of pride, self-esteem, security, and even your sense of personal identity. Finally, the right to privacy is essential for the protection of other moral rights such as the right to think freely, to act freely, to pursue happiness, and to speak freely. Environments and societies that ignore people's privacy invariably infringe upon these important moral rights.

The Right to Free Expression

This is the right to express your opinion without being penalized for doing so. It is not, however, the right to harm, libel, or slander your employer. An employer may justifiably demote or even fire an employee who repeatedly or purposefully does significant harm to a company. The right to free expression includes the right not to be penalized merely because you said something that displeases your employer. In order for penalties to be justified, the effect of your statements must be to cause (or at least be likely to cause) significant and unjustified harm to the employer.

Your intentions can also play an important role in deciding whether or not you have the right to express yourself freely about your employer or others. This right does not justify slander or libel. Slander, a legal concept, is saying things that are false and damaging, while libel is publishing such comments in print. It is especially unethical if your intentions are to harm the person you slander or libel. The Supreme

Court has ruled that, even if your comments are true, they might be slanderous or libelous if your primary intent was to harm the subject of those comments; in short, truth might no longer be a defense against slander and libel.

To become an employee is generally to agree to perform your work to a certain level of productivity. To interfere with that productivity is objectionable on two grounds. First, it violates the work contract between employer and employee. Second, it damages the goals of the employer. It is for these reasons that an employer can be justified in taking reprisal against employees who make statements that irresponsibly damage the employer's interests.

It is the intent or effects of your stated opinions, not their content alone, which justifies reprisal. Of course, divulging corporate trade secrets to outsiders can justify your being fired. Because such secrets are essential to successful company business and because it is your duty to honor this, you should keep them confidential. If you violate the policies of your employer, this may warrant the employer's response on the grounds that you have proven to be no longer trustworthy. Again, claiming a right to free expression is not sufficient justification for your actions in these cases.

Suppose, however, that a company has a policy that no employees are to state their personal religious or political beliefs at work. If such a policy is not job-related, violation of it will do no significant harm to the company's business. In such a case, the policy itself violates the employees' right to free expression.

The right to free expression is justified by the principles of autonomy and do no harm. It is fundamental for the health of any democratic society, and the citizens' right to pursue happiness. Free expression should not be denied at the workplace unless it is essential to furthering the legitimate purposes of the employer.

The Right to Due Process

In the workplace, this is the right of an employee to appeal a decision by management to an impartial third party with the power to correct the decision if it is wrong. The body empowered to render a decision must be composed of individuals who do not stand to gain or suffer from the decision. There must also be appropriate procedures to guarantee that the employee receives a fair hearing.

This right protects employees against the arbitrary use of managerial power. If an employer takes no steps to guarantee this right, then employees who want due process must appeal to the civil courts. However, civil procedures are slow and cumbersome and often discourage those who have been wronged from seeking redress. Consequently, many unions have established practices of arbitration which protect employees accordingly. Governments may require government contractors to implement appropriate procedures.

Due process is considered an ethical right for a number of reasons. First, recognition of this right is necessary to protect all the rights and ethical rules mentioned above. Due process is important to the same extent as these rights or rules. Second, it is based on a combination of the principles of autonomy and do no harm. Employees are not the property of their employers, but are autonomous persons with the right to pursue their life goals so long as they do not infringe on the similar pursuit by others. Employees can be wronged by unjust treatment. Due process gives employees the chance to seek justice when an employer has acted unfairly or arbitrarily.

Third, people have a right to some influence over the decisions that affect them. They have a right to protection from arbitrary power over their lives, and to work in environments in which there is a balance of certain powers. Fourth, businesses are licensed by society to provide services and products that benefit society. As such, businesses should implement the values of society, without being allowed to create their own despotic subcultures.

Although some businesses have opposed the formal recognition of the right to due process in the workplace, few individuals advocate unlimited power over them exercised by their superiors. The principle of equal consideration of interests also provides a justification of the right to due process.

The Right to Workplace Safety

Employees have a right to expect that their employer has taken reasonable precautions to protect them from bodily harm. What counts as reasonable is, of course, not easy to state. However, there are certain general factors which should be considered. Employees should be informed of known risks, encouraged to take care to avoid them, and trained in ways of doing so. But difficult questions of degree can arise. How thoroughly employees should be educated and how much care they should take are matters requiring much consideration. These questions must be answered in the contexts of varying workplaces, and as a result of a more lengthy analysis than is presently appropriate. However, that there is some basic right to safety is an important ethical consideration based on the principles of do no harm, autonomy, fidelity, lawfulness, and other rights.

Additionally, the right to a safe workplace protects employees from negligence on the job from whatever source. Safety procedures that guard against injury due to negligence are reasonable measures for a company to take and for employees to expect. To neglect worker safety may constitute legal neglect and be illegal.

2.5 CODES OF ETHICS AND PROFESSIONALISM

Organizations of professionals issue codes of ethics that require special attention. Professional organizations exist for physicians, attorneys, teachers, clergy, certified public accountants, registered nurses, licensed engineers, licensed psychologists, licensed social workers, and journalists. Their codes usually state a strong commitment, when relevant, to the principles of do no harm, confidentiality, honesty, fidelity to clients, autonomy, and lawfulness, as well as to many of the rights stated in the foregoing. Violations of these ethical principles, when brought before a peer review board, may lead to disciplinary actions, including loss of the professional license to practice. The ethical principles of professional associations are enforced as if they were law, and some U.S. states legally recognize the power of professional associations to act in this manner.

Most professions have five major characteristics. First, members of a profession have certified knowledge of a body of information that is identified and defined by an elected group of the practitioners. Second, membership in the profession requires specialized training and certification of mastery of the information and standards set by the professional association. Third, there is a code of ethics governing the profession created by the members of the profession. Fourth, the primary, accepted goal of the practitioners is promoting the well-being of their clients and society. Fifth, practicing professionals make day-to-day decisions more to follow the code of ethics and promote the well-being of their clients than to benefit or enrich them personally. Professionals want to be paid, but not at the expense of their values.

Professionals seek to develop the virtues of competence, autonomy, and beneficence in their colleagues. They understand that practicing the profession involves the competence, willingness, and confidence to make independent judgments and to accept responsibility for them. They educate those new to the field in the importance of the ideal of service to clients and society.

Professionals are paid primarily for their professional opinions. A professional opinion is a person's best use of good judgment and professional knowledge. Professionals in the same field can disagree without their opinions being considered mistaken or irresponsible. A professional opinion is not simply an opinion by a professional or an expert; rather, it is an opinion based on the current standards of knowledge and mastery set by the profession. These are often referred to as "standard practices" or "commonly accepted practices" of a profession.

Standards of professional competency change as time passes, and are not always easy to determine. They are stated in textbooks, taught in schools, learned by newcomers to the profession, or established by case law. Courts may determine standards when they examine and decide between conflicting testimonies of professionals testifying as expert witnesses.

Professionals usually have a contractual relationship with their clients to provide services meeting current standards, in exchange for reimbursement. This contractual relationship is entered freely by both parties, and can be dissolved by either one. However, the contract requires far more of the professional than of the client. The client owes little more than money, but the professional must act in a way that protects the interests of the client. A professional cannot ethically abandon the relationship with the client if doing so would significantly harm the client. On the other hand, a client is expected to be truthful, and to pay for the services rendered. That is, it is wrong of clients to lie or mislead professionals working with or for them, for the same reasons it is wrong to lie and mislead others in general. But it is not wrong for a client to decide to terminate a relationship with a professional for virtually any reason.

Professionals have a special relationship with one another, as indicated by the term *collegiality*. It is important to note that not all coworkers are professional colleagues. Those who lack most of the five characteristics listed above cannot be professional colleagues. Professional colleagues have different expectations of each other than of nonprofessionals, including a rough equality of competency and shared ethical values. Because they each have certified knowledge and competency in their fields, professionals assume, initially, the competency and good intentions of their colleagues.

Making the assumptions above has important implications for professional disagreements. Fidelity normally requires you to confront colleagues first, before reporting them to a higher authority, when you believe they are mistaken. Since our colleagues are competent and trustworthy, they should be given a chance to correct any problems in their performance before going higher. If a colleague nevertheless fails to correct the problem, that colleague demonstrates that he is either not competent or not trustworthy, thus failing to exhibit the autonomy and integrity required of a professional. Reporting such a colleague to a higher authority is not a violation of fidelity. Rather, in doing so, you are acting in a professional manner.

In summary, to act professionally is to act in a way that upholds the main ethical principles of the profession. To act unprofessionally is to act in a manner that violates some of those principles. Professionals who confront a compromising situation that unavoidably violates some of the ethical principles of the profession may have to defend their actions. The clearest and most reliable defenses usually involve ethical reasoning and decision-making strategies of the sort presented and explored in this book.

2.6 JUSTICE

Justice concerns the ways in which people are treated in social contexts. Thus, we normally refer to a society as having an unjust penal system or a corporation as having a just system of employee protections. But we would less likely refer to a thief, con artist, or a poor worker as acting unjustly.

Justice is embodied in the idea of fairness to all. We might even call justice the right to fair treatment, or to be treated as one has earned or deserves. The most common notions of justice mandate following the principles that similar cases should receive similar treatment, dissimilar cases treated differently, and that equals should be treated equally and proportionally. Thus punishments and rewards should vary according to the severity of the offense or worthiness of the accomplishment.

Institutions are the primary instruments of justice. These institutions are most often governments, but also include corporations, educational institutions, and others. Appropriately and defensibly implementing justice outside of institutions is less common. As noted in the section on capitalism in Chapter 1, a notion of justice or fairness is presupposed by an economic system. Of course, individuals within institutions are instrumental in implementing justice.

Because all people have equal value in a fundamental moral sense, everyone should be treated justly. All people should be recognized as having equal moral rights and should be treated equally in accord with ethical rules. Justice demands moral treatment of all in accord with the principle of equal consideration of interests.

There are four main kinds of justice. ***Procedural justice*** includes the equal chance of all people to receive a fair hearing in any disputes. Procedures designed to implement due process are attempts to implement procedural justice. This kind of justice is fundamental to a just, democratic society, and essential for a humane workplace.

Compensatory justice refers to the justice of decisions designed to compensate those who have been harmed by others. If you have been fired unjustly, slandered, or robbed, you might appeal to a court of law for compensation. Awarding monetary damages is the court's attempt to achieve compensatory justice. To do so, the court attempts to determine the harm to you and the monetary or other reparations necessary to restore you to your former state of well-being. In order to treat equals equally, the court would compare similar cases to determine the level of appropriate compensation.

Retributive justice refers primarily to the administering of punishment. It is based on the very old, traditional view that those who have done wrong deserve to be punished. That is, simply the fact that they did something wrong justifies having something bad done to them. Justice here means that the punishment should be fair, uniform, and fit the crime. If you have done wrong and deserve to be punished, the punishment should be appropriate and similar to fair punishment for similar wrongs by others. Retributive justice is an old concept repudiated by some who argue that retribution itself cannot be rationally justified. The idea behind retribution is the belief captured in the ancient expression "An eye for an eye and a tooth for a tooth." Opponents argue that two wrongs cannot make a right, and that harming a wrongdoer is merely another wrong deed.

Opponents of retributive justice also argue that only four considerations can justify fines and other penalties. Punishment can be justified as deference for others, prevention so the wrongdoer will not commit other crimes, protection for others from further harm by the perpetrator, or as education for the perpetrator about the wrongness of the deed. But none of these justifies retribution, and thus none of them proves that a culprit deserves to suffer, so it is argued. This viewpoint became increasingly popular during the twentieth century, but has not by any means eliminated the concept of retributive justice from the minds of most people. There are regularly popular outcries against those believed to be criminals who succeed in evading the justice system.

Distributive justice refers to the distribution of goods and services or benefits and burdens in a society. Here, questions of equality and just desert are important. How should we distribute the benefits and burdens of our society? The central issue is how we determine which segments of society should be rewarded or burdened. The criteria by which we make this determination are hotly disputed and constitute the basis for distinguishing between liberals, moderates, socialists, and conservatives in the political arena.

Those on the far left of the political spectrum, known as *socialists*, maintain that society exists in order to benefit its members. Since the lives of all people have equal ethical value, all people have equal ethical rights. It is the role of government to guarantee equal rights for everyone. Those on the far right, known as *libertarians*, view ethical rights as options, and maintain that only ethical rights are properly equal among all people. Everyone has an equal right to participate freely in trading, and thus the marketplace. But individuals' success in the market may differ, and should be allowed to differ. The right to own should be interpreted broadly, so that people are allowed to keep whatever profits they have legally acquired or have been given by those who have legally earned them. Moreover, government should provide people with nothing beyond what they obtain in these two ways.

Closer to the middle of the spectrum are liberal and conservative views of distributive justice. *Conservatives* are located a little to the right and *liberals* a little to the left of center of the political spectrum. Liberals maintain that the equality central to the concept of justice includes both rights and, within rather moderate limits, goods and services. They hold that those who are rich are freer than those who are not, and that society should strive to provide a certain minimum degree of freedom for all. They favor the existence of a free market, but believe that it is best that no one be allowed to perish from extreme misfortune or poverty. Therefore, they favor redistributing to the poor some of the excess wealth of the rich. Such redistribution should, however, permit the rich to remain relatively rich. The distributions should provide a minimally decent life for the poor, including a decent minimum level of freedom and opportunity for them.

The conservative view of distributive justice maintains that all of one's important moral rights can be maintained even though one is poor. According to the conservative position, the wisdom of the ages shows that poverty does not diminish human dignity. It is not the job of government to ensure that all have sufficient means to live. Rather, the job of government is to maintain the openness and freedom of the marketplace, preventing monopolies from taking over and protecting individuals from being harmed by others. To do this, government should maintain a few public institutions such as a system of law enforcement and courts, and perhaps public education.

2.7 SELF-INTEREST

Self-interest is not often thought of as an ethical principle. An ethical principle must be consistent with the principle of the equal consideration of interests, which imposes a limitation on self-interest. ECI demands that you pursue your self-interest only so long as you do not treat the interests of others as less important than your own. However, even granting that limitation, self-interest in some contexts may have some ethical justification.

There are reasons to believe that each of us has an ethical duty to take care of ourselves. First, to fail to do so is to act in a way that impoverishes a small part of society: you. Second, a society in which people ignore their duties to themselves would soon disintegrate and its members die off. Third is the fact that most people are happiest, most well-adjusted emotionally, when they take care of themselves. Fourth is the argument from tradition. This is the argument that values that have stood the test of time must have some real importance.

One approach to the argument from tradition is embodied in the ***principle of conservatism***. This is the principle, recognized in the law, that one should not interfere with an ongoing practice without an obviously good reason to do so. The mere fact that an ongoing practice may be doubted, or may have disadvantages, is not sufficient to warrant interference with it. The critic bears the burden of proving that altering the practice will do more good than following it. It is not the responsibility of those who favor the practice to establish its worth. The fact that it has become a traditional practice does count as one significant reason to think that it has some value. This is often called "passing the test of time." Those who want to alter the practice are justified in doing so only if they can provide sufficient reason to believe that the alteration truly does more good than harm.

One traditional, ongoing human practice is teaching children to take care of themselves and to pursue their own self-interest. Moreover, many of the great religions of the world teach that we have responsibilities to ourselves. Thus, a concern for our own interests reflects the considered judgment of humankind over time. These are significant reasons to think that the pursuit of self-interest, as long as it does not contradict ECI or religious law, is an ethical, fit, and proper endeavor for human beings.

2.8 THE NETWORK OF ETHICAL VALUE

It is important to recognize that the ethical principles presented here are all interrelated in meaning, in their import for our lives, and in their justifications. The system of ideas here may be thought of as a network, with each intersection of lines an ethical principle connected to the others directly or indirectly. Ethical values are not neat, isolated units to be adopted or ignored at will. Rather, each one has extensive implications for others. To develop an understanding of one principle will often lead to further insights regarding others.

The "material" constituting the strands of the network is the principle of equal consideration of interests (ECI), which is the common thread running through them all. If you follow the other principles carefully, you will generally be acting so as to treat the interests and well-being of others as equally important to your own. If this principle defines the ethical point of view, then each of the other principles assists us in applying that point of view to concrete, specific situations.

The network of value is flexible. The flexibility applies to the relationship of the various principles in different concrete situations. In some situations, two or more principles may be closely intertwined such that a given decision may violate several at once. In others, a decision may violate only one. In one situation, the best decision may be one that upholds one principle but violates another; in another situation, the best decision may do the exact opposite. Taken together, the principles in the network of ethical value comprise what is sometimes referred to as an ethical world view. They offer counsel on a wide variety of life's problems. The list of ethical principles discussed here is certainly not exhaustive. However, any expansion of this list would likely include the addition of principles and concepts that partially include and are partially defined and justified by reference to those described above.

The ethical principles presented here need not be viewed as beyond question. None of them need be viewed as absolute, or unexceptionable. They have limitations, and might perhaps be justifiably reformulated for various purposes. The importance of these principles must be distinguished from their exceptions. An ethical principle may be extremely important even though it has some ethically justifiable exceptions.

At the basis of every society is broad agreement among most members on the content of major ethical principles, such as those presented here. Most disagreement arises in the application of the principles to specific situations. Indeed, some of the most important and challenging work in ethics occurs in the application of these ethical principles to specific, concrete, day-to-day situations. This is what makes personal ethical problems so challenging. The next chapter shows you how to use the RESOLVEDD strategy of decision making to help you work through some difficult ethical problems. It develops a sample analysis of the case outlined in Chapter 1 that applies some of the ethical principles explained here.

CHAPTER 3

THE RESOLVEDD STRATEGY OF MAKING ETHICAL DECISIONS

The RESOLVEDD strategy is a process for thinking through a personal ethical problem in order to arrive at the best decision you can. The best decision in a specific case is one that upholds your most important values to the greatest extent possible or is most consistent with your ethical character, all things considered. Because your ethical values are often the most important values you hold, the best decision is usually an ethical decision that upholds these values to the greatest extent possible.

An ethical decision also upholds the principle of equal consideration of interests, treating the interests or well-being of others as at least equal to your own. Ethical decisions are reached as objectively as possible, as well. If an ethical decision violates any ethical principles, it does so only in order to uphold or to avoid violating other, more important, ethical principles. It is, then, essential in ethical decision making to determine which ethical principles or values are the most important in the case at hand.

An ethical decision is normally a decision upon which you would be willing to stake your reputation. It is one that you think is right on the basis of ethical principles that you try to follow, believe others should follow, and believe is right for people of good character to make in such cases. Ethical decisions are usually decisions in which you can take pride, knowing that you have tried to apply your ethical principles honestly, and knowing you have done your best to be a good person. You can identify with the decision you have made, believing that it is a decision suitable for a good person. Thus, your conscience is clear; you can readily enact the decision and willingly live with its consequences.

At times none of this is easy, none of the available options is clearly ethical, and all the foreseeable consequences of the best solution are unfortunate. Herein lies the challenge of ethical decision making: Often there are no simple solutions. The RESOLVEDD strategy does not remove the difficulties of ethical decision making. However, it can help you clarify those difficulties, examine them from several perspectives, work through them systematically, and make a well-informed choice. The strategy will help you organize your thinking about things that responsible people ought to consider when thinking through an ethical problem to reach a good decision.

3.1 AN OVERVIEW OF THE RESOLVEDD STRATEGY

The RESOLVEDD strategy presents a series of steps to follow to develop your analysis and decision, though your thinking need not follow these steps in exactly this order. Normally, our minds jump back and forth among the different parts of a RESOLVEDD analysis, and new ideas in one part will generate new ideas in another. The main parts of an analysis are described below as steps for the sake of the initial presentation of the strategy and in a useful order for written analysis.

Step 1—R: *Review* the history, background, and details of the case.

Step 2—E$_1$: State the main *ethical problem or issue* present in the case.

Step 3—S: List the main *possible solutions* to the case.

Step 4—O: State the important and probable *outcomes* or consequences of each main solution.

Step 5—L: Describe the *likely impact* of each main solution on people's lives.

Step 6—V: Explain the *values* upheld and those violated by each main solution.

Step 7—E$_2$: *Evaluate* each main solution and its outcomes, likely impact, and the values upheld and violated by it. Compare the possible solutions to each other and weigh them.

Step 8—D$_1$: *Decide* which solution is the best; state it, clarify its details, and justify it.

Step 9—D$_2$: *Defend* the decision against objections to its main weaknesses.

Step 1 begins the analysis with a careful review of the context, facts, and background of the case. The important details that create the ethical problem should be clearly understood. It is essential to know the facts of the case so well that one can envision oneself in the situation described.

Step 2 should state your initial thoughts about the nature of the ethical problems you face in the case. The understanding gained in this initial estimation may later change as you develop the analysis. The first two steps lay the groundwork for the following considerations.

In step 3, you state concisely the main possible solutions to the case. Before stating these solutions, start by making a long list of many possible solutions. Once all the imaginable ones have been listed, you can then begin the process of reducing them to fewer, more general, and realistic main solutions. Proceed by grouping the many together and then narrowing down the list to a more manageable size by combining specific variations. It is important not to eliminate any solutions too quickly in this step, and to identify lessons that may be learned and possible options to take as a result of those you do eliminate. The main solutions must be fully analyzed in the next three steps and evaluated in the seventh. These are the backbone of your analysis, and omitting any main possible solutions in this third step may lead to a decision that is short-sighted.

In step 4, you identify the most likely and important possible outcomes or consequences of each main solution. Consider the question "If I choose solution A, then the following things might happen," and then go on to list them. Answers to this question will ordinarily lead you to think of considerations that constitute part of the fifth step. The outcomes, as opposed to likely impacts in step 5, are the very general consequences of your choice. These could include what might happen to the company, society, or a competitor.

Step 5 states the likely impact of each main solution on people's lives, an especially important aspect of ethical analyses. Will a solution hurt or help people, and in what ways? Here, you are trying to determine how individuals are affected by the general consequences of each possible main solution. You might ask a question such as "If the company is sued (an outcome from step 4), how will the workers, managers, I, or members of the community be affected?" You might also ask at this point, "How likely are each of these consequences?" These fourth and fifth steps identify consequences that are essential to your overall analysis. Thinking them through should suggest to you the ethical principles upheld and violated by each main solution.

In step 6, you identify, explain, and clarify the main values or ethical principles at issue in each main solution. The task here is to clarify which values or principles are upheld and which are violated by each main solution. Simply naming or listing these principles is not enough. It is essential to explain how and why each main solution violates or upholds the appropriate principles.

To this point, you have described the facts of the case, noted the main options, listed the important outcomes and likely impact of those solutions, and clarified the values at stake. Now, in step 7, it is time to evaluate the main solutions, compare and contrast them, weigh them to determine which are better, which worse, and why. In this seventh step, you make value judgments about the seriousness of the violations of values and the importance of upholding the values described in step 6. That is, you state your own views on the nature and significance of the ethical issues, and present your reasons for holding these views. This step also requires you to make value judgments about the outcomes and likely impacts that you listed in steps 4 and 5. You must indicate which of these are most important, which less important, which can be ignored and which not, and why.

In addition to making value judgments, you also evaluate by indicating your opinion of the likelihood of the outcomes and impacts listed in steps 4 and 5. Indicate what you think is likely to happen, what is unlikely and can be ignored for now, and why. Indicate why some outcomes are more likely to occur than others, and why some likely impacts of main solutions are more significant than others.

This seventh step may well be the longest, most involved, and most difficult of all. It requires you to review and state your own personal viewpoints on all of the matters considered in the earlier steps. You must take a stand on various issues, formulate reasons for your opinions, and question and evaluate them. You are here weighing and comparing probabilities and value judgments. As you work through the seventh step, you will eliminate all but one main solution from further consideration. You will state why those eliminated are best avoided. You will lay the groundwork for the arguments that justify your conclusions. Your work in this step will be drawing to a close when one main solution remains.

It is important to realize that you might think of new possible solutions during this seventh step. You could discover that you had neglected an option early on and that it looks very promising now. You must be open to the possibility that the solutions you identified earlier in the analysis do not exhaust all of the possibilities. In-depth analysis in this seventh step can lead you to a new possible solution that turns out to be the best decision. You might have to rewrite some earlier steps.

Step 8 begins when it is clear that you favor a particular main solution. In this step you will develop and support your decision. A number of things need to be done in this step. First, refine your preferred main solution and describe the specific course of action you think is best. The details of your decision are important. You cannot determine whether the decision will really work unless you consider these details carefully. So, where you eliminated details in the third step above, you now state and clarify them in this eighth step. Second, explain or summarize directly why you favor the main solution that you do, and why it is ethically preferable to the others. Third, examine the specific course of action you have decided upon, and show why you think it will work and why it accomplishes the goals you seek in the case. Fourth, justify your view that this specific decision is the best one in the case, taking all important values, outcomes, and other considerations into account. This might require you to summarize the most important parts of some of your analysis from steps 4 through 7. Although repetition is not necessary, it is often essential to clarify the many reasons your preferred decision is the best one.

The ninth step is to defend your decision against the main objections to it. Whether or not you have formulated the perfect decision, someone else still might object to your decision and cite one or more significant weaknesses in it. Your job in this step is to anticipate, state, and explain these weaknesses, then to defend your decision against them. That is, you need to provide answers to those objections that show why your decision is still the best one, despite its alleged disadvantages or weaknesses. You are anticipating your critics and answering them before they can raise their objections. Doing so usually indicates that you have done a thorough and balanced job of analyzing the situation.

Some parts of the RESOLVEDD strategy could be covered in a slightly different order than discussed above. Some steps can appropriately be mixed in with the others. For example, you could combine the O and L stages into a consideration of consequences, both general and as they affect individuals. Or you might do some evaluation immediately after listing some outcomes or likely impacts of main solutions, and after clarifying the values upheld and violated by main solutions. But it would be jumping the gun to cover step 8, one's decision, before stating, analyzing, and evaluating the main solutions, their outcomes, likely impacts, and value implications. There are important reasons why the parts of the analysis are suggested in the order they are. But this order need not be viewed as rigid and unalterable.

3.2 APPLYING THE **RESOLVEDD**
STRATEGY TO THE CASE OF "THE NOT SO GREAT GATSBY"

A description of the case of "The Not So Great Gatsby" is found on page 1. What follows is an analysis of this case as might be done by a student. Although far more can be said about the case than is included here, the analysis does illustrate an application of the RESOLVEDD strategy. The steps of this analysis are in the following order:

Review of the case

Ethical problem in the case

Solutions 1 and 2

Outcomes 1 (outcomes of solution 1)

Likely impact 1 (likely impact of solution 1)

Values 1 (values upheld and violated by solution 1)

Outcomes 2 (outcomes of solution 2)

Likely impact 2 (likely impact of solution 2)

Values 2 (values upheld and violated by solution 2)

Evaluation

Decision

Defense

A RESOLVEDD Analysis of the Case of "The Not So Great Gatsby"

REVIEW   This case arose due to pressure from my boss to take unusual steps with an employee who is a marginal but rather troublesome worker. However, it seems clear that although Gatsby's work is sometimes below average, it is minimally competent, not substandard, and offers no clear grounds for firing him. He is not really doing anything wrong, although he may be one of the worst employees I have, due to his attitude, nastiness, and other traits. Management has decided to force me to help them get rid of Gatsby.

Higher-level managers are not supposed to make decisions for lower-level managers, even though they outrank them. My boss should not be giving me orders about what to do, nor should he expect that I will necessarily carry out this suggestion. But he probably expects that I will, so I must be very sensitive to this suggestion and not accidentally offend my boss by flagrantly ignoring it.

ETHICAL PROBLEM OR ISSUE   It is clear that my problem is not Gatsby—at least not in terms of my immediate decision. My problem comes from my boss's suggestion that I do something that is sneaky, mean, and not entirely ethical. My actual problem is how to react to my boss's suggestion in light of the fact that what I do may violate the principle of do no harm as it applies to Gatsby.

According to the case description, my boss only suggested a solution to the situation, but did not order it. I am under no clear obligation to do exactly as he suggested. But does the principle of fidelity mean that I owe it to my employer to try, within the limits of acting ethically and legally, to find a way to raise productivity and morale? I will have to find a way to communicate to my boss effectively the rationale for my decision. That decision will need to be one that my boss agrees with and that is best for the company.

Thus, it seems my main problem concerns whether to violate the principle of do no harm to Gatsby in order to uphold the principle of fidelity to my boss, or vice versa.

SOLUTIONS   I could (1) do as my boss suggests, rotating Gatsby among the most undesirable jobs, or (2) resist my boss's suggestion and handle the case in my own way. If I choose this second approach, I have several options. These include my continuing to counsel Gatsby, giving him time off and requiring that he attend training sessions, or persuading the union to put pressure on him.

OUTCOMES 1   If I rotate Gatsby among the most undesirable jobs and shifts on the production floor, my boss will be pleased that I am following his suggestion. On the other hand, Gatsby might figure out what is going on and fight back in order to stop it. If he took the case to the union, he might win a grievance on the grounds that his work is acceptable and my strategy is harassment and seems to violate the spirit, if not the letter, of the union agreement. If he didn't figure it out, he might quit.

LIKELY IMPACT 1   Following my boss's suggestion might upset Gatsby, even to the point of quitting or filing a grievance. This, in turn, could backfire on me if Gatsby was successful in gaining the attention and sympathy of his fellow workers. The whole thing could turn into a nasty, demoralizing, and efficiency-reducing labor–management conflict. Not only can Gatsby be harmed, but I can be harmed, the workers can be harmed, and the company can be harmed by this conflict.

On the other hand, Gatsby might get the message and straighten out. His coworkers would surely like to avoid his nastiness, my boss would be happy, and there might be no grievance filed or other troubles caused for me. His productivity might even improve. But I wonder, given Gatsby's history, if this is realistic.

VALUES 1   Doing as my boss suggests would be a way of upholding the principle of fidelity toward my boss and the company. I would be respecting the chain of command and taking steps to address a personnel problem and increase efficiency. It could also alleviate some of the harm to the company and other workers the boss sees Gatsby causing by his poor performance and attitude.

This first solution would violate the principle of autonomy toward Gatsby. Merely shifting him around to the worst jobs without informing him of my motives would make it impossible for him to face the challenge squarely, effectively, and responsibly. It violates his right to know about conditions directly affecting his job, performance, and life. The shifting might cause him to become confused and demoralized, thereby inhibiting him from thinking positively in terms of the real choice he in fact has. Although I would be happy if he were to quit, he does have a right to understand that he need not do so, and a right to consider seriously the possibility that he might shape up instead. It clearly violates the principle of do no harm by causing him this mental anguish. It also violates the right to due process by depriving him of the information he needs to appeal my actions.

I also violate the principle of honesty toward Gatsby by hiding my true motives from him. The principle of fidelity toward Gatsby is violated since I would be acting in a way that is hardly faithful to him, thus acting against his best interests and violating the spirit of the union contract. Rather than helping production run smoothly, this solution sabotages, manipulates, and harms one person by making his life miserable.

OUTCOMES 2   If I ignore my boss's suggestion and handle the case in my own way, my boss could view me as stubborn, inflexible, and insubordinate. He may just get someone else to do what he wants. But if not, I can handle the situation more fairly.

LIKELY IMPACT 2   If I ignore my boss, I could get a poor job performance review (JPR). But if my own method of handling the case is effective, this might redeem me to my boss. Gatsby may not suffer as much if I handle the situation well. Of course, Gatsby could still be harmed and might take it out on me personally. If the other workers see it his way, I will have to deal with their resentment and anger every day at work. However, the other workers might be more understanding if they see me dealing directly and honestly with Gatsby. The other workers might welcome a change in Gatsby's attitude, too, if my plan works.

VALUES 2   Ignoring my boss's suggestion violates the principle of fidelity toward my boss and employer by ignoring the lines of authority I agreed to follow when I was hired and am therefore obligated to uphold. However, there is some room for debate here, since my boss only made a suggestion, and it is not completely clear that I am expected to follow it as if it were an order. If the boss holds me responsible, though, I can be harmed by losing his support and receiving a bad JPR.

This solution upholds the principle of do no harm if I can handle it so that Gatsby feels he has been treated fairly. The principles of autonomy, right to know, right to due process, truth, and fidelity will all be upheld because following the boss's suggestion so clearly violates them with respect to Gatsby. My handling of the situation, if done well, will not violate these values as solution 1 did, but rather uphold them by treating Gatsby fairly, with respect, giving him a chance to react, and in a way that preserves his autonomy. I will not be harmed, either, by the negative reactions of Gatsby and his fellow workers. Finally, the other workers will no longer be harmed by Gatsby's constant mistreatment of them, and morale will improve.

EVALUATION   The main problem with ignoring my boss's suggestion is that doing so would jeopardize my boss's high opinion of me and thus my JPR. It is not a significant violation of the principle of fidelity, as my boss merely made a suggestion, but did not order me. However, there is reason to doubt that any effort I make to solve the problem on my own would be successful. This makes the importance of all the values upheld by solution 2 unclear, since if I cannot find an equitable solution, I will end up violating them anyway. Given Gatsby's personality and my total failure to get him to cooperate so far, it seems unlikely that I will have much luck in my efforts to reform him. This second solution would be personally risky, although not ethically problematic. But what good is a decent solution if you can't actually pull it off?

The first solution, following my boss's suggestion, has some advantages. It might be best for Gatsby if it motivates him to shape up rather than shipping out.

However, knowing him and knowing the meanness of such an approach, I do not believe it is likely to have such a positive effect on Gatsby.

This solution would be treating Gatsby in an underhanded and inconsiderate way, failing to respect his need to know why he is being treated in this way, and violating his autonomy and right to know. Such treatment of any employee is clearly not ethical, and cannot be justified by the fact that Gatsby himself has not acted cooperatively or fairly. In reality, two wrongs do not make a right; one cannot counter one wrong with another. Moreover, this solution has the serious potential to create significant practical management problems that waste large amounts of time and energy, reduce morale and productivity, and might hurt my career. Following this choice seriously violates the principle of do no harm for Gatsby, me, the other workers, and the company itself. This option is the worst choice on all important grounds.

The main problem with the second solution is that it threatens my career and causes me harm. There must be some personally less threatening ways to deal with the casual suggestions of my boss, and thus avoid the negative consequences. If I followed such a solution, I would be free to address the problem with Gatsby in a way that is creative, ethical, and less objectionable in practice. Here I might be able to respect Gatsby's autonomy and right to know, avoid harming him, and be truthful toward him, at the same time maintaining the fidelity I owe to my boss and the other workers. These values are all important to me and outweigh the fidelity to my boss to follow his suggestion to the letter.

Once my boss realizes the significance of the union–management conflict that could result from shifting Gatsby around, he may well be willing to admit that we should just turn our backs on Gatsby. If so, he might then suggest that I simply drop all concern with Gatsby. But I think I can take steps that have not yet been tried with Gatsby, may have some hope of success, and would cost the company very little.

DECISION   My decision would be to handle the situation in my own way. In implementing the decision, I first need to have a serious, in-depth, heart-to-heart talk with my boss, explaining to him in a very diplomatic way all the disadvantages of shifting Gatsby around. I would make it obvious that upper management would likely disapprove of his initial suggestion. I would then explain the ethically acceptable alternatives available, and explain my plan to act on them. This would show him that I have taken his suggestions seriously, value his opinions, and want to address the problem in the best way for the company overall. I would stress the principle of doing no harm to the company, but also the need to respect Gatsby's rights.

DEFENSE   One objection to my approach is that my boss might be bullheaded and insist that I defer to his experience and authority. If I don't, I am setting myself up for a very bad JPR and reducing my chances for advancement. However, if my boss takes such autocratic measures, there would be no solution that would be good for me personally. My best approach, then, is to use every means at my disposal to convince him of the benefits of my handling the case in the best manner I know how. I think there's a good chance he would listen.

Second, what if, no matter what I do, Gatsby doesn't respond? If this happened, then I'd have failed, my boss could hold me responsible for the failure, and Gatsby would still be hurting the company. However, this is true whenever we try to influence others' behavior. Anyone, anytime, could become irrational and not listen. If this happened with Gatsby, I think my boss would be open-minded enough to see that it wasn't my fault. After all, he had failed with Gatsby, too. Even if I am held responsible, I can take some comfort in the fact that I did the best I could and treated Gatsby fairly. His unfair or irrational reactions are not under my control. All I can do is my best. However, I don't think Gatsby will get totally irrational, nor do I think my boss would miss the fact that I cannot simply order Gatsby to behave better.

3.3 UNKNOWN FACTS

Relevant factual information might be omitted in a case, even if you might be aware of it in an actual situation. The case description of "The Not So Great Gatsby" offers little clear information about the context—neither the nuances of the suggestion made to you by your boss, nor the strength of your personal relationships at work with the boss and other workers. In actuality, you would have such information, and it could play an important role in your decision. However, when such information is not stated in the case description, you should assume it is unknown and develop your analysis and decision with as little reference to it as possible.

In practice, most decisions are made in the presence of significant factual uncertainty. There are *always* important facts that decision makers simply do not have. All decisions are based on a degree of speculation. If we waited until we knew every possible fact, we would never decide or act. In the above analysis, the author speculates about how likely it is, if you follow your boss's suggestion, that Gatsby would cause trouble once he figured out what was going on. There is also speculation about how likely it is that you could persuade your boss to accept your point of view. Decision making in ethics, as in all fields, requires that you respond thoughtfully to unknown facts. Of course, a miscalculation on such questions can lead you to make a decision with disastrous consequences. It is part of the art of effective critical thinking and decision making to learn how to address and work with such uncertainties. Try to be as realistic, objective, and honest with yourself as you can about what can and cannot be assumed.

3.4 LACKING TIME

It takes considerable time and concentration to develop an analysis of a personal ethical problem. Yet such a conflict may occur in a complex situation demanding a quick decision. The RESOLVEDD strategy can be of help in such high-pressure situations.

There may, of course, be times when you cannot work out a complete RESOLVEDD analysis. In these cases, you have no choice but to rely on various habits of thought that you have developed in advance. Such habits are developed by practicing the RESOLVEDD strategy on cases such as those presented in this book. Practice helps you become more familiar with applying ethical principles, such as those presented in Chapter 2. With practice, you will be better able to detect situations in which these principles play important parts. You may be able to determine immediately that a certain possible decision upholds or violates an important principle. This quick grasp of the important ethical factors is sometimes described as intuition or insight. Practice in using the RESOLVEDD strategy can help develop and sharpen your intuition and insight.

In time, and with practice using the RESOLVEDD strategy, you will more quickly develop your ethical analyses. The routine steps of the strategy will take less time. This, in turn, will give you longer to consider the most trying issues of a conflict.

Practice helps you establish your value judgments, further reducing the time needed to analyze future conflicts. In future, unfamiliar, cases you can apply the same principles and methods, thus further saving time. On the other hand, earlier mistakes may well have taught you important lessons useful in future conflicts. With increased practice, each new ethical conflict will become less novel, and need less time for analysis.

There is no denying that the pressures of time can increase the likelihood of making questionable decisions. Ideally, it is best to take as much time as necessary to analyze ethical conflicts. Realistically, however, this is not always possible. Through practicing the RESOLVEDD strategy, you should learn to make better decisions in less time. The more practice you have, the more the whole process becomes "second nature" to you. When you reach this point, your ethical analysis can be done more quickly, even though it might not be easier to cut through difficult issues and conflicts. Do not, however, sacrifice the quality of your thought process for speed. A good analysis is more important than a quick one. Where the situation demands a quick solution, having practiced and followed the RESOLVEDD strategy will be an asset.

3.5 A CHECKLIST

Review

____ What are the particularly important relevant details of the case?

____ How did the situation come about?

____ Is something wrong? What? Why?

____ Is anyone at fault? Why?

____ Is there likely to be disagreement over the case from people related differently to it? Why? What are the different perspectives people may have on the case?

____ What information would you like to have that is missing, and that you must decide without having?

Ethical Problem

____ What options do *you* have in the situation?

____ Why is it difficult to make a decision in the case?

____ Initially, what do you think is the main ethical conflict in the case?

____ What main points will you need to consider in making the decision?

Solutions

___ Group the options into a small, manageable number of main solutions. Remember that you may end up deciding to do something that is not exactly like any of the solutions with which you began.

Outcomes

___ List the significant possible consequences of each main solution that you will be evaluating later because they are essential to effective decision making in the case.

Likely Impact

___ List the ways each main solution is likely to affect people's lives by hurting or helping them.

Values

___ List the important ethical principles upheld by each main solution, and explain briefly how each one is upheld by it.

___ List the important ethical principles violated by each main solution, and explain briefly how they are violated by it.

___ A list of values upheld and violated without explanations is largely useless. A principle may be violated or upheld in a way that is important as well as in a way that is not. The way a principle is upheld or violated is far more important and useful than simply being told it is upheld or violated.

Evaluation

___ Are some possible consequences of some possible solutions more important than others? Why?

___ Are some possible consequences of some possible solutions more likely to occur than others? Why?

___ Does one solution uphold or violate certain values in more or less important ways than another? Why?

___ Why is one possible main solution better or worse than another?

___ Have you made it clear why you have rejected the main solutions other than the one you choose as your decision?

___ If all main solutions are unsatisfactory, have you searched for other possibilities? Have you considered that new, unthought-of possibilities may be hidden in your main solutions and that you might find a variation of one that is satisfactory?

Decision

___ Exactly how will you carry out your decision? Explain the details.

___ Just why is this decision the best, all things considered? Explain.

Defense

___ What are the main weaknesses of your decision? Why might someone object to your decision?

___ If these weaknesses have not been stated and addressed previously, do so here.

___ What are the best answers to these weaknesses? Why do you still think your decision is the best? Explain.

CHAPTER 4

THE RESOLVEDD
STRATEGY IN DEPTH

The previous chapter offered the initial presentation of the RESOLVEDD strategy and an analysis of the case of "The Not So Great Gatsby." The present chapter addresses, in more depth, some of the questions that often arise in developing a RESOLVEDD analysis.

4.1 WHEN IS AN ETHICAL PRINCIPLE UPHELD BY A GIVEN SOLUTION?

The mere fact that a solution does not violate an ethical principle does not show that the solution upholds the principle. Consider, in the case of "The Not So Great Gatsby," the solution of ignoring my boss's suggestion and moving ahead to handle the case as I prefer. This approach clearly does not violate the principle of confidentiality. But neither does it uphold that principle in any significant way. Rather, that principle is irrelevant to the decision simply because the principle of confidentiality does not offer a reason either to follow that solution or not. It is irrelevant, and perhaps confusing, then, to mention that principle in step 6, the values portion of your analysis.

Consider, however, whether or not the principle of do no harm is relevant to your decision on this same solution. Since following the suggestion may do harm to Gatsby, refusing to do so may avoid doing harm to him, and so may be said to uphold the principle of do no harm. Just why is this so?

Following your boss's suggestion is an important possible solution to the case. That doing so violates a particular ethical principle and not doing so does not are both relevant and important ethical aspects of the situation; therefore, this should be considered by any reasonable person deciding on a solution. We say the solution upholds the principle of do no harm in order to express the importance of the fact that not following your boss's suggestion does not violate the principle of do no harm. To say that an ethical principle is upheld is to say that it is not violated but also counts in favor of, or justifies, that solution. If a principle is upheld, it means you could use the principle as a reason in support of your decision.

The following is a condition that must be present in order for a given ethical principle or value to be upheld by a given solution: For a solution to uphold a value, there must be some other solution to the problem at hand that would violate that value. If a given value is not violated by any possible solution, even if it is one you have already dismissed, then the value need not be mentioned in your analysis. Such a value is not relevant to any significant decision regarding the conflict, and should probably not play a major role in your analysis. There could be a possible, but extremely unattractive, solution that violates a certain ethical principle. In such a case, there would be no significant reason to state that the alternative solutions uphold this ethical principle. In this case, the principle plays only a minor role in the decision at hand.

Consider a possible (but outrageous) solution to the case of "The Not So Great Gatsby." You could simply hire someone to give Gatsby a beating and deliver a warning to shape up or it will be worse the next time! Such a solution would violate the principle of do no harm! But this hardly justifies your citing as an advantage of the other possible solutions that they uphold the principle of do no harm since they do not include beating Gatsby. Making such a point is generally unnecessary because this is obviously an extremely bad solution. Citing this application of the principle of do no harm as an advantage of other solutions is unnecessary for anyone taking the ethical point of view.

A second condition for a value to be upheld is that the alternative solution that violates it is worth being considered by an ethical person. Such a solution is one that an ethical or moral person might, in some circumstances and in good conscience, follow. These two requirements for a value to be upheld can be combined into one:

> For a possible solution to uphold a value, there must be some other possible solution that would violate the value. The other solution must be worth consideration by an ethical person.

Another way of thinking about whether or not a principle or value is upheld by your solution is to ask, "Could I use the principle or value in question to support or to justify my decision?" A principle or value is upheld by a solution if you could use that principle or value as a significant reason in favor of your solution. If the principle or value offers good reason for another person to accept your solution as the right one, then it is upheld by your solution. Remember, to uphold a principle or value means that the principle or value can be used as a reason to support your particular solution.

On the other hand, for a principle or value to be violated or sacrificed by your solution means that it could be used as a reason to reject your solution. If your solution violates a principle or value, then that principle or value could be used by someone who disagrees with your solution as a good reason for saying your solution is not justified. That principle or value, then, could be cited as justification for others to see your solution as wrong, and as a reason to ask for another alternative solution. The question here is, "Could someone use the principle or value in question to reject or criticize my solution?" If the answer is yes, then the principle or value is violated to some extent by your solution.

4.2 A SOLUTION CAN UPHOLD AND VIOLATE THE SAME ETHICAL PRINCIPLE

A given solution to a personal ethical conflict can both uphold a particular ethical principle and violate it at the same time. This is possible because of the broad and general nature of major ethical principles. As you may have noted already in the case of "The Not So Great Gatsby," failing to carry out your boss's suggestion may both uphold and violate the principle of do no harm. It may uphold the principle in avoiding doing harm to Gatsby, and violate it in causing problems for you, your boss, and the company.

These considerations help clarify the importance of explaining, in the values section, just how a main solution violates a given ethical principle. The important point is not that an ethical principle is violated by a solution. It is the specific way in which it is violated that you must consider and stress in the evaluation stage. The fact that an ethical principle is violated by a solution does not prove the solution is ethically wrong. Recognizing the violation is merely one reason to think the solution is wrong. But there may be other, more important, reasons why it is the best solution given the circumstances. These can only be understood and evaluated by examining the specific way and context in which the ethical principle is violated.

Ethical principles are general in nature. Each concrete situation pertains to a given principle in a slightly different manner, depending upon the particulars of the situation. Ethical decision making requires that you look very carefully into those particulars and understand each situation as a unique instance of the relevant ethical principles. Each instance will embody the ethical importance of a principle in its own unique way, and to a greater or lesser extent. Your decision must emerge from careful consideration of the ethical values uniquely present in the case at hand and the various alternative main solutions.

This is not to say that ethical principles are purely relative or subjective. The principles and values themselves are not changed by considering each unique application of them on a case-by-case basis. The same principle may apply differently to different situations. So each situation requires a reevaluation of the relevance of ethical values. Some of the most influential ethicists of our age, such as W. D. Ross, have long recognized this point. In contrast, one form of relativism involves the view that the very principles and values themselves are changed or re-created by the unique aspects of each situation. Relativists of this sort maintain that each person, each time, each place, and each new element of a situation create the need to revise or manufacture new ethical principles or values. This view is sometimes referred to as *situation ethics*. This theory offers little hope for the prospect of learning from our ethical successes and mistakes. Other forms of relativism, such as cultural relativism, differ but tend to suffer from similar flaws.

The standard view of ethicists is that our principles and values commonly remain the same although they affect our decision making in different ways in various situations. This view does not imply that every new situation requires that we adopt new principles. Rather, we should analyze and evaluate each new situation and our relevant principles before we understand fully how or whether they apply to that situation. As time and experience pass, we learn more about our principles and how they relate to the world, and thus develop moral wisdom.

4.3 WHO SHOULD I CONSIDER WHEN DOING THE O AND L STAGES?

Students often ask, concerning the O and L sections of the RESOLVEDD strategy, "Who should I consider when I look at outcomes and the likely impact on people's lives?" Usually this question arises as a result of either looking too narrowly or too broadly at the O and L sections. That is, sometimes we tend to focus only on ourselves, people we are directly concerned about, and perhaps the company employing us.

Other times we look at absolutely everyone and anyone when we consider moral decisions. Both approaches can lead us into errors. Either we leave important consequences and individuals out of our analysis, or we get bogged down trying to imagine how our decisions affect people beyond those who are actually involved and relevant to our analysis. But how do we answer the question of just who needs to be considered?

A good suggestion would be to do a *stakeholder analysis*, a method of analyzing consequences of business decisions that has lately become widely accepted. A *stakeholder* is anyone who has a stake, a reasonable interest, in the actions of a company or individual employed by the company. Stakeholders are people who can be affected by a company's actions or by the choices made by individuals working for the company. Stakeholders have reason to care about how the company or its employees act because those actions affect the stakeholders in some way. Therefore, we can say that, when doing the O and L sections of the RESOLVEDD strategy, a good rule to follow would be to consider the outcomes and likely impacts of our choices on all stakeholders.

Exactly who might qualify as a stakeholder can vary from case to case, depending upon the circumstances and effects of the chosen action. In general, stakeholder analyses are meant to broaden the scope of people to consider when making an ethical decision in business beyond the owners or stockholders, employees, and consumers of the company's product. Many corporate actions affect the public, whether or not the public holds stock in the company, works for the company, or purchases the company's product. To limit our consideration of consequences to stockholders, employees, and customers no longer seems acceptable to many ethicists, though it remains a popular practice for businesses.

Some choices may affect only a few people in a small department of the company, while others may affect a large number of people outside the company. An example of the first sort might be the choice of whether or not to require all the machine shop personnel to take their lunch at the same time, even though the employees want to be free to choose their own lunch schedules. This decision will not affect production or the operation of other areas in the plant. While it is conceivable that other employees might be affected if the lunchroom became too crowded, we will assume this is not a problem, nor is there a problem with the shop's being closed for the half-hour lunch period. Here the only people who have a stake in the decision are those managers and workers in the machine shop, so these two groups are the only stakeholders.

An example of the second type would be a decision to ignore updated warnings about safe levels of a toxic pollutant discharged into the local river and to stick to the now outmoded guidelines the EPA applies to the company. Here the company's choice affects everyone living downriver from the plant because they could be adversely affected by the toxic waste, especially if drinking water is drawn from the river. Negative publicity might outrage consumers and cause a drop in sales. Layoffs could follow if sales drop too low, so the workers are affected. Stockholders will lose money if the stock price drops as a result of lower sales and negative publicity. Managers, especially those who chose to ignore the warnings, might be fired or transferred. Even politicians who failed to enact stricter controls can be affected if the public votes them out of office. Thus, this decision affects a large number and wide range of people, all of whom are stakeholders with an interest in the company's choice of pollution controls.

It would be wrong and a violation of the principle of equal consideration of interests to ignore these people if you were making this decision.

Stakeholders, then, include every person who has some interest in or reason to care about an ethical decision made in the workplace. The principle of equal consideration of interests requires us to take all stakeholders into account when solving personal ethical problems. Anyone *reasonably* affected by your choice should be considered. Stakeholder analysis broadens our perspective so that we include everyone who is *justifiably* said to have reason to care about a corporation's or individual's actions. You should not limit your analysis to those who have a monetary interest in a company or decisions (stockholders, for example) since many of the effects of ethical decisions are not monetary. Health effects, psychological effects, effects on family relations, and other societal effects are often important whether or not those affected have a monetary interest in the company.

Thus, a workable answer to the question "Who should I consider in the O and L sections of the RESOLVEDD strategy?" is "Consider all the stakeholders." If you do this, you will be considering the consequences of your actions for those who are actually affected by your choices. Be careful not to limit your scope to employees and stockholders, nor to broaden your scope too much by considering absolutely everyone (even those in no way affected) in your analysis. The important thing to remember is that many choices you make will affect even those who have no monetary interests in the decision. Asking whether or not a person has a stake in your choice can help ensure that your analysis will be reasonable and follow ECI.

4.4 UNDERSTANDING EVALUATION

It is important to understand the difference between describing the outcomes, likely impacts, and values upheld and violated by the main solutions and the evaluation of these three. The evaluation is not simply a summary or combination of the other steps. It involves some fundamentally different kinds of thinking and is essential for arriving at a well-considered decision.

Statements that are characteristically part of the solutions, outcomes, likely impact, and value steps are all objective and descriptive. They present the basic, ethically relevant facts of the case. They do not assert that you believe that something is likely or unlikely to happen, or that it is right or wrong, good or bad, or should or should not be done.

To state "I could do as my boss suggested" is to say that this is a possibility. It is not to state a value judgment regarding how good or bad the solution is. Nor is it to assert that you think something will probably happen or probably not happen.

There are two main kinds of evaluations you can make. The first is to evaluate the likelihood or probability that something may happen. You may state "This is unlikely" or "This would probably lead to a certain consequence." Notice how it is different to state "I could do as my boss suggested." You make no evaluation in this last statement, but make evaluations of probability in the first two.

The second kind of evaluation involves the assertion of a value judgment. That is, you state that you believe something is good or bad, right or wrong, or ought or ought not be done. A value judgment asserts whether your own values support this judgment. To state "I ought to do as suggested" or "The suggestion is a good one" is to assert that one's values give strong reason to think that following the suggestion is appropriate.

To state an outcome or likely impact of a solution is to describe one or more possible consequences of it. It is not to state how likely or unlikely it is that the consequence will occur, how important the outcome or likely impact is, or whether it is desirable or not. In addition, it is not to suggest that, or how, or why, you weighed alternative principles or values to decide which were most important to you. To indicate your opinions on such matters is to evaluate them and belongs in the evaluation stage of your analysis.

The distinction between applying concepts and your own value judgments is essential. Consider the following from the case "The Not So Great Gatsby": "For me to tell Gatsby that my boss has suggested we get rough with him would be to violate the principle of confidentiality by disclosing a private conversation with my boss." This asserts that the solution violates an ethical principle. But it does not present your evaluation of the violation. It does not indicate, for example, whether in your view it is ethically significant in comparison with other ethical principles at stake in the case. The statement does not indicate whether you think the harm done is serious, and how serious it is. It does not indicate whether the harm done by telling this to Gatsby is as serious as the harm that would result from dropping the issue altogether. Nor does it indicate whether you think the violation of confidentiality is ethically justifiable. In other words, it does not explain how you weigh the values in importance. These are matters of evaluation that need to be stated and supported with reasons and that constitute the seventh, evaluation stage of the RESOLVEDD strategy.

To evaluate, then, is to present your opinion either of what is likely or unlikely to happen or of what is right, wrong, good, bad, important, insignificant, or ethically justifiable or unjustifiable and why. It is to begin to develop your own point of view after you have clarified the facts and principles that are relevant to the case. It requires that you make judgments of probability and value judgments and then present the reasoning or evidence in support of them.

It is essential to note that every decision requires that you state reasons why you reject certain possible main solutions or options in the case. These reasons support evaluations of why you think some options are less preferable than others. You cannot make a decision to do something without first having good reasons why the alternatives are less satisfactory. Every decision requires more than simply some reasons why it is best. You must show why the alternatives are not as good. A decision that fails to establish why the alternatives are less satisfactory is fundamentally irresponsible and untrustworthy. This point is addressed further in section 4.9.

4.5 AVOIDING MORAL ARITHMETIC: ETHICS IS QUALITATIVE

In the process of evaluating, you may be tempted to take a shortcut that is best viewed as unhelpful and misleading. The temptation is to count the values upheld and the values violated by each main solution and then decide that the solution that upholds the most values or violates the fewest values, or upholds the greatest number of net values, is the best. This procedure, which may be described as ***moral arithmetic***, is seriously misleading.

To simply count the number of values upheld and the number violated assumes that each value upheld or violated is of equal importance in ethical and other relevant ways. This, however, is not usually the case. In a particular situation, a violation of confidentiality might not be as ethically significant as a violation of some other value. Indeed, it is possible that one solution could violate a single ethical principle while another violates many, and that the first solution is still the worse of the two. Which is worse will depend upon the context, how and why each value or set of values is violated, and the significance of that value or set of values to you.

Ethics, like many subjects, is a *qualitative* discipline. This means that ethics cannot be quantified. That is, mathematical methods of analysis cannot be applied to it with any advantage. The reason this is true is that right and wrong, good and bad, are not comprised of equal units that can be numbered. Questions of finance and economics are answered by reference to amounts of money, where every dollar is equal in value. Something that is wrong is not wrong because it is lacking in quantities of anything that can be counted in such discrete units.

4.6 MORAL AND OTHER IDEALS ARE RARELY HELPFUL

The discussion of ethical values in Chapter 2 omits consideration of a whole group of important ethical principles described by the philosopher Bernard Gert as ***ideals***.* An ideal is a moral principle that encourages us to seek to improve the world by striving to reduce the presence of evil. Ideals express high values to which some people aspire, yet which they recognize as difficult to realize fully. For every moral or ethical rule, there is a corresponding ideal. For the moral rule that one should not harm people (the principle of do no harm), there is a moral ideal that you should try to help people (the principle of beneficence), and thus act to relieve pain. For the moral rule that you should not break your promises (the principle of fidelity), there is the moral ideal that you should act to help people resist breaking their promises. For the moral rule that you should not deceive people (the principle of honesty), there is the ideal that you should act to prevent deception. In general, rules require you to avoid doing wrong, whereas ideals encourage you to try to perform good deeds.

Advocates of an ideal take it very seriously, often to the point of believing that it embodies the very highest value to which a human being can aspire. They may even view it as essential to a meaningful life. Ideals may be important sources of personal motivation.

Ideals may be thought of as defining a moral maximum, while rules define a moral minimum. To violate a moral rule is to do something that is, ordinarily, wrong. However, you cannot, properly speaking, violate a moral ideal. You may fail to live up to its strong demands, and thus fall short of a high and worthy goal. But in doing so, you do not necessarily act wrongly. You can sometimes avoid opportunities to

---

*Bernard Gert, *Morality: A New Justification of the Moral Rules* (New York: Oxford University Press, 1988).

help others without actually hurting them. From an ethical perspective, it is bad to hurt people, but not always bad not to help them. To this extent, you are ethically required to follow moral rules, but not moral ideals.

Although moral ideals may express our highest moral aspirations, they do not necessarily express more important values than moral rules. It may be worse to violate a moral rule than a moral ideal. If it is wrong to murder people, then it may not be justifiable to do so in order to make the world a better place by eliminating a terrorist. Acting to uphold a moral ideal ordinarily does not negate the wrong done by violating a moral rule. In the end, a deed that violates a moral rule usually does more harm than the amount of good that results from the extent to which the deed upholds a moral ideal.

There are, of course, other kinds of ideals, such as religious or political ideals. Some of the relationships among these other ideals and other corresponding religious, political, and other principles are similar to the relationship among moral ideals and moral rules mentioned here. Consider the Christian ideal expressed in the Golden Rule (do unto others as you would have them do unto you). Although a Christian believes that people should strive to follow the Golden Rule, Christians generally do not view the failure to do so as being seriously wrong to the level of murder or stealing (both forbidden by the Ten Commandments).

Osama bin Laden serves as a case in point. He stated in a speech to his followers in 1998, three years before the attacks on the World Trade Center of 9/11/01, "The call to wage war against America was made because America has spearheaded the crusade against the Islamic nation." His denomination of Wahabi radical Islam maintained that terrorist acts were a fully justified means of striking back against aggression by Western nations aimed at Islamic peoples. He and his followers elevated these terrorist attacks to the level of a religious and moral ideal, based on noble motives, maintaining that Allah, their god, would reward the attackers as martyrs.

Moderate Moslem leaders pointed out the extremist and unjustifiable nature of bin Laden's position. An ideal, no matter how strongly believed, and based on the most extreme self-sacrifice, cannot justify violations of the law, moral rules, and other ethical principles. There is no denying that religious, moral, or political ideals may be more important for some individuals than their moral or other corresponding rules. However, those who violate moral rules in order to uphold their cherished ideals often seem to do so from a partly blind enthusiasm that disregards the value of other individuals.

Those who seek to uphold an ideal, and in doing so violate a moral rule, are sometimes referred to as **fanatics**. A fanatic is a person who does what is ethically wrong in order to uphold some ideal or cause in a way that is not ethically justifiable. Fanatics are willing to sacrifice anything for their ideals, no matter how extreme the ideal or how terrible the sacrifice.

Although your ideals may be important to you, this should not reduce your respect for the interests of others embodied in the principle of equal consideration of interests, that we should not treat the interests of others as less important than our own. This most basic principle of ethics is both an ideal and a requirement of all who seek to live good lives. There has been no coherent basis offered for the view that ideals provide sound justification for violating ECI.

Consideration of moral and other ideals has been deferred until now because they are rarely helpful in resolving personal ethical problems. People differ greatly in their interpretations of such ideals, and in their views of proper implementation. Such diversity does not prove any one version of these ideals to be mistaken, or less important than another. However, the ideals should be treated with caution and not assumed, without careful consideration, to justify violation of other moral or ethical principles or ECI. Insofar as rules, rights, and other values effectively implement ECI, these should be taken very seriously before they are sacrificed to do what appears to follow some moral, religious, political, or other ideal.

There is one kind of situation in which you may find it helpful to consider the extent to which a given decision fulfills one of your important ideals. This may occur when you find that all other ethical considerations in the case are evenly balanced for and against two or more alternatives. That is, if there is no other compelling reason to do one thing or another, but one of your important ideals favors a certain decision, and does so in a way consistent with ECI, then that ideal gives you good reason to choose that decision.

4.7 CONSCIENCE AND INTUITIONS

Most people who truly desire to act ethically have a conscience. To have a conscience is to have the inclination to feel guilty for doing something wrong. A conscience can play an important role in your life, in that you probably want to avoid violating what it tells you. Your conscience at times serves you as an indicator of right and wrong. That is, you sometimes have a clear intuition, feeling, or sense that a certain course of action is wrong, although you do not yet clearly or consciously know why. Such intuitions are useful, as they help us make up our minds in situations when there is too little time and a split-second decision is needed. However, it is important not to rely too heavily on our conscience or intuitions, because they are not foolproof. Many times the content of intuitions and "pangs of conscience" are not clear or coherent, and other times such hunches are misleading.

Conscience may be thought of as a red flag, a warning sign that perhaps something is not quite right. You should take the warning flag seriously as an indicator that you need to consider carefully the situation in which it was raised. However, you must still decide for yourself what to do, and whether conscience truly does indicate the best course of action. Further reflection and analysis may be necessary in order to determine just what your "pang of conscience" really does indicate, and if the verdict of your conscience or intuitions is correct.

The best way to make a decision is to consider all sides of the case, weigh the import of all possible outcomes, likely impacts on people's lives, and relevant values, then choose in light of these. The RESOLVEDD strategy will help you to conduct that investigation on your own, given adequate time. Use of the strategy will likely help you develop your ability to analyze personal ethical problems, and thus strengthen your powers of intuition and conscience.

It is important, however, that you do not cite your conscience or intuitions as reasons that favor or oppose a given decision. Conscience and intuitions are vague; their apparent content needs to be questioned, analyzed, and evaluated as much as any other voice to which we listen. Moreover, reliance upon your personal intuitions can lead you into relativism and subjectivism, both of which are questionable sources of moral justification. Use of the RESOLVEDD strategy should sharpen your powers of intuition and conscience, and teach you not to be guided blindly by them.

4.8 DEFENDING YOUR DECISION AGAINST REMAINING OBJECTIONS

The last step in your analysis is to state the most significant weaknesses of your decision and defend that decision against them. The specific nature of a significant weakness depends upon the particulars of the case. Perhaps you have been overly optimistic in thinking your decision will resolve a certain practical problem in the case. Or perhaps your decision violates some important principle for a less important reason. You may have underrated the odds that a given outcome would materialize or that a person's life would be affected in a certain way. On the other hand, you may have overlooked another solution offering more advantages than your stated decision.

If you identify an objection to your decision that is so serious that you cannot adequately defend your decision, you may need to go back and reconsider other possible options, reformulate your decision, or possibly reexamine your evaluations. Your task is not finished until you have established, to the best of your ability, that your decision is the best one possible in the case, all things considered. You should try to show that the weakness either is not as significant as it seemed or is outweighed by the strengths of your solution. But if you cannot do either, you must reconsider your options.

This final step is in many ways the most difficult for students who are not used to questioning their own conclusions. Once you have formulated and defended your decision, you probably feel confident about it, and even proud that you have come this far and done so well. It can be emotionally difficult to switch to the role of critic of your own work. Before taking on the task of critic, it is often helpful to let some time elapse after completing the eighth step—let your analysis sit overnight before critiquing it. Time helps give you a better perspective on your work, enabling you to admit that your analysis may have limitations and that others may reasonably disagree with many things you do or believe. Such disagreements need not reflect negatively upon you. Rather, they may offer valuable insights and suggest ways to broaden and strengthen your own thinking.

Another helpful strategy is to tell someone else about the case, show him/her your written analysis, and ask for suggestions. Others could have thoughts, insights, perspectives, or objections you could not have imagined, given your different points of view. They may raise questions you should address. Talking to others helps you be more objective about the case and your analysis. In the effort to carry out this ninth step, you can learn important lessons about yourself and your thinking, as well as the case at hand.

4.9 EVALUATION IS ESSENTIAL: AN EXERCISE

Evaluating is an essential part of decision making. A decision that has been made without evaluation of the alternatives, their outcomes, and the values upheld and violated by them is arbitrary, spurious, and weakly justified. Consider the following decision to be made: Should I report my coworker for her recent violation of company policy? Let's assume that there are two main solutions possible in the case: I can either report her or not.

Now consider a decision made after the following outcome and values statements:

"If I report her, I might look bad, or she might be investigated, or some other bad thing might happen. If I report her, I would violate the principle of fidelity by not first giving her a chance to address the problem. But I would uphold the principle of do no harm by taking steps to protect the company in the future.

"However, if I do not report her, she may make more mistakes, create more dislike of our company, or maybe not make another mistake because she learned from this last one. If I do not report her, I would violate the principles of fidelity and do no harm by not taking steps to do my best for the company. I would uphold the principle of fidelity to my coworker by not doing something to get her in trouble."

Suppose that the evaluation stage is omitted, so that you simply go directly from the outcome and value statements to the decision. You decide, "The best thing to do is not to report her. By not reporting her, I will give her more time to correct her ways, I will avoid violating the principle of fidelity to her, I can talk to her and help her learn from her mistake, I will avoid making her angry at me, I will avoid making myself look like a 'snitch' in the eyes of the boss, and I will promote harmony among our work team, thus promoting workplace efficiency."

There is something very wrong with this decision. Something essential is missing. The decision is based on a failure to evaluate the evidence for the main solution that the writer rejects. It is therefore unjustified, based on inadequate reasoning, and weak. Specifically, you have given some reasons not to report the coworker. But you have given *no reasons* showing that it is worse to report her. And if it is not worse to report her, then your justification for the decision accomplishes nothing.

It is not responsible decision making simply to make a decision and then cite no reasons to think it is a good one. No decision is best unless it is better than its alternatives. Critical evaluation of the alternatives is essential for any decision to be a good one.

Specifically what, then, should be evaluated? *The outcomes, likely impact, and values violated and upheld by each main solution should be evaluated, and so should each main solution.* Consider the following evaluations added to the decision, and note how they add the necessary ingredients for a good analysis:

"The principle of do no harm, which includes the duty to act to protect the well-being of the company, is the most important principle in the case. This principle determines the way in which I should apply the principle of fidelity to the case. I have a stronger duty to uphold fidelity to the company than to my coworker.

"On the other hand, if I report her, this is likely to produce anger and resentment on her part, and thus on the part of other coworkers. This, in turn, will likely isolate and alienate me from the others, and will promote an air of distrust and conflict. It is very unlikely that such a hostile act will in the long run actually lead to better company performance. Employees who feel attacked are well known to make more mistakes in their work. Hostile environments produce low morale and poor work performance.

"In this case, it is likely that not reporting my coworker but counseling her instead would more successfully obtain the best results. After all, I have a good relationship with her, I can discuss my concerns with her, and this can help her to understand the gravity of the problem without her feeling threatened or hostile. So not reporting her buys us more time, creates a more cooperative environment, and opens possibilities and options that would be closed off by reporting."

Exercise: Distinguishing Evaluation Statements

Of the following statements, which are most properly found in the values section (mark these with a V), which in the outcomes section (mark with an O), and which in the evaluation section (mark with an E)? Answers are supplied for the first three.

1. To report my coworker violates the principle of fidelity because coworkers owe it to one another to give one another a chance to learn from their mistakes. (V)

2. If I report my coworker to my supervisor, nothing might happen, or she might be watched. (O)

3. It is wrong to act in such an untrusting manner toward a coworker because an effective work environment requires effective teamwork. (E)

4. Reporting my coworker is likely to alienate me from her and other coworkers.

5. Ignoring the problem violates the principle of do no harm by allowing such damaging behavior to continue.

6. The most important thing to do in the case is to act in a way most likely to protect the company's interests.

7. Company reputation is more important than congeniality with coworkers because the basic purpose of the job is to promote the company.

8. I have a stronger duty to prevent harm from coming to the company than to protect coworkers from trouble because the harm that may come to the company is likely to be a more serious harm.

9. Reporting my coworker to my supervisor would uphold fidelity to the company by my taking steps to protect its interests.

10. Reporting my coworker is less likely to benefit the company than just talking to her in a kind, understanding, and sympathetic way.

11. A good employee would not ignore such a threat to the company's reputation.

12. It would be better under the circumstances not to act too hastily or brashly.

13. I have a good relationship with my coworker.

14. Reporting my coworker may result in a hostile environment.

15. Hostile environments at work cause worker conflicts.

16. A hostile environment may result in a lot of poor performance by other workers.

17. Hostile environments at work make poor workplaces.

4.10 TIPS AND REMINDERS FOR WRITING A CASE ANALYSIS

When you are writing a fully developed RESOLVEDD paper, keep the following in mind:

1. In the *review* section, be sure to state important and relevant facts that contribute to the ethical problem in the case. Do not try merely to paraphrase the case study. List and clarify the significant facts that the reader needs to know to understand how and why the conflict occurs.

2. In the *ethical conflict or problem* stage, be sure to state the main principles that conflict in order to clarify the ethical aspects of the problem. State at least one main value or principle upheld and one violated by each main solution. For example, it is worth asking, "Should I uphold fidelity to my boss by carrying out the suggestion, or should I find some other course of action that does not violate Gatsby's autonomy?" It is less helpful to say simply, "Should I carry out the suggestion or not?" Recognizing some of the ethical considerations here will be useful later when you work on the values stage.

3. For the *solutions* stage, it is important to understand that you are merely listing the main options available without all of the possible details. Given variations of detail, each main solution might be divided into many specific possible solutions. Such detail would quickly become unmanageable and too complex to facilitate well-reasoned decisions. The main solutions are just broad, general, and realistic ones that will help you begin your analysis. However, it is crucial to remember that you may well end up with a decision that is different in some ways from all of the main solutions stated in this third step. In the evaluation stage you should bring in important details that can be used to create later, in the decision stage, the best specific solution overall.

4. For the *outcomes and likely impact* stages, be sure to be complete and specific. Take account of all parties affected, including you and such parties as the general public and other companies and organizations. Performing a stakeholder analysis may help you include all relevant parties in your analysis.

5. In the *values* stage, be sure to explain how and why each principle is upheld or violated by each main solution. A list of such values or principles without clarification of how they are upheld and violated is of little or no value. It does not contribute to understanding the nature of the ethical problem at issue or of the advantages and disadvantages of the many different options available.

  In practice, it is often the case that directly opposite solutions will have reversed sets of values upheld and sacrificed. That is, for solution 1 the values upheld will be identical to the values sacrificed for solution 2. When running over the relevant values in your mind, you should start by asking if this is the case, even though other values may be involved. This gives you a working base from which to expand your lists of values upheld and sacrificed. For example, if I were considering not following my boss's orders in the Gatsby case, and considering following them exactly, fidelity to my boss would be upheld by the first solution and violated by the second. The same is often true for the other values involved, though this is not an absolute rule.

6.   In the *evaluation* stage, be specific and detailed about your reasoning. How and why you decide which values are most important must be explained fully. State and defend your own personal views on the importance of both the principles you have clarified in the values stage and the consequences clarified in the outcomes and likely impact stages. It is essential to explain to the reader the reasoning that you used to arrive at your own personal viewpoint as to the most important values and consequences in the case.

7.   In the *decision* stage, summarize the values and other reasons that support your decision. You need not repeat most of what you have stated in the evaluation stage, but you might need to summarize it briefly and perhaps state some additional reasons. Explain in detail how your decision will be carried out. These details are essential to determine how workable and realistic your decision is.

8.   In the *defense* stage, you should state the main weaknesses of your decision and then provide a defense against each weakness. In doing so, you are answering an objection to your decision, not simply repeating your main justification. To do this, you should first, in your own mind, put yourself in a critic's position and focus on the weaknesses of your own analysis. Then reply or answer the objections to show why they are not strong enough to cause you to abandon your decision. If there are truly no objections possible, say so. However, such a finding usually occurs because of your own lack of imagination or perspective more than because you have formulated the perfect decision!

Keeping these tips in mind while you think through your analysis and write it out will help avoid some common faults. Such faults usually result from a lack of depth or detail in thinking and writing. Effective use of the RESOLVEDD strategy requires attention to conceptual detail and to the reasoning you develop. Think of your job as that of providing an argument for your position to someone who will initially disagree with the conclusion. By clarifying certain crucial points listed by the RESOLVEDD strategy, you are presenting the reader with enough reasons to change his or her mind and accept your conclusion. Attention to the details of your position and your thinking will help you develop a strong, justified position that can withstand even the most serious criticism.

CHAPTER 5

TWO ANALYSES OF PERSONAL ETHICAL PROBLEMS

Following are two personal ethical problems accompanied by analyses illustrating some different applications of the RESOLVEDD strategy. The first analysis includes the titles for each stage of the RESOLVEDD strategy; the second shows how an analysis need not include the headings, but can use transition sentences to indicate to the reader the stage of the analysis. The use of titles is perhaps useful for students beginning to use the RESOLVEDD strategy, and a straight narrative style without titles may be more suitable for advanced writers.

The reader will notice that in both analyses, O, L, and V are grouped together for each main solution. That is, we have listed O, L, and V for the first main solution and then for the second, rather than listing O for the first main solution and then for the second, L for the first and then for the second, and V for the first and then for the second. Because this latter order is too confusing to read, we suggest the order exemplified here and in Chapter 3.

5.1 MUST A REPORTER BE A GHOUL?

You have been hired as a new trainee for the local newspaper, the *Ripton Daily Centurion*. Ripton is a rural town of 12,000 people, and the *Centurion* has a readership of just over 15,000 in the broader area. Surely not the *New York Times*, the *Centurion* is a good small-town paper with a fine record of covering the news and some journalism awards to its credit.

It was your interest in writing that led you to consider journalism as a first full-time job after finishing college. Your father had introduced you to a golf partner who was the editor of the *Centurion*. An interview, examination of your records, and letters of recommendation led to your opportunity to experience journalism in action.

Your first few days on the job were filled with basic orientation: meeting people, learning how the paper was put together, and talking to reporters. You were next assigned to accompany a veteran reporter, Carl Woodside, on his beat. You will work with Woodside for two weeks, and then move on to other reporters who cover different areas. Joining various reporters was designed to give you a broad view of journalism that might motivate you further. In reality, however, it created an unpleasant problem for you.

Your stint with Woodside began with two days covering a political rally, a town council meeting, and interviews with three firefighters who had been injured in a fire at a gas station. None of this prepared you for that third day on the beat.

While driving through town, you heard a loud crash nearby. You both turned to look as Woodside yelled, "Look! Big accident!" He swung around to race back to the scene. There were three cars tangled in the middle of an intersection. As soon as he parked, you both ran to the scene. Two of the drivers were just crawling out of their cars, shaken and bruised, but not seriously injured. The driver of the third car was on the pavement, still on her knees beside the back seat, head in hands, crying and screaming. A quick look, and Woodside sent you back to the car for the camera.

When you returned, he pointed to the back seat where there appeared to be an injured child, about four years old. The woman was apparently the child's mother. She was screaming over and over, "Call an ambulance!" A lady on the lawn of a nearby house yelled that she had done so. You were not prepared, however, for what happened next.

Woodside ordered you to poke your head into the car's open window and take pictures of the injured child. The mother apparently overheard the instruction and yelled at you, "Stay away from him, you ghoul! If you get near him, I'll kill you! Just leave him alone!" At that, she rose and threw herself between you and the car.

Woodside yelled at you, "Get the picture! Get it now!" You hesitated, caught in a conflict.

"What's your problem, can't you do your job? Snap the damn thing!" As he yelled this, Woodside actually tried to pull the woman out of your way.

Coldly and insistently, Woodside began firing questions at her. "How did this happen? Whose fault was it?"

You just stood there, stunned. As the ambulance arrived, Woodside told you to photograph the transfer of the child to the ambulance. At this point, you managed to carry out his orders. The ambulance raced away, and you spent an hour observing Woodside's questioning of the other drivers, witnesses, and police. Then you both headed back to the office to write up the story.

In the car on the way, Woodside lashed out at you. He said that your job was to follow his orders. As a journalist, you had to cover tough stories. The public had a right and a need to see the details of such a nasty accident. Woodside went on and on, making related remarks.

When you protested that the woman had asked you not to take the pictures, Woodside screamed, "What does she care about the public's right to know? It isn't her job to cover the news. But it is ours. Next time, do what I say or quit this job if you can't hack it, kid."

That night Woodside's words echoed in your mind, bringing out the problem you face: What should a reporter do in such a situation? Did Woodside do the right thing? Does the job of a reporter really require one to violate the wishes of a distraught victim, as he thought? Would a reporter be shirking his duty to act in a more restrained and less intrusive manner? You now must consider these questions and decide whether you can stay on the job.

What is the duty of a newspaper reporter in a society with freedom of the press? You will need to consider the question of the social benefit of reporting the details of an automobile accident and the obligation to your employer. You must also consider the question of an accident victim's rights to privacy. And finally, for this question to be fully RESOLVEDD, you must decide the weight of the personal preferences of the individual who is a reporter. Can you handle this job? Should you stay on? Quit? Is there some other solution to consider?

5.2 AN ANALYSIS OF "MUST A REPORTER BE A GHOUL?"

REVIEW   I am a new employee working for a local newspaper and have been assigned to work with one of the reporters to learn how to develop stories. We came across an accident that he wanted to cover just after it had occurred. There were three people who had minor injuries, but one woman who was screaming about her injured child still in the car. She wanted us to call an ambulance, but instead the reporter told me to grab my camera and snap photos of the child in the car. The woman was very upset and called us ghouls. I hesitated because of this, but the reporter kept yelling "Get the pictures!!" We did nothing really to help either her or the child, but other people had called the ambulance and it took the child away before I could get any pictures in the car, though I did get some of the transfer to the ambulance. The reporter, Carl Woodside, yelled at me on the way to the office and suggested I quit journalism if I couldn't stand doing the job. He maintains that journalism requires being callous and focusing on the story. Is he right about this, and must I be an insensitive ghoul to be a journalist?

ETHICAL PROBLEM OR ISSUE   The main ethical problem or choice I face is whether I should continue to learn journalism or not. Of course, underlying this is the question of whether Woodside is right in thinking that a reporter must sometimes act in a disrespectful and inconsiderate manner in order to report news to the public. Do I have an obligation to the profession and to my employer to be callous and uncaring in the name of the public's right to know? Do no harm seems to conflict with fidelity and the public's right to know.

SOLUTIONS   (1) I can quit and find another job, or (2) I can stay and try to develop the right attitude about stories and focus on the public's right to know and my duty to inform them. There are of course many different ways I might develop the second main option, and the analysis will lead to careful consideration of these. On the one hand, the editor might help me resolve my concerns, and on the other, a further talk with Woodside might help. Further thought and analysis on my own might well lead to a resolution. (3) I could confront Woodside and try to straighten this out with him.

Confronting Woodside might be an effective approach if I were sure it would make a difference. But not knowing him well, and wanting to keep my job for now, it is better not to risk a confrontation. It is unlikely that a confrontation now will do any good. After all, Woodside does have a lot more to teach me. It is unlikely that this sort of incident will repeat itself, and if it does, I will be ready for it. So I will not consider (3) now.

OUTCOMES 1 If I quit, I may or may not find another summer job, and I would have to search for another career. I would not have to do any disagreeable tasks for Woodside or the paper, and I would avoid any potentially damaging further conflict with Woodside or other reporters. My father might be upset if I quit, as would the editor who arranged the job for me in the first place. And it could take months to find a steady job.

If I quit, then I would simply avoid the question of whether or not it is the duty of journalists to act in such disrespectful ways in some circumstances. By leaving the profession now, I might never find the answer to the ethical question about the proper role of journalists.

LIKELY IMPACT 1 My quitting might not affect Woodside or the paper very much, but it might make me look bad in the eyes of my father. It could also cost me considerable income, requiring months to find a new job and a new career.

VALUES 1 Quitting so soon after agreeing to take the job amounts to a violation of the principle of fidelity. I violate the principle of do no harm by depriving the newspaper staff of an assistant and forcing the paper to initiate another search for a new employee. The same principles are sacrificed in regard to my father, too, since I promised him I would do the job and he now looks bad to the editor, which harms his reputation.

If I quit and leave journalism, I would uphold the principle of fidelity since I am not trying to do a job for the paper that I perhaps cannot do well. I would also be honest with the others on the staff by not trying to cover up the problem and my inability to do the job. By quitting, I am not denying the editor and newspaper staff the right to know about my own incompetence. Quitting also upholds the principle of do no harm by helping Woodside and the newspaper staff to avoid a difficult personnel problem.

OUTCOMES 2 If I stay and try to adjust as Woodside describes, I can keep my summer job, earn some money, get some experience, and stay in journalism. On the other hand, I might be even more miserable and find I can't handle the work of a reporter. I might have to do more unsavory assignments and upset more people. Woodside might attack me further, or even try to make life difficult for me.

LIKELY IMPACT 2 If I stay on and try to get used to the job, accepting and taking Woodside's approach, I might learn how to adjust and overcome my reservations. Woodside could realize I was inexperienced and come to accept me. However, I might have to act in more disrespectful ways and become callous and insensitive. But I would be on a career path, and would avoid embarrassing my father.

If I stay on but reject Woodside's crude style of reporting, he might find out and work against me. Conflict might grow between me and other reporters, and it might all lead to a damaging end to my new career. But I can take pride in myself for not giving up, and might be able to overcome such risks and develop a career in journalism without embarrassing my father.

VALUES 2 If I stay on while knowing I cannot do the job well, I am violating the principle of do no harm to the paper by my substandard performance, and the principle of fidelity by giving it less than the quality of performance I promised to give. I would be violating the principle of honesty by concealing the inadequacy of my work.

If I stay and try to adjust to the demands of the job, I uphold the principle of fidelity to the paper, the editor, and my father by giving a second chance to the opportunity they gave me. I would avoid violating the principle of do no harm by not quitting and by continuing to contribute as an assistant to the work of the paper. As long as I try to overcome my problems, I am being honest with the paper, too. If, for example, I stay on and decide to confront Woodside, trying to get him to see my side, I am being honest and forthright.

On the other hand, if I stay on but conflict develops between me and Woodside or some other reporters, my actions might violate the principle of do no harm to the newspaper. If I end up fighting with Woodside, this would violate the principle of fidelity by ignoring the rules of seniority or the chain of command by quarreling with my superior or senior.

EVALUATION   I recognize clearly that until now this whole disturbing experience has in fact caused me little harm, which is an important consideration. The whole thing has been little more than a bruise to my ego! It is likely that others would say the same thing of it. I need to make my decision in this case on the basis of what is most important, not on the basis of emotional impact.

As I look back at the consequences and values involved in the main options, it seems very clear to me that just quitting and walking away would do significant harm to me, the paper, and my father. Quitting and running is generally best avoided unless it is absolutely necessary. It is just too easy to quit. I need to learn to handle tough situations and benefit from my mistakes. I wouldn't want to live in a world where everyone just quit when things got tough. I mean, who could you count on? How would any of us ever improve ourselves? I certainly don't want others to treat me that way. And so I cannot honestly treat them that way, either. Therefore, I will try to formulate a way to stay and still be honest, be faithful, and make a worthwhile contribution to the operation of the paper.

What is especially important to me is the principle of fidelity, to honor my commitments. I uphold this principle best by trying to keep my commitment to the paper, the editor, and myself. It is clear that I have made a strong commitment to contribute in a constructive way to the newspaper while I learn the profession. The principle of fidelity here covers my duty to do so and to adjust, as well as not to confront superiors. I think I can learn and adjust and then, later on, let Woodside know I did not appreciate being treated so badly. This, however, will take time; I need to know him better. Therefore, it seems to me that my best choice is to stay, swallow my pride for the moment, and adjust.

Giving up at this point is not the way people should act in such circumstances. If I were an editor, I surely would not want any new journalists to give up so easily. Nor would I, if I were the editor, want my staff to quit just because of one incident. I know my father would want me to stay, too.

DECISION   I will stay at the paper for the summer and meet my commitments. I will have to get used to Woodside and any other staffers who might criticize my work. But then that's true of any job, isn't it? My plan will be to try to learn from everyone, get to know Woodside, and figure out how to express carefully my feelings about Woodside's handling of this situation. This will happen only after I've been around him awhile, even if in the end I never do actually talk to him about it again. The fidelity I owe to the paper, the editor, Woodside, my father, and to do my best are the overriding considerations now. The harm done by quitting or confronting Woodside just isn't worth the benefit I would get out of doing either. If similar situations arise, I will deal with them by being honest and expressing my objections after I have brought my feelings under control.

It is perhaps an irony of this decision that it is clearly the best even though it does not answer the underlying ethical question that motivated my consideration of the whole case. That is, my decision is not based on an answer to the question of whether or not journalists should sometimes act disrespectfully toward innocent bystanders in order to "scoop the story." I can now see clearly that my decision in the case does not in the end require an answer to that question. It is a question that is in this case best postponed and answered later.

DEFENSE Suppose Woodside remains nasty to me and I cannot adjust to him? Perhaps I will be miserable. But there is no reason that this should prevent me from learning! I have learned from teachers and professors I did not like, and surely I can learn much from Woodside. My father, moreover, indicated that Woodside is fair even if he does have a temper. And I surely need not like everything about someone to work and learn.

Another objection is that it might turn out that Woodside was right and I do not have what it takes to be a good journalist. It is too soon to draw such a conclusion at this point. I need to give journalism a fair chance before admitting defeat. I need to avoid creating a self-fulfilling prophecy.

5.3 SIN OF OMISSION

You live in a city of about 50,000 people and sell real estate for a local Realtor. Your client, Ms. Bayotic, is single, middle-aged, and a new arrival in town. She is looking for a small house suitable for her to live in alone. You have shown her several houses in her price range, one of which appeals to her because it is attractive, well cared for, and located in a pleasant neighborhood.

Despite its appeal, the house does, to her mind, have a drawback. It is older than she had wanted, and she is concerned about buying an older home. She is afraid of hidden problems in its plumbing, electrical service, or structure that might cost her more in the next few years than she can afford.

You have a strong desire to make a sale. The market has been depressed for several months now, and you have not sold a house in more than a month. Your bills have been mounting, and there is pressure from home to "bring home the bacon."

In mulling over the problem, one thought occurs to you that might offer a solution. You could suggest to Ms. Bayotic that she call the City Hall and request one of their housing inspectors to check out the house and give her a report. Although the city does not advertise this service, it does allow its inspectors to inspect houses for individuals for a fee of $60. The unbiased opinion of an impartial third party might well allay Ms. Bayotic's worries and secure the sale.

The problem with such an approach is that the city inspectors are famous for the trivial nature of many of their observations. When you bought your own house last year and had it inspected, they turned in a long list of very petty violations of city codes. They listed the lack of a handrail on the stairway to the basement, the lack of an overhead light in a hallway, and the lack of an exhaust fan in a bathroom. Although they did not require you to remedy such infractions, you are afraid that a similar list might scare off Ms. Bayotic for insignificant reasons.

You have no clear legal obligation to suggest that Ms. Bayotic look into this city service, nor to inform her that there is such a service. The National Association of Realtors Code of Ethics does not specifically state that one should inform one's clients of such a service. Article 9 of the code states, "The Realtor shall avoid exaggeration, misrepresentation, or concealment of pertinent facts relating to the property or the transaction. The Realtor shall not, however, be obligated to discover latent defects in the property or to advise on matters outside the scope of his real estate license." It does not require Realtors to inform clients of all possible ways in which they may obtain opinions about a house. Article 9 is broadly interpreted to refer to the condition of a house itself and services that the Realtor offers the client. Local Realtors interpret it to refer to facts about the house rather than facts about what one may do to gather further information about a house. Indeed, it is standard practice among local Realtors to avoid mentioning the inspection service to clients, and to sell houses that have not been inspected.

It is clear at this point that in order to sell the house, you will have to promote it strongly. You believe honestly that the house is in "good condition." But you now wonder if you have any ethical obligation to inform Ms. Bayotic about the city inspection service. What should you do? Analyze the case until it is RESOLVEDD.

5.4 AN ANALYSIS OF "SIN OF OMISSION"

I have a client who is hesitant to buy what looks like "the perfect house" for her because it is old. I want to make the sale, but also satisfy the customer. I could tell her about the city's available service for inspecting houses and perhaps set her mind at ease; however, it could lead to her seeing a list of trivial violations and scare her away from the sale. The house seems in good condition.

This is a case that is clearly irrelevant to the law and on the fringe of professional ethics. Ethics does play a role in the case, however, for I must consider Ms. Bayotic's well-being as well as my own. To satisfy my own needs should not be my only goal as a salesperson. In making a sale, I also have a responsibility to help my client.

The fact that other real estate salespersons do not inform their clients of such information does not make it right. Established practice may be a reason to do something, but should not be the only reason. In my analysis, I will need to consider very carefully the relevance of the principle of equal consideration of interests, as I do have an obligation to treat my client in a manner in which I would be willing to be treated myself.

The principal ethical issue in the case is whether or not I owe it to Ms. Bayotic to give her this information. It is the proper relationship between real estate salespersons and their clients that needs to be considered. Do I have a duty of fidelity to tell her? Is not telling her violating that duty or a right to know?

There are three main solutions to the case. First, I could do as my competitors do and not tell Ms. Bayotic about the city inspection service. Second, I could inform her of the service and take the accompanying risks. Third, I could have the inspection done without her knowledge and decide what to do with the information later.

The results of choosing the first solution and not informing her of the service are that she may or may not buy the house, and it is not clear at this point which is more likely. If I try to promote the house strongly, this might work, or scare her off. On the other hand, if she finds out about the service from someone else, she may wonder why I did not tell her, and she may lose trust in me.

The only reason I would choose to withhold the information from Ms. Bayotic would be to facilitate the sale of the house. Doing so would be motivated partly by the desire to benefit myself. But since I think the house is a good buy for her, withholding the information may benefit her. So withholding would uphold my own well-being and also hers, although it is far from clear whether this is the best thing to do in the circumstances.

My withholding this information from Ms. Bayotic would be a violation of the principles of autonomy and fidelity. I would be deliberately withholding information that could enhance her ability to make a more informed choice. I would be making this decision partly for egoistic reasons and partly to promote her best interests. But I would be withholding information that she could use, and would be doing so without her consent. Therefore, withholding would be a breach of trust and would violate the principle of fidelity.

On the other hand, if I choose the second solution and tell Ms. Bayotic about the service, she may or may not decide to use it. And it is not at all clear whether her using it would or would not have a strong influence on her decision. If I explain to her the pettiness in the inspectors' reports, this might neutralize some of her concern. She might also have more respect for me and more trust in me. Whether or not she buys the house, informing her could in turn lead her to recommend me to future clients.

Telling her would uphold the principles of autonomy and fidelity by enhancing her ability to make a well-informed decision and by giving her this relevant and possibly helpful information. It would not violate any important ethical values, although it might arguably be a sacrifice of my own egoistic value.

If I choose the third solution and order the inspection done without telling her, I may have to pay for it myself. But I might be able to persuade the owner of the house, or even Ms. Bayotic, to pay for it afterwards. If the inspection came out well, it might be a significant selling point for Ms. Bayotic. If it did not come out well, I could drop it or decide to show it to Ms. Bayotic anyway. Several options would still be open.

Ordering the inspection without telling Ms. Bayotic might uphold my own self-interest and might help Ms. Bayotic if it helped her to realize what a good house it really is. It might thus uphold the principles of autonomy and fidelity by helping her to decide and by my doing my best for her. The fact that it might cost me some money shows that I am willing to take a risk for her benefit.

Ordering the inspection on my own violates the principles of autonomy and fidelity in different ways. First, ordering the inspection is done primarily for my benefit. She would not be in a position to make any decision about the inspection report unless I decide to tell her about it. So this solution might well be motivated primarily by my own desires, and secondarily by concern for her well-being. And I would be acting faithfully to her only after I had determined that telling her would benefit me.

The third solution, ordering the inspection myself, has serious disadvantages. First, doing so places my own well-being above that of Ms. Bayotic. There would be no good reason to inform her of the inspection unless it turned out well. If it turned out poorly and I informed her I had it done, it would simply scare her off. Second, if I told her about the inspection after it was done, she might wonder why I had not told her first. She might think that I was simply pulling strings behind her back, and lose trust in me. This solution would violate the principles of autonomy and fidelity and risk my reputation. It is best avoided.

Evaluation of the outcomes and likely impact of the first two solutions provides little help in resolving the case. The consequences of neither decision are more likely to occur than those of the other. The ethical values at stake in the case are somewhat more helpful, for the failure to inform Ms. Bayotic would violate the principles of autonomy and fidelity. However, I do not think that either principle is seriously violated by withholding the information. Salespeople are not expected to inform their clients of every possible avenue they might pursue to arrive at a decision. Both the lack of clarity on the matter in the Realtors' Code of Ethics and the standard practice of other salespeople support this point. Moreover, the city does not advertise the availability of the service and seems unconcerned about encouraging people to use it.

The facts that I very much need to make a sale and Ms. Bayotic needs a house are important aspects of this case. My own desire to make the sale together with my knowledge of her needs incline me to be extremely positive about the house. But this worries me. I might be too positive and apply too much pressure and thereby scare her off. I need to be aware of the limitations of my own ability to influence her, and the possibility that the "hard sell" might backfire. The point here is that even my own egoistic needs do not clearly show that withholding the information is the most effective way to make the sale or to benefit myself or her.

On balance, then, there are only two considerations that reveal a significant difference between the two best choices of telling or not telling: the principles of autonomy and fidelity. Withholding the information is a violation (even if only a weak one) of these ethical principles, and informing her of the inspection service is not. These two principles are the outstanding considerations in the case, and convince me that I should indeed tell her about the city inspection service.

I would tell her about the service and explain to her carefully the nature of the report that would result. In doing so, I would not try to scare her, but would simply try to be straightforward, working toward the single goal of helping her as best I can. That way, she can decide for herself whether she wants to use the service. And if she makes the decision herself, she is less likely to be shocked by the results of the inspection.

My decision to tell her does have a number of advantages. First of all, my telling her is more clearly ethical than not telling her. Furthermore, in doing so, there are advantages for me personally. For one thing, I will have no doubts that I am doing my best for her. For another, this can only help my reputation in the long run. Finally, even if she does not choose to buy the house, she may come to trust me and develop a sense of loyalty to me, and ask me to show her other houses. I may end up selling her a house after all, even if not this one.

The only serious objection to this decision is the possibility that she may, as a result, buy neither this house nor another one from me. But the disadvantage of this decision does not point to a corresponding advantage of the alternate decisions. For there is no good reason to think that withholding the information or ordering the inspection myself would be any more likely to secure the sale.

CHAPTER 6

PERSONAL ETHICAL PROBLEMS FOR ANALYSIS

1. VIGILANT OR VIGILANTE?
Is Your Coworker a Clear and Present Danger?

For the past two months you have worked stocking shelves at a local discount store, and you hope to keep the job for the rest of the year. The job pays fairly well and initially seemed to be restful and relaxing. Unfortunately, that all changed last week. You had watched a news channel that was showing a speech by the Director of Homeland Security. He had encouraged the population to follow the advice of the President and maintain special vigilance in light of the latest terrorist warnings and be willing to report suspicious individuals and activities.

The problem you now face centers around Zahir. He is another employee who also stocks shelves during your shift. He has worked in the store three months longer than you and was hired during a time when there were very few applicants for the job. However, unemployment in your area has recently increased, and you know that there is now a long line of people who have applications on file, waiting for an opening. At your store stock clerks are protected by no union contracts; they can be hired and fired at the will of management. Such employees do not even have access to a grievance procedure.

Zahir has caused you no problems personally. He is hardworking but rather quiet, reticent, shy, removed, and reluctant to communicate with you even during your breaks. You have no ill will toward him, but you find it somewhat disappointing that he is unwilling to relate to you. Zahir speaks with a thick foreign accent and appears to be from a Middle Eastern country.

There are two things about him that now arouse your suspicion. First, whenever you both arrive at the store at the same time, you notice that he is dropped off by two other men in a five-year-old car. They also look Middle Eastern to you. Second, at break times when you are waiting at the machine to buy a drink, Zahir often pulls out a thick wad of bills, peels one off the top and puts it in the machine. He then returns the thick wad to his pocket and works with it bulging there throughout the shift. The wad is there every day even if he does not buy anything with it. He seems to have a lot of cash for a store clerk.

A current article you read on terrorism said that a couple of recently identified terrorists have been known to behave in exactly the manner Zahir behaves—lots of cash, Middle Eastern friends, and very quiet. You wonder if he might be a terrorist! You realize that whether he is can be discerned only if he is reported to the local FBI for investigation. You also remember that the Director of Homeland Security encouraged "good Americans" to report people they might consider suspicious. But you feel squeamish about reporting Zahir.

One problem is your immediate supervisor, an assistant manager named Jon Bertch. He surely does not like Zahir; you can tell by his tone of voice and body language when Zahir is around. Moreover, he makes many derogatory comments about "camel jockeys," "towel heads," and "foreigners." There's no doubt that, if he is given the least opportunity, Bertch would gladly fire Zahir and hire one of the applicants waiting for such jobs.

You are so troubled by these thoughts that you actually called the FBI to find out how they would proceed if you reported someone to them. The agent explained that the FBI cannot make any promises about how it would proceed in some hypothetical case, but that they never begin by actually asking an employer any questions about the person reported. That would likely occur only if other attempts to obtain information about his immigration status, work status, or other factors raised questions. They reassured you that if you gave them a name, the person might never learn that it was you who did so.

On the other hand, you know that an investigation might well cause Zahir all manner of inconvenience and that if Jon Bertch became involved in any way, Zahir would almost certainly lose his job. Moreover, Zahir has in fact done nothing you think is wrong. His unidentified friends do not seem like evidence, and you have heard that carrying a wad of bills is actually not uncommon for foreigners coming to America from underdeveloped countries where the banks cannot be trusted.

Yet, will we ever break the many terrorist cells now believed to be hiding in the country if we do not report all our suspicions? But what, exactly, counts as a suspicion worth reporting? After all, it is oppressive and frightening to be investigated, and knowing that the authorities have a file on you often causes resentment and paranoia in the best of people. If Zahir merits being reported, are you going to report every person of Middle Eastern appearance with a little cash? Should we freely make such suggestions to the FBI? You also recall that the article you read indicated that of the last four thousand tips given the FBI in the past couple of years, not one has produced any evidence of a link to any terrorist organization.

So you now have a lot of thinking to do about a problem caused by what you had thought was a relaxing, stress-free job. Which considerations are most important and decisive for you in deciding what to do and get this all RESOLVEDD?

2. IT'S NOT MY UNION
Crossing a Picket Line

The strike at Carbon Manufacturing Company had been going on for about four weeks when you saw the ad in the paper that read: "Jobs, jobs, jobs! Carbon Manufacturing is looking for employees in all departments. High pay, benefits, no union dues. Apply at the personnel department."

Knowing that the Carbon plant was a union shop and that the strike was under way, you figured this was a temporary position with no future. Then a friend informed you that he had applied and was told that the company planned to replace the union strikers permanently. He explained that the pay was at current union levels and benefits were pretty good. The only catch was that the company expected you never to join a union.

Because you needed a job, this all sounded very interesting. However, you were bothered by the prospect of being a scab, and also by the nonunion clause. Your father had been a strong union man and had taught you about the good that unions had done for working Americans. Before unions existed, the pay was low, hours long, benefits few, and there was no job security.

Such poor working conditions, you believe, are a thing of the past, and it does not seem to you that there is still a need for unions. In fact, they seem outdated and, because of their constant unreasonable demands on management, part of the cause of our falling behind countries like Japan, where unions do not exist or have little influence. So, lacking your father's strong commitment to unionism, you are seriously tempted to apply for a job at Carbon Manufacturing.

On the other hand, you recognize that the local union has done good things for your neighbors and that you are a part of the community that has benefited from the union's activities. Indeed, many of your family and friends are members of the union. Moreover, if you sign up as a scab, you could find yourself in the middle of some violence when crossing the picket lines. Should you apply for the job and thus undermine the union?

Your problem stems in part from the fact that you have had nothing but low-paying jobs in local burger joints and grocery stores for the past six months. Your employment problem arose after the closing of the plant where you worked as a maintenance mechanic. You are trained to fix many different kinds of machines, from lathes to punch presses and more, and genuinely resent having to sling burgers or pack bags of groceries. Lately your self-esteem has dropped in direct proportion to your time out of work. Your wife and two children have been very understanding, but you feel as though you are not doing as well for them as you were when you brought home a larger paycheck. The job you are eligible for at Carbon would pay almost as much as you were getting after three years in your previous position.

Although you have not yet made up your mind, you visit Carbon's personnel office, where your interview goes well and you are offered a job. The personnel manager explains that if the strike is settled, you will be kept on in the same position, regardless of whether the union workers return. However, the job does require that you sign a statement agreeing not to join a union as long as you are employed at Carbon.

Where do your loyalties lie? What are your priorities and obligations? Make the decision, analyzing the issues until they are RESOLVEDD.

3. IS THE CUSTOMER ALWAYS RIGHT?
Accommodating a Customer's Political Views
(based on a Business Round Table discussion)

Scenario A. The Vice President

Jessye King was your best corporate business manager, having worked for your company, Woollard Accounts Management, for more than fifteen years. His knowledge of accounting, finances, and the economics of corporations was exemplary. Over the years he had handled some of your most profitable and demanding clients.

Your position as the senior vice president in charge of client accounts puts you in the position of having to handle the first complaint you had ever had about Jessye. It wasn't just a simple complaint, such as "He muffed the figures and we lost money," but rather one that called into question the borders between private and professional activities.

Jessye's job as a corporate business manager was to help keep the books, plan and advise corporate investments, manage a corporation's stock portfolio, and handle other such financial matters for your clients. He had always received the highest praise for his managerial acumen and had a reputation for his expertise. That was why you had assigned him to the newest, and potentially most profitable, account your company handled.

Queen Victoria, Inc. (QV), was a company that initially specialized in women's products of all sorts, from makeup to hygiene. It had recently gone multinational and acquired a number of smaller corporations, some related to its initial product line, others ranging far afield, from the manufacture of campers to children's toys. In all, it had acquired seven different companies in the last three years. Because of its sudden growth and prosperity, QV hired your firm of financial managers to direct its financial operations and accounting. Given its prominence and high-profile success, you assigned Jessye King, your best corporate manager, to head the QV team. It looked like a match made in heaven, until you received a distressing phone call.

Dispepsia Burden, known jokingly as Lady Di, the QV executive acting as liaison between QV and Woollard, phoned you early one Monday morning in a confrontational mood.

"Hello, Woollard Management, what can I do for you?" you said.

"Well, for one, you could can that ass, Jessye King. How's that for a Monday morning wake-up call?" was Di's initial greeting. You recognized her voice immediately, and all those stories you had heard about her being notoriously difficult echoed in your head. So far, you had never dealt with her anger, mainly because Jessye had been so skillful with the account, but it looked as if the time had come for you to do so.

"Well, well, Ms. Burden, to what do I owe this unexpected call? How's the account going?"

"Hi, sorry to sound so nasty on a Monday morning. In fact, the account is going very well, Jessye has done a fine job—financially," was Di's response.

"Do I detect some nonfinancial issues here?" you asked.

"Most definitely. And then some. I cannot work with this guy any longer. Either you replace him, or we take our account elsewhere," she countered.

"Whoa, whoa, what in the world could he have done? He's done a good job, you say, but you want him off the account? Am I missing something here?" You were glad Dispepsia could not see the look of shock on your face as you replied.

"Let me explain. You know that I am very active in the Association of Women in Business and a number of feminist organizations locally and nationally," Dispepsia paused for a response.

"Yes, quite aware. But what could this have to do with Jessye?"

"You must have heard about the march and picketing of the Mistral Club this Saturday? It was in all the papers."

Indeed, you knew of it. The Mistral Club was an old and respected club for men. Most of the prominent men in your community had been members during the 100 years of its existence. "Respectable" was the only word you could think of to describe its history. As a social club, it had taken many liberal political stances over the years in favor of civil rights (it had many members from minority groups) and various political causes. It also took conservative viewpoints on other issues. You had always thought that one of its virtues was that it could not be classified as liberal, conservative, or any other political stripe. It had always seemed that for this club, fairness and objectivity outweighed ideology. So what was your client's problem?

"Listen, I was at that march carrying a sign protesting the 'men only' status of the club. We were marching around the club when what do I see? There's Jessye King sitting on the veranda, sipping a martini! I couldn't believe it. So, I waited around after the protest and caught him coming out of the 'members only' door."

This was shaping up badly, you thought. But you reserved judgment until you heard the whole story.

"'Hey, King, what are you doing here?' I shouted," Dispepsia said. "Are you a member? Well, what do you know? The guy says, 'Yes, I'm a member. My dad was a member, and he got me in.' What do you think about that?" Dispepsia was shouting now.

"I never knew he was a member. It's a private social club that does a lot of good, Ms. Burden, including good for women. I think they sponsored a breast cancer march last year and other . . ." Before you could finish, Dispepsia cut you off.

"Look, that's all window dressing. The fact remains, King belongs to a chauvinist, discriminatory club. I cannot deal with such a person, no matter how well he manages our account. You must have other equally good account managers there who can take it over. Get King off our account—now!"

"I'll talk with Jessye. If he resigns from the club, would that satisfy you?" You crossed your fingers as you waited for the response.

"I guess it would. It would show where his heart really lies. If he did that, I would have to think his professionalism and dedication to QV were beyond doubt. I might still wonder why he was in the club in the first place, but I wouldn't think it affected his professional responsibilities," Dispepsia said, with a hint of hopefulness in her voice.

Later that day you called Jessye into your office and explained all that had gone on during your phone call with Ms. Burden. You stressed that all she needed was a sign from Jessye that he could put business ahead of his membership in the club. Was that too much to ask? you queried.

"Hey, boss, you know me. I do my job well. I'm professional, and I'm good. The clients always prosper with me at the head of their accounts. QV is no different. Did anyone say it was?" Jessye waited for your answer.

"No, Jessye, in fact, Ms Burden was pleased with the account and your handling of it."

"OK. That's it then, right? I am doing my job, doing it well, and the client agrees. I don't see the issue here," Jessye said.

"The issue is that Ms. Burden thinks that she cannot relate to you personally, and thus professionally, as long as you belong to what she considers a 'politically incorrect' club. I mean, Jessye, it's the twenty-first century and this is a restricted club. Can you blame her? I know it's not a company matter and it is a private membership, but would you consider quitting the club? It's for the good of the company and the account, after all."

"No chance. Sorry," Jessye replied immediately. "Don't mean to be difficult. It's just that, first, my dad was a member and got me into the club even before I had anything to recommend me. The club helped me a lot through school, with encouragement, and even a scholarship at one point. I can't quit and say I reject them. Second, it's a social club and not business-related at all. There are women's clubs, sororities, and other such organizations for women that don't admit men, so why is my club any different? Finally, the club rules prohibit doing business at the club." Jessye crossed his arms and looked directly at you.

"I see your point, but the customer is always right, don't you agree? Whether or not you think it's business-related, your club membership includes many of the top male executives in town and gives you an 'in' with them, a place to talk with them, and a comradeship that just isn't there for women in business in our town, even if you never do business at the club. And as an executive, your personal actions reflect on the company's reputation. Social or not, the club gives you access to people who can help you professionally and excludes women like Dispepsia. I don't necessarily agree with her, but I see her point. I think you have to resign, or else I am going to have to consider her request to remove you." You were anxious and hoped that Jessye would see the logic of your point.

"Sorry. I can't and won't do it. The family expects me to remain a member. Even my mother is proud of our relations with the club. It doesn't have anything to do with the company. It's purely social, and if Ms. Burden thinks otherwise, she should ask herself if she's gone too far. No matter what anyone thinks about the rest of it, even the client says I've done a good job professionally. As near as I can see, that ends the discussion. I hope you don't take it personally, but I cannot and will not resign," Jessye said clearly, slowly, and very honestly.

What should you do? Should you remove Jessye from the account? The client says you must, even though he has discharged his professional duties well. Does this matter, though, if the client is willing to take a multimillion dollar account elsewhere if you refuse her request? She does, after all, have complete veto power over the whole account. Or is this a matter of principle? That is, does Jessye have a right to his own private life and associations? Suppose Dispepsia were a Catholic who refused to work with someone who was a Lutheran? Would you remove that person? This is a thorny issue you must get RESOLVEDD and soon, with the account hanging in the balance.

Scenario B. The Account Manager

You are Jessye King. You have just been raked over the coals, as you see it, for non-business-related reasons. Your boss has related to you the discussion with Dispepsia Burden from scenario A and has asked you to quit the Mistral Club you have belonged to for many years. This was after both he and Dispepsia praised your handling of the account!

Mistral is a private social club, long respected, well known, and one that has done a lot of good for the community. In fact, the club helped pay for your college education with a substantial scholarship, as it has for many other nonmembers. Moreover, your father and family all take pride in their relation to the club and would feel betrayed if you quit. You feel as though you owe the club much and want to remain a member.

However, you are faced with an adamant client who has pressured your boss with threats of voiding a very lucrative relationship with your company. Part of you acknowledges that the customer is always right, but part of you knows that your private life is no business of that client or any other. As a private club, Mistral has the right to admit or not admit anyone it chooses, just like the Augusta National Golf Club.

Moreover, the club is not a place where business is conducted, even if you have gotten to know many prominent businessmen there. There is an unwritten rule that club participation is purely social and that business is never to be discussed or conducted at club functions.

But you might now be removed from the QV account against your will. This could harm your future with the Woollard company and with prospective clients. If you fight it, it might even garner public notice. If it happens, of course, you would have to consider a lawsuit to keep your job, claiming reverse discrimination and a violation of your privacy. That, surely, would hit the papers and harm you, the client's company, and the Woollard corporation. For the good of the company, resigning seems best. But from your personal view, your autonomy is being violated, your private life is being used against you in an unfair way, and none of it has anything to do with your handling of the account. Does any client have the right to make such demands? you wonder. You believe Ms. Burden is using her position as the QV account executive to force her political views on you and your company. But she and QV also have the right to take their business elsewhere for any reason whatsoever.

Your boss has given you a couple of days to think it over. One way or the other, he expects this issue to be RESOLVEDD soon. What should you do as a responsible executive and a loyal member of your family, and why?

4. LOYALTY TO WHOM?
Health Insurance for the Few or the Many?

Your company has grown steadily in twenty years from a small machine shop to one employing more than 150 people. Of the original fifteen people you started with, ten are still with the company. It felt like family for many years, and you continued to operate by the same rules that stressed loyalty, job security, family leaves, and a good benefits package for all your people. This reputation was one of the factors that made it easy to hire the best people, keep them for so long, and produce the highest-quality product.

Lately, however, a serious problem has arisen concerning the benefits package you offer your workers. With the costs of health care rising, the move to HMOs, and increased insurance costs for employers, you have run into a monetary and ethical problem. In the past eight years your treasurer, who handles all the benefits contracts, has turned to eight different insurers in order to get decent health care coverage for your employees. Whenever he tried to renew a contract for coverage, the current insurer always backed down and refused to continue coverage. The reason was always the same: you had too many "high-risk, high-cost" employees working for your company.

When the treasurer first told you of this problem, you thought it was just the one insurer who would drop coverage. However, each year for the past eight it has been the same. In looking over your workforce, the insurers picked out anywhere from eight to fourteen workers who fell into the "uninsurable" category due in part to their preexisting conditions. The advice each insurer had given was to release the high-risk people and institute a hiring policy that required full disclosure of every new hiree's past medical records as well as the usual physical exam. This way, each said, you would eliminate the high-risk employees who had either cost the insurers enormous sums of money for coverage, or who were likely to do so in the near future.

The problem is that four of the employees identified by each insurer were among the original fifteen workers who had gotten the company off the ground with you twenty years before. It was true, though, that each had existing medical conditions that had required very expensive care or very clearly would sooner or later. One man suffered from diabetes and kidney damage that required dialysis. His medical bills last year were close to $30,000. Another high-risk worker was a woman who had recurring cancer, requiring a hysterectomy, two other operations, chemotherapy, and continual monitoring. Over the years her care had run over $100,000. The other two employees were in similar situations. According to the insurers, these four people had used up more than anyone's fair share of the health care dollars. The insurers did not want to take the risk again.

Apart from these four workers, there are about ten others that insurers have identified as falling into the high-risk category. Of this group, time on the job ranges from four years to sixteen. Some haven't yet needed care, but have conditions that indicate they might very well become high-cost patients.

This year, your treasurer told you, it had been almost impossible to find reasonably good coverage. He spent months searching the country trying to find equivalent coverage. The best he could do was another slightly downgraded package that meant employees, to stay at the same level of coverage they had, would have to pay an average of $750 a year out of their own pockets. No insurer would offer the same coverage package as the year before. This had happened four times before. The treasurer thinks it may be impossible to find any coverage next year. In any case, the costs to the company of each new package have gone up 40 to 300 percent each year. Next year it could triple again! The company might not be able to afford anything like a decent package, even if an insurer willing to write the package could be found.

This was not something you wanted to happen. Your workers had always shown admirable loyalty to your company, and you had repaid it in kind with the best benefits package available. But these downgrades and the looming insurability problem has you worried. You would really hate having to cut coverage back even more since many workers cannot afford the $750 this year, let alone more next year. Besides, your coverage was always what you thought was owed to your employees. After all, they had made you a success. Without them, you could not have stayed in business.

Discussion of the problem with various managers and workers brought suggestions aimed at those few employees whose conditions had scared off previous insurers. The younger workers, especially, often commented that it seemed wrong for them to lose coverage and have to pay extra just because six or eight other employees had special medical problems. One young worker had asked directly, "How come 140 people have to suffer for the good of 10? Is that fair?" This was the crux of the issue. What is fair?

Some of the younger employees thought you should look into easing the high-risk employees out of the company. They believed it could be done humanely but firmly and quickly. Their position boiled down to the old saying, "The good of the few is outweighed by the good of the many." Others said why wait, just give the employees in question two weeks' notice and a month's severance pay, and that's that.

These suggestions struck you as cruel and discriminatory. You understood the resentment, but not the vehemence many younger workers felt toward the older workers. The older workers knew how their coworkers felt, and a couple had even asked if you wanted their resignations. One of those asking was LeJohn Williams, the diabetic, who had worked side by side with you from the beginning and was now head bookkeeper. This showed you how serious the problem had become. Your treasurer also said other "old-timers" had hinted that they would rather quit than cause the company this kind of problem. Two had recognized that a tripling of health coverage costs would jeopardize the company's stability.

When you spoke to the older workers privately, they all confessed that they had no real desire to leave the company and were worried that they would never find another comparable job given their ages and conditions. But is it fair to penalize every worker just because of the few? The cost of the benefits was fast approaching the cost of the wages in the company's budget.

In the end, the decision is totally yours. You could accept the resignations, ease out the rest of the employees in question who did not offer to resign, and then find decent health care coverage for the remaining workers. This might entail demanding access to everyone's medical records to identify all those "high-risk" workers, and making such access a condition of employment in the future. All of these measures seem to be a major violation of privacy, all just to convince some insurer that your company is worth the risk. It would put quite a few good workers on the street, as well. You still think you owe them better. Yet what comes first: the few, the many, the monetary status of the company, profits, loyalty, or privacy? You need answers to these questions to see this problem RESOLVEDD.

5. SO, WHAT ARE THE STANDARDS?
Hidden Promotion Requirements and Whistle-Blowing

You work for Utopia Manufacturing, a medium-size company employing about 375 people, with sales around $35 million annually. Utopia produces various sorts of electrical supplies for the construction industry. Utopia prides itself on its fairness and generosity toward its employees. Until now, you had thought this pride was well justified. However, you now have doubts about Utopia's claim of fairness and openness. You have discovered that Utopia's stated policy for determining wage increases seems to be very different from the actual practices of evaluating employees. While the stated policy is objective and open, the actual practices make use of unstated and supposedly prohibited standards.

You are presently employed at Utopia as a skilled blue-collar worker in the machine shop, where you have worked for eight years. Following Utopia's creation of a student aid co-op program, you returned to school to finish your B.A. in business, which you had begun many years ago before dropping out. Later you completed Utopia's machinist's training program. Utopia is now paying your way toward your M.B.A. and wants to employ you in a midlevel management position once you complete your degree.

One of the classes you were required to take was business ethics. During the course, you decided to write a paper on Utopia's wage evaluation policy as an example of a fair, honest, and ethical business practice. While researching this paper, your views about fairness at Utopia had crumbled.

You had decided to analyze Utopia's guidelines for raises in Area Six, the area where you work. Three friends of yours in management agreed to help your research. You began by interviewing Danny Rose, Area Six day shift supervisor, who was personally responsible for initiating pay raises there. During your taped interview, Danny stated, "The most important thing I look for is attitude and initiative. If an employee has those two, then I will probably grant a raise. I evaluate progress and potential, as well as productivity. But if an employee's attitude and initiative are good, though there may be problems in other areas, I wouldn't hold the employee back."

You also interviewed Celia Weinstein, plant superintendent and former Area Six supervisor. She said, "The supervisor really knows how capable employees are. Unless I have specific knowledge to indicate that the supervisor's opinion is wrong, I approve wage increases. I don't have detailed enough information on any one employee to do a complete evaluation. But I do look for employee dependability. If I know I can count on someone's willingness to be called to work 24 hours a day, they'll get the raise."

Jamaal Rashid, director of human resources, works with upper management, especially the vice president of production, to determine guidelines for hiring, firing, promotions, and raises. He showed you the employee review sheet that he developed with other managers during a brainstorming session, which is used to determine all wage increases. But Jamaal pointed out that no two people are the same. Although the sheet lists only objective factors, he looks for a good attitude and desire to work as the two most important elements in determining raises. Thus, you have concluded that the three people most directly involved in the wage increase process use initiative, attitude, willingness to work, and dependability as the key factors in granting raises.

Although all this sounds fine, the problem arises from the content of the policy guidelines themselves. Listed on the evaluation sheet are (1) Time of Service, (2) Production Rate, (3) Quality of Production, (4) Knowledge of Production Methods, and (5) Continued Training. Each factor is to be rated on a scale of 1 to 10. Each of the five, moreover, is fairly easy to judge, since each involves easily quantifiable and objective factors. Nowhere on the sheet do you find the subjective factors of attitude, initiative, willingness to work, or dependability, none of which can be clearly determined on the basis of observation. However, your main worry is that these standards are all unstated. Moreover, the union contract for Area Six employees states that such subjective considerations are *not* to be taken into account when considering wage increases.

Aided further by other friends in the office, you uncovered a confidential memo from the vice president of production to all evaluators. The memo explicitly approved the *unstated* standards, and emphasized that they should be the most important factors in determining raises or promotions. On the other hand, the policy statement given to the union and distributed to all employees clearly states that to move from pay rate 4 up to rate 3, all that is required is four years of experience. To move from rate 3 to rate 2, one must have, in addition to six years of experience, a job proficiency rating of 8 or higher. To move from rate 2 to rate 1 requires, besides seven years of experience and a proficiency rating of 8, a rating of 8 or higher in job knowledge and evidence of continued training. None of the subjective factors is mentioned.

It became clear to you by the time you finished this research that the company uses a completely hidden set of standards, misleads the union and workers, and does so with the approval of all the managers involved in the evaluation process. There is no question that this practice is entirely unethical.

The question, however, is what you should do about it. You have taped interviews and a confidential memo as evidence. But the memo was obtained secretly, the interviews given by people you went to as friends and who trust you, and the whole project was a result of Utopia's willingness to help pay for your schooling to advance your career. On the other hand, all the blue-collar workers have been systematically lied to and are being evaluated using hidden standards to which they cannot object nor reply should their raises be denied.

To whom do you owe your allegiance? How can you take steps to correct the situation without betraying the trust or jeopardizing the jobs of those who helped you? What, moreover, would be the best steps for the company to take? How could you proceed without losing your job and the education Utopia is providing you? Analyze the situation until it is RESOLVEDD.

6. DECEPTION OR SHREWD BARGAINING?
What Constitutes Unfair Contract Negotiating?

Having been a legal secretary for nearly nine years, you are familiar with many of the provisions of the American Bar Association's code of ethics and various definitions of what is considered fair bargaining in negotiations. Specifically, you know that no material facts should be withheld by either side in negotiating salaries and payments for services. Rule 4.1 of the ABA Model Rules states, "Under generally accepted conventions in negotiation, certain types of statements ordinarily are not taken as statements of material fact. Estimates of price or value placed on the subject of transaction and a party's intention as to an acceptable settlement of a claim are in this category."* You looked this up because you were bothered by the present course of your negotiations with your boss regarding your salary and bonuses for the new fiscal year. In particular, you wondered if it was really fair for you to tell him that you would not accept anything less than an 8 percent raise and a bonus of $1,000 (10% more than your previous bonus), although in fact you know that you would be quite happy to get a 4 percent raise and the same bonus.

Is it a material fact that you are in reality willing to accept much less than what you told him last week? According to your grasp of the law, a material fact is one that, if known to the ignorant party, would reasonably be expected to cause that party to behave differently. It seems to you that if your boss knew you'd settle for less than you said, he would negotiate differently with you and the other partners in the law firm who must approve all raises and bonuses. Legally, fraud is involved if one party has "superior knowledge." Superior knowledge is the grasp of material facts that the other party lacks and that, without being told, the other party would be unlikely to discover.

---

*American Bar Association, 1987, p. 185 in the West Publishing edition.

"Surely," you think, "I am in that position when it comes to knowing that I'll settle for less. My boss can't possibly get inside my head to find this out."

To double-check, you asked Vera Browning, an associate in the firm and a close personal friend of yours, what she thought about all of this. She acknowledged that the ABA's code seemed to exclude your intentions as material facts. However, she pointed out that, according to common law, "If one party to a contract . . . has superior knowledge that is not within the fair and reasonable reach of the other party and which the second could not discover by the exercise of reasonable diligence, or [if the first party has] means of knowledge which are not open to both parties alike, he [the first party] is under a legal obligation to speak."*

Then she added, "But look, we women have been too easy in negotiating here. These senior partners have been taking advantage of us because we are too polite, too timid to play the game the way they do. So my advice is that, where the law seems ambiguous, go for it, play it tough. Bluff and negotiate hard. You don't owe them a peek into your head. Would they give you one into theirs?"

All in all, you are bothered by the conflicting ethics and legality of your negotiations. On the other hand, isn't this all just part of shrewd bargaining? Surely any good salesperson keeps this kind of information under the table when haggling over prices. When you bought your house, the real estate salesman quoted a price that was higher than the seller was willing to accept. You didn't see any ethical or legal problem there. In fact, when you sold some property last year, you had the same salesman handle the account because of his shrewd sales techniques.

In addition, you feel sure that your boss's initial offer is less than he is willing to pay you. So aren't you both just playing the same game? Where does shrewd but ethical negotiating end and fraud or unethical deception begin? According to what you know about the ABA's guidelines and legal definitions, this *could* be unethical or even fraudulent negotiating. Yet, as Vera said, the whole question of what is legal is unclear. Besides, you are sure you're worth the money you asked for, and you are sure your boss thinks so, too. Then again, he's not just a stranger; you've worked with him for seven years and gotten to know him quite well. So don't you owe it to him to be honest? Hasn't that been the key to your successful working relationship? The question that nags you now is whether he has been honest with you.

Tomorrow you have a crucial meeting with him to hammer out the final details of the raise and bonus proposal he will take to the next partners' meeting. What should you tell him? What offer should you make? You want to be fair and ethical, but also want to avoid being the pushover Vera hinted you would be if you didn't stick to your first ultimatum. The problem needs to be RESOLVEDD before the meeting at 9:00 A.M. tomorrow.

7. THE PRICE OF HONESTY
Using Your Position to Dump an Unpleasant Employee

You are the personnel manager for a manufacturing company employing 110 workers. You have held the position for two years and, except for one problem, have

---

American Jurisprudence 2d, Fraud and Deceit, section 148.

enjoyed the job. That problem is a worker, Davis Meany, nicknamed "the lawyer," who falls into the category you like to call the "if only" group, meaning "If only there were some way to get rid of this guy, I'd do it in a minute."

"The lawyer" has been with the company for almost ten years, works as a warehouse clerk, and is protected by a strong union contract. He has an annoying mastery of the details of that contract. It seems that whenever he's given an order he doesn't like, he cites some clause in the contract that gives him a way out. Often he is right, although careful scrutiny would reveal that some of his claims are misreadings of the contract. Rarely does anyone challenge him, however, because of his nasty temper and the fact that it is usually easier to assign the task to someone else.

Meany's attitude and the fact that he stands up to the bosses with impunity has lowered morale among the other warehouse employees. They think they are being forced to work harder to cover for him. On the other hand, whenever management has tried to correct the problem, the other union workers unite firmly behind "the lawyer" and assert his rights "under the terms of the contract." You suspect they are afraid that if the company forces Meany to follow orders, they will all lose some of their guaranteed protections. So they seem willing to put up with all the problems rather than compromise the contract.

Recently, Meany has been coming to work late, leaving for long washroom breaks, and sometimes going home early. The terms of the contract do not allow you to cut his pay unless he misses more than a half hour a day, which he never does. This "five minutes here, ten minutes there" practice has also affected the attitudes of some workers, even outside of the warehouse. They seem to admire his nerve in standing up to you and the bosses, and their work habits seem to have slipped a bit, too. Other workers seem to resent his practices. But since no one will file a grievance, you are unable to do anything other than talk to him about his behavior.

Your attempts to counsel him and help improve his work habits have largely failed. Predictably, he has answered, "Show me the exact clause in the contract that says you can discipline me" or "Where does it say that I have to see a shrink about coming in late once in a while?" You have often felt humiliated by such discussions and spend a lot of time after each confrontation thinking, "If only there were a way . . . ."

The plant manager, following your last discussion about the problem, shouted, "Get rid of this guy! I don't care how. I don't even want to know."

Later that week, you received a phone call that presented a tempting opportunity. Sajid Singh, the personnel manager from a comparably sized company located in the same town, with which you do a small amount of business, wanted some information about a prospective employee. He told you that one of the clerks from your company had applied for a job as the warehouse supervisor at his plant. Singh asks if you or your company would mind if he offered this clerk a job that included a raise and promotion. He is concerned that you not feel that they had "stolen one of your best workers." You are overjoyed when you learn that the clerk in question is none other than Davis Meany, "the lawyer"! You respond by saying, "We would never stand in the way of one of our employees' leaving for greener pastures."

Singh says he appreciates your understanding and hopes you can help him with one final detail. He says that his company has no doubts about the man's capabilities, since he's been working in various warehouse positions for close to twenty years. He has shown that he's a steady and trustworthy worker employed by your company for almost ten years. Moreover, he claims that your company has never had a single complaint about him. However, they need to have a strong letter of recommendation to back up their hiring him because there are two other qualified candidates still in the running, although they're the second and third choices behind Meany.

"What I need," Singh says, "is an honest evaluation of his capabilities, attitudes, and work habits to go along with his excellent resume and successful interview." Once he receives the letter, which is really a technicality, Singh tells you, they'll be making the man "an offer he can't refuse."

Having told Singh you would get to work immediately checking out all the details and talking to everyone who would have knowledge of Meany's performance, you hang up the phone and lean back in your chair, thinking, "'If only' time is here!" Then you wonder, "Can it really be this easy? Should I really do this?" Well, should you? If they're so impressed with him and believe his representations of himself, isn't that their problem? Analyze the case until it is RESOLVEDD.

8. IT'S YOUR CHOICE
Forcing Employees to Leave a Company

You are a midlevel manager working for a giant multinational corporation that has been going through some rough economic times. Out of a total worldwide workforce of 350,000, the company has lost 34,000 employees during the past five years. The company's annual earnings estimate has fallen to below $7 a share, from last year's $10.45 a share, on earnings of $6.02 billion. New estimates for the second quarter earnings are now below $1 a share, compared to last year's $2.45, or $1.41 billion. This continues a trend begun almost five years earlier.

During the tough economic period, the company set up a voluntary program that gave incentives to employees who sought work at other companies. This was done in order to honor a "no firings" pledge the company had upheld ever since its founding decades before. The voluntary program included incentives for early retirement, quitting, and for expenses incurred if an employee took a job with another noncompetitive company.

Upper management now believes there is a problem with the voluntary program. It seems that too many of the company's good workers have taken advantage of the incentives, while many weaker employees have remained. An internal study done by the company's industrial psychology department concluded that productivity was down 20 percent among remaining workers, mainly due to the fact that many of the best employees had left the company.

The accounting department has recommended reducing the workforce by another 14,000 in order to reduce further profit loss. This has created a problem for the company: how to cut the workforce while honoring the "no firing" pledge and still hang onto the best workers.

On your desk is a memo from the highest level stating that a new policy is in effect. The memo outlines a program that allows managers to "encourage" certain targeted employees to leave the company. The memo also notes that many of the weaker employees have been laid off indefinitely, thereby technically adhering to the no-firing policy. However, there are a certain number of targeted employees who, under the terms of their contracts, cannot be laid off. It is these employees that you are being told to "encourage" to leave. Attached to the memo is a list of four expendable employees who work in your department. The list ends with the statement, "You are to convince said employees that seeking employment elsewhere would be in their best interest."

Through the managers' grapevine, you learn that a dim view will be taken of midlevel managers who cannot "encourage" the targeted employees to move on. As you contemplate the memo and the pressure being put on you and the other managers, it strikes you that at least two of the employees named on your list are people whose work you have always considered to be well above average. Not on the list are two people whose work you believe is marginal. No guidelines or reasons are given explaining how the company decided who would be placed on the list and who would not.

The whole situation has you deeply troubled. You think that this is a violation of the spirit of the no-firing policy. Yet you are aware that the best hope for the company's continued economic survival is to cut back its workforce. You are also bothered by the two people on the list who do not deserve to be eliminated and who have considerable value to the company. Finally, you have no real idea of how to go about "encouraging" people to leave jobs they have held, in all four cases, for at least five years.

After speaking to the head of personnel about the policy and your questions, you are still unsure of how to proceed. She told you that it was really up to you how to convince the employees to leave. Furthermore, if you feel that some of the people on your list are there by mistake, you must prepare a memo outlining your objections and suggesting alternate names that might replace them on the list. She also notes that those employees who leave will be given two weeks' severance pay for every year they've worked at the company. But this offer is good only for those who leave voluntarily before the end of the next month. After that, there will be no severance pay for employees who leave voluntarily or who are fired. Your job is to inform marginal employees who want to stay that their pay may be cut or that they may be fired eventually.

It seems clear to you that the company is not simply encouraging voluntary participation. Rather, it is pressuring certain employees into quitting. The token adherence to the no-firing policy seems to be a mere sham. On the other hand, should you fail to carry out company orders, you may well be looked upon as marginal.

There are a number of options. You may adhere to the list, refuse to do the company's dirty work, or come up with some better way of handling your situation. Which is best, and for what reasons? Analyze the case until it is RESOLVEDD.

9. SPYING ON OUR TEAM?
Leaking Trade Secrets

It was a meeting of Gannon Data Corporation's department managers that weakened your trust in the six members of your own research group. At the meeting, the evidence indicated that someone was leaking new product information to your competitor, Plusdata Corporation. It had just come out with a new software application that could do everything your group had planned for your next product—four months ahead of you! This wasn't coincidence.

Gannon designs custom software for specialized business applications. If a competitor hits the market even two months ahead of you, it can deprive you of significant market share. It seemed clear that three years of work by your development group had gone for nothing. Feeling angry and determined, you now began to review the personnel files of the people who work for you.

The third file narrowed your focus to Marcy Patton. There in the file it identified her husband, Terry, as working for Plusdata. At that earlier time, it had not been thought of as a rival company, but one that had previously developed some products related to your group's research. Terry Patton is listed as a "data systems specialist," someone who develops new software referred to as "data systems."

On the other hand, Marcy has been working with you for four years, two before she married Terry, and throughout the present but now failed project. She always seemed completely trustworthy, and you can hardly imagine her telling trade secrets to Terry.

Perhaps it is someone else in the group, a disgruntled employee like Zeke Lesser, who had been turned down for promotion and was job-searching for a while, but with no success. Had he interviewed at Plusdata? You don't know. You wonder, "Should I ask Zeke where he interviewed? Do I have the right to know? What if he tells me to bug off? But what if he says he did interview there? What can I conclude from that?" It didn't seem likely that Zeke would be that sneaky or that upset about his job. But it also didn't seem possible that Marcy could be giving away the information Plusdata must have used to develop their software. Your review of the files indicated that nobody else in the group was really a possibility since they just didn't have access to the right kind of information.

You wondered how you could handle this so you didn't insult anyone, create a climate of distrust, or give away your suspicions. You decided to call everyone, one by one, into your office over the next few days, explain the situation, and see what you could pick up on the matter. Perhaps you would detect some telltale signs of uneasiness in Marcy or Zeke.

During your interview with Zeke, you decided that he was in the clear. He pointed out that he had never interviewed with Plusdata because he had had a bad experience with them during an interview years before. "A bunch of SOBs! Only an idiot would work there," were his exact words. You wondered if he knew about Marcy's husband, but just chuckled to yourself and let it pass. But this did seem to leave Marcy as the only likely source of the leak.

The next day you met with Marcy. After explaining the problem, you asked, "Is there any possibility that you know who could be leaking the information?" She answered that she had no idea at all.

"Doesn't your husband work for Plusdata? What exactly does he do there?" you asked.

"Yes, he works there as a data systems analyst, but you don't think I'd tell him anything about the details of our work here, do you? Sure, I complain about this or that and tell him whether the work is going well or not, but no technical details."

"Could he be putting two and two together and figuring out what we're doing here?"

"Look, Terry's not like that, he'd never do things that way. Look somewhere else. I don't like the insinuation that I'm leaking information or he's spying on us. Do you think he's some sort of secret agent who married me to pry out our trade secrets?"

After apologizing for being too blunt, you explained that this is the only explanation that makes sense, and that you never thought Marcy was leaking secrets or doing anything deliberately wrong. But if Marcy and Terry talk about work at home, couldn't Terry remember a good idea, forget where it came from, and think it was his own idea? "Maybe you'd better just not talk about work at all," you suggest.

Marcy replied angrily, "That's crossing the line. You can't tell me what to say to my husband at home. We relax by talking about our days. If we couldn't do that, we'd go nuts with all this secrecy to worry about. We think of each other as one person, parts of the same whole, and I'm not going to stop talking about my problems with Terry. I don't tell him anything technical about our work. And he does not try to figure out what I'm doing. Zip, zero, end of discussion. If you bring it up again, I'll quit and really take my trade secrets with me. There's no law against that, is there?"

In fact, Marcy may be wrong; her contract contains a "trade secrets clause" forbidding her to take trade secrets to a new employer. But you are getting ahead of yourself; you still need to decide the next step. What are your options? How will the situation be RESOLVEDD?

10. SPYING THE SPIES
Do You Report a Coworker's Personal Discussions?

You had worked at Galesburg Data for almost six years without anything like this happening. It struck you as very odd. Your supervisor had talked to four other workers from your area in the last two days, all very "hush-hush." The supervisor had never called you in for a "heart-to-heart talk" before, but today that changed.

As you left your supervisor's office, you wondered why she had asked you whether you discuss work-related problems with anyone. What was going on? Why did she ask you about your knowledge of what the other people in your area were working on? The supervisor had never raised such questions before. And then she rambled on about company loyalty for almost ten minutes. It just seemed weird.

Sitting at your desk near the supervisor's office, you kept thinking about events during the past month or so. It was pretty obvious something was going wrong. Then all those interviews and questions. Company loyalty? Was someone quitting, taking their knowledge of trade secrets with them?

That's it! That's what it's all about—the new project, Plusdata's newly announced retrieval system. It all fit. Someone had leaked information.

Just as you reached that conclusion, you saw Marcia Poston going into the supervisor's office. Something clicked. You recalled a lunch you had with Marcia and her husband about three months ago. At the time, Marcia had gone on and on about the developments in her work on Galesburg's new retrieval system. She kept asking you about your role in the project, too. You recalled nothing out of the ordinary, just the usual "shop talk." But her husband, Tony, was there, and you now realize that she had told you he worked for Plusdata!

Other conversations ran through your mind, and you remembered at least three other times that Marcia talked about confidential information in front of her husband. None of it was anything more than harmless talk between coworkers, and she probably wasn't even aware of doing it. But there was no denying that Tony was there and probably heard more than he should have. Did Marcia talk to Tony about work-related things when they were alone? How much detail might she have given him? You can't imagine her "selling out" Galesburg, and Tony did not seem like the kind of guy who would be trying to steal trade secrets from his own wife. But it still seems to fit.

Should you tell the supervisor about your suspicions? Is there enough evidence? All you have are impressions and unreliable memories about casual conversations. Suppose you're wrong about what's going on? Suppose you're right about the problem, but wrong about Marcia? Won't this hurt her both professionally and personally? How much do you owe Galesburg or your supervisor? How much do you owe Marcia, your colleague and friend? Perhaps it's best to let the supervisor do the digging and to stay out of it altogether. You are just not sure. To make a decision, you should analyze the issue until RESOLVEDD.

11. A MARTINI FOR ROSSI
Alcohol on the Job and Whistle-Blowing

Edgar Rossi could have no way of knowing that you were looking for him, nor that the reassembly of an important piece of machinery for the production line was being delayed by his absence. The boss did not know that Rossi had not returned from lunch, as he was in a production meeting that had started during your lunch hour. But you had noticed Rossi's absence about fifteen minutes after your lunch was over.

You had just finished working on the roller bearings of the plastic molding machine. Rossi was supposed to help you on the next step when you realized that he wasn't back. This was the last step in the repair, and the other shop workers had moved temporarily to other jobs in the plant. As a result, there was no one available to ask about Rossi's whereabouts. In addition, there was no one present to fill in for Rossi, and you weren't able to do the complicated rewiring that was his specialty.

At this point, your only choice was to search the plant for him. After looking for about twenty minutes, you bumped into Jane Howard, a good friend of Rossi's.

"Have you seen Ed lately, Jane?"

"Not since lunch. I left early, but Ed stayed over at Gillard's with a friend he met there, a guy he hadn't seen for five years, who just walked in as we were leaving."

You decided that you had to check out Gillard's, a local bar and grill that is a popular lunch spot with the plant workers. You trotted down the block, entered Gillard's, and found Rossi sitting at the bar with another man.

"Rossi, come on, we've got work to do—now," you said, after exchanging greetings with both men.

"Oh geez, is it that late?" Rossi answered, with his words slightly slurred and the smell of liquor on his breath.

"Yeah, but Mr. Locus isn't back from his meeting yet, so he hasn't noticed you were gone."

You both ran back to the shop and completed the work before Mr. Locus, the boss, returned from his meeting. However, Rossi was in no shape to do the work as well or as quickly as he should have. So you took over a lot of it and just followed his instructions. As a result, it took much longer than usual. Although the machine was back on line by four o'clock, you knew it would have been there at least an hour earlier if Rossi had not taken his long lunch. As everyone at the plant knows, every hour the line is down costs the company about $80,000. You felt guilty about the delay, though you realized it was not your fault.

Normally, this sort of thing would not have bothered you. But Rossi had been missing last week, and you covered for him then, too. Moreover, other workers had been complaining about Rossi's erratic behavior for the last six months. You had smelled liquor on his breath more than once, a couple of times at the beginning of the day. Although none of the managers had noticed Rossi's absences, your coworkers figured it was just a matter of time.

As you talked this over with your wife, a psychologist, she frowned and then said that it sounded like Ed Rossi was either an alcoholic or well on his way to becoming one. When she listed the symptoms of alcoholism, you pointed out that Rossi's recent behavior fit the mold pretty well. She then said that the most recent statistics she had seen, which were somewhat outdated, indicated that alcoholics cost American businesses close to $55 billion a year in lost production, health coverage, accidents, crime, and welfare costs. Part of the problem, she explained, was that other workers try to cover up for their friends, and the problems continue longer than they should.

The next day at work you confronted Rossi tactfully about his behavior and his drinking. You stated that you didn't know for sure that he had a drinking problem, but that everyone suspected it. He vehemently denied having a problem with alcohol and said you were just "uptight" because of yesterday's close call. He reassured you that it would not happen again.

Things went well for about three weeks. Rossi was always on time, you did not smell any liquor on his breath, and he took no more long lunches. But then, when you were assigned, along with Nick Battle and Rossi, to fix a hydraulic lift, Rossi was absent again. There was no way the two of you could do the job, as it involved holding a large hydraulic piston in place while someone tightened the clamps that held the assembly. Weighing 300 pounds and awkwardly positioned, the piston required two strong workers to hold it.

"Where's Rossi?" Nick practically bellowed.

"I'll see if I can find him," you responded. This time you went immediately to Jane to ask if Ed had been at lunch with her. She said he hadn't, but she had heard him say he was going over to Gillard's with Paul. Paul said he had had lunch with Ed over an hour ago, but that Ed had stayed at Gillard's, saying he was entitled to a three-martini lunch just like the executives. A quick call to Gillard's confirmed Rossi's presence. But this time, speaking on the phone, he refused to return to work, claiming he was sick. By the slurring of his words and his belligerent tone, you figured he was drunk.

"Well, I say it's time to blow the whistle on Mr. Rossi. I'm sick of people covering up for him," Nick said seriously when you told him the situation. "What do you say, are you with me? After all, you've got the facts. Let's get Mr. Locus and get it over with."

Should you go along with Nick? So far, none of the bosses knows about Rossi, and they may ignore your complaint. Perhaps you owe Rossi one more chance, since you can't be sure he's an alcoholic. On the other hand, his behavior is starting to affect morale and has put you in a bad position. He is definitely costing the company money in lost production time. Consider the options available, the values at stake, and address the problem until it is RESOLVEDD.

12. TO REWARD OR RETIRE?
Does Past Contribution Count for Nothing?

You work at a small manufacturing facility as a middle manager responsible for three teams of employees, each with its shop floor manager in charge of minute-by-minute operations. In an effort to eliminate all questions of age discrimination, your parent company, which owns the facility, has eliminated all mandatory retirement policies. It has instituted a rigorous system of regular evaluations of all employees to be carried out quarterly. The local union has approved the evaluations, which are causing considerable extra work for management at all levels.

For the past year, you have heard disturbing rumors about your oldest shop supervisor, Milton Bailey. Last spring, some workers complained that he had lost a number of their completed job assignment worksheets and had then blamed them for not turning in the completed forms after finishing their jobs. This fall, three of his workers have expressed to you in an informal way the concern that he seems a little out of touch, rambling on while giving out work assignments and often losing track of which workers are performing which jobs. Such criticisms have reached your immediate superior, Marlene Burley, the plant superintendent, who has asked you to investigate.

At 68 years old, Milt has spent his entire career at this facility. When he began nearly 45 years ago, it was a small, independent operation that employed less than one-fifth the number of workers it does now. In those days, it produced only one-tenth of its present volume and demanded little technical skill of its managers. Milt worked his way to the supervisory level on the strength of his ability to work well individually with small groups of employees. Since he became a supervisor, Milt's team has doubled in size and his job has grown to require more technical expertise.

Milt's first love is his personal involvement with each job. As he says, "I'm a hands-on guy, not some desk jockey." But the increased team size and technical nature of his work have reduced the impact of his personal touch. In the past, he had always received above average performance reviews and enjoyed the loyalty of his workers. Lately, however, his performance reviews have generally rated his work as "adequate," and complaints from his subordinates, especially the more recently hired skilled workers, have increased.

Milt has been a model employee throughout his career, always willing to work overtime and use his considerable human relations skills to mediate between management and employees during labor disputes. Moreover, when your company was purchased by a conglomerate three years ago, Milt was a moving force in making the transition from independent company to corporate subdivision. It was he who calmed the fears of many workers who worried that the takeover meant the loss of their jobs. He strongly supported retaining you in your position after the merger. In fact, he wrote glowing reviews of your work for the new management. In your opinion, the company, the employees, and you personally owe this man a debt of gratitude. Perhaps it was a sense of this that led management to grant Milt an exception to the mandatory retirement policy still in effect two years ago.

But that was then and now is now, Marlene Burley points out. Gratitude and efficiency are two different things. She has ordered you to do a thorough evaluation of Milt and give her a recommendation next week on just what to do in his particular case.

When you paid a surprise visit to his area last week, you found his performance competent enough, although he did seem to be a little annoyed and unresponsive to a worker's suggestions about whom to assign to a particular job. He also seemed a little distracted and absent-minded, which reminded you of the time last month when he gave rather vague reasons for missing an entire scheduled meeting with you.

You later mentioned the topic of retirement in the course of a casual conversation with Milt, and he was visibly distressed. At first he insisted, rather defensively, that he himself would know when he no longer had the ability or energy to do his job. He also indicated in subdued tones that his job had been the most essential part of his daily life since his wife had died two years ago. For him, he said, retirement was not something he ever thought about or wanted.

Your report is nearing completion, and your findings are clear: Milt's performance is declining, although he has made no serious mistakes as yet. As his absent-mindedness, unresponsiveness, and moments of annoyance increase, he will clearly be losing the confidence of his subordinates. And as they complain more and he ultimately makes a costly mistake or two, the cost of removing him too late will increase.

Marlene has already made her ideas clear to you, saying that it is better to trim dead wood sooner than later. Of course, she has only worked here for two years, arriving well after the takeover. She lacks your understanding of what Milt has given to this facility and your sense of loyalty to Milt, as do his young, technically trained subordinates. Indeed, like many companies in the era of takeovers, restructuring, and downsizing, this one has clearly deemphasized the importance of loyalty both to employees and to the company.

So now you have a problem in deciding what to recommend to Marlene. She has already given you excellent evaluations and has hinted that she will be recommending you for a raise if your good work continues. But what is the best way to handle a case like that of Milton Bailey? Should there be a place in employee policy for appreciation of past contribution and loyalty? And how could one make such a case to today's managers who are under world-competitive pressure to promote the bottom line? These are value questions with important ethical components which need careful analysis and evaluation if the case is to be best RESOLVEDD.

13. THE COST OF HIRING A DISABLED WORKER
Can You Afford Not to Do So?

Marcia Begay, a Navajo woman, was clearly the best-qualified applicant you had interviewed in the last two weeks. You were looking for a good architect to add to your construction company, but you also knew the costs of hiring her.

Marcia was the first candidate you interviewed. She impressed you with her resume and letters of recommendation. She had an M.A. from one of the top three schools of architecture in the nation, six years of experience with two well-known architects, and training in structural engineering beyond what most architects possessed. None of the other candidates came close to these qualifications.

However, there was a drawback. Marcia was unable to walk and sat in a wheelchair. She explained that she could use her crutches, but that she seldom bothered as she was fully mobile in her wheelchair. You did not see this as a problem. The problem was, ironically, architectural.

When Marcia said that she had a very hard time getting into your office for her interview, she expressed some surprise that a construction company would occupy a building that did not have any access for wheelchairs. You explained that the building was more than sixty years old and that you had never employed anyone who used a wheelchair before. She understood, but also said that if she were to accept this job, there would have to be an elevator and other structural changes made. Without such changes she would not accept a job with your firm.

Being an architect, she was able to explain exactly what was needed. As the owner of a small construction company, you knew exactly what such modifications would cost. To install the elevator and alter the existing building to accommodate it, plus the other necessary adaptations, would run over $200,000. When you asked Marcia if she would consider starting before the modifications were made, she said yes. But unless they were done within a few months, she added, she would have to quit.

At that point in the interview process you told her you would weigh her requests when considering who to hire, but that she was still one of your top candidates. Now, however, it was clear that she was the only candidate any reasonable employer would consider. The other three candidates were good, but nowhere near Marcia in ability or experience.

Without the need to modify your building, which you own, there would be no doubt about who to hire. And any outsider such as the EEOC would easily realize that, according to your published and actual criteria, Marcia was your best candidate. Indeed, not hiring her might open you to a charge of discrimination based on her physical condition or even her ethnic status.

It is clear in your mind that if you do not hire Marcia, the reason would be solely because she uses a wheelchair. On the other hand, perhaps it is the fact that she is disabled that makes you unable to afford to hire her. But aren't these really the same? Discrimination for any reason is still discrimination, is it not? The Americans with Disabilities Act also seems to require the modifications to your building if Marcia works there.

The question here appears to be whether you should do what is right at a potentially disastrous cost or avoid what is right in order to secure the future of your business. But it is in fact not so clear that the cost of hiring her would be disastrous or that not hiring her would secure the future of your business. After all, if you do not hire her, you will hire someone else who is less able to do the job effectively. It will take careful evaluation of the alternatives in order to get this problem successfully RESOLVEDD.

14. IT'S HIS COMPANY, BUT . . .
Gender Discrimination and a Promotion

John Damien is the president of a medium-sized printing company that he started from scratch more than twenty years ago. Rachel Lesser has worked for John's company for the last four years and has reached a turning point in her career. At the present executive meeting, she is being considered for promotion to vice president. If promoted, she would be the first woman to reach that level in the company. However, a struggle is brewing.

Rachel began four years ago as a salesperson, dealing mostly with small clients and companies that were placing a single order. She prided herself on treating everyone as if they were long-time customers. As a result, many of the new clients did become steady customers. Rachel's sales expertise increased John's business substantially in the next two years.

During the last two years, Rachel continued to sell printing but also took over a good deal of the office management at the print shop. John had always been a bit disorganized when it came to the details of everyday operations. Rachel began helping with one or two loose ends and went on to cover more and more of the everyday business of the company. John was increasingly able to work with the printers and graphics art department, his two specialties.

Eventually, on your recommendation, John made her sales manager, with a raise and bonus. Although she rarely worked directly with John, who was hardly ever in the office, John trusted your judgment enough to promote her. The company is now running much more efficiently.

You are now vice president in charge of accounts, personnel, and purchasing, having risen to that position over the past ten years. You have a good working relationship with John and feel as though you understand and trust him well. This is one reason for your success in the firm. Now, however, you are faced with an extremely touchy situation.

At the last executive meeting, you proposed that Rachel be promoted to the rank of vice president. You gave a positive presentation that the other three executives found convincing. John, however, spoke up, abruptly opposing it. Due to his position as president, John's opposition was a veto. To your satisfaction, the other executives joined you in objecting to John's veto. As a result, John said that he would consider it for a week and announce his decision at the next meeting. That meeting took place earlier today, and you are still reeling from it all.

John began the current meeting by explaining that he just could not promote Rachel. He was not, he insisted, biased against women. He explained, however, that he had never been able to work closely with women without becoming nervous and inhibited in his job. That was the reason there had never been another female executive. He apologized for seeming to be sexist, explaining that it was not a prejudice, but a simple fact—a phobia, according to his therapist. Indeed, he explained, his feelings ran so deep that even therapy had failed to improve his ability to work with women. Since he would have to work closely with any vice president on major issues, he could not take the chance of promoting Rachel. If he could not work effectively, the business would suffer.

You had argued, at the meeting, that in her new capacity Rachel would not be doing much more than in the past. John had responded that she would be at weekly meetings, be consulted on all major contracts and negotiations, and meet with him regularly for all kinds of things that vice presidents do. At that point, you had suggested just giving her the promotion and raise, without any new responsibilities and without her having to attend the weekly meetings. John pointed out that it would be bad business to pay for a vice president who did no more than a sales manager. In addition, it would be bad for her morale to promote her to executive level without executive responsibilities or privileges. It was better, he said, not to promote her, especially since she didn't know that she was being considered. "No harm, no foul," was the way he put it. "Just keep the whole thing confidential and no one gets upset."

Nothing you said would change John's mind. Although you think this is unfair to Rachel, you can hardly blame John. After all, you think, it isn't exactly his fault. It's a psychological problem he is trying to overcome, and he deserves credit for that much. At first, you accepted John's explanation that he is not prejudiced—he is going on past experience. And the business surely would suffer if John couldn't do his job efficiently. But you were still troubled by your conviction that Rachel deserved the promotion and could do more for the company if she received it.

As you were walking out of the meeting, Rachel stopped you and asked to speak with you in private.

"I heard a rumor that something big concerning me was coming up at the meeting today," she said.

"I can't discuss the meeting at all, Rachel," you said. "These meetings are private. Execs only, you know," the excuse sounded weak as you said it.

Rachel picked up on your uneasiness and kept asking about what went on and how it affected her. She said that if she was being discussed, for better or worse, she had a right to know. What should you say to her—today, tomorrow, or later?

She does not accept the claim of confidentiality. She pointed out that you yourself hinted strongly that something important would happen to her. Should you tell her what happened? How could you explain it if you did? Could she have grounds for a lawsuit? Suppose she asked you to testify against John? There are so many awkward and troublesome angles that you could be caught up in. And how would John react to what might appear as a "betrayal"? What do you owe John, the company, and Rachel? Much will have to be sorted through before you can make a responsible decision and have the situation RESOLVEDD.

15. LOSE IT OR MOVE IT
Is Being Overweight a Reason for Discharge?

Becky Darrien worked as an emergency room nurse at Bigtown Hospital until she was suspended pending the decision by a three-member board of review. The hospital has arranged for a hearing to help the board determine whether or not she should be terminated. You have been asked to serve on the board of review as the representative of Becky's peer group.

You have been a registered nurse at Bigtown for almost eight years and have a nodding acquaintance with Becky. You do not, however, work with her or know her except to say "hi" in the halls. The other members of the board are Dr. Lord, a staff surgeon, and Mrs. Hines, a senior administrator from the personnel department.

The problem before the board involves Becky's weight. She is 5'5" tall and weighs 330 pounds. When she began at Bigtown Hospital four years ago, she weighed 240 pounds. During her preemployment interviews, she stated that she had lost 30 pounds during her senior year as a nursing student because her school had a limit on how much a nursing student could weigh. The school had taken the position that some nursing functions require that nurses be physically fit. Moving patients and administering cardiopulmonary resuscitation (CPR), for example, require strength and agility. Becky had failed to pass her physical during her senior year and had agreed to go on a school-supervised weight loss program, during which she lost the 30 pounds the school regulations required.

Following her graduation, she joined the nursing staff at Bigtown and began to put on the weight she had lost. Now, four years later, she weighs 330 pounds, despite being put on a hospital-administered weight control program more than nine months before.

The hospital, like the school of nursing, has strict physical fitness requirements for its staff. Becky is nowhere near the weight guidelines for someone her height. The hospital rules require her to weigh 230 pounds or less, and she had been hired with the understanding that she would lose weight. During her weight loss program, however, she gained 45 pounds. The hospital administration has decided that Becky cannot perform her job effectively due to the limits on her physical endurance and mobility caused by her weight. The administration has stated that Becky was granted sufficient time to lose the necessary weight, has failed, and it is now appropriate that she be terminated. The termination order has been submitted to the three-member board of review as required by the nurses' contract.

During the early testimony to the board, the hospital lawyer argued that Becky had violated her contractual obligations to maintain her fitness for duty and that therefore the hospital no longer had any obligation to honor her contract, which runs for another eight months. Furthermore, the lawyer pointed out that her weight prevents her from performing her duties adequately in the Emergency Room, where she works. She had, on a couple of occasions, become faint and breathless during particularly long emergency CPR sessions, which lasted almost an hour each. In each case, another nurse had taken over her job while she rested.

The hospital lawyer further argued that the hospital has an obligation to its patients to maintain high standards of performance for its staff. Additionally, some nurses who testified thought that it might be best for Becky to avoid work that makes such heavy physical demands. Thus, perhaps everyone would benefit in the long run from her being released.

Becky argues, on the other hand, that she is fit for her job and is being discriminated against because of a social stigma attached to overweight people. She claims that 45 minutes of CPR would exhaust any of the members of the board, and that many trim, fit nurses cannot go that long without a break. Becky maintains that she has substantially performed her contractual obligations. As far as the violation of her obligation to lose weight, Becky believes that she is an addictive personality and cannot stop eating because of a genetic condition that is beyond her control. You are aware of recent studies that indicate that some people suffer from the sort of condition Becky describes. Moreover, some researchers have described such a condition and classified it as a disease like alcoholism. She believes that since she has no control over her weight, the hospital is punishing her for something she is not responsible for, thus violating her right to just and fair treatment. But you are not at all sure that Becky falls into this category since she has not presented any evidence to back up her claim.

After the hearings and discussion, Dr. Lord votes to keep Becky on staff until the end of her eight-month contract. If she loses the weight, he will vote to give her a new contract; if not, he recommends another hearing. Mrs. Hines votes for termination, rejecting the idea that Becky has no control over her weight. Even if the claim were true, Mrs. Hines says, the fact remains that Becky had not passed the physical required for continued employment. She adds, "Our obligations are to the patients first, and if she isn't fit enough to do her job, the patients suffer." You ask for some time to think before voting.

Yours will be the deciding vote, and you have the evening to think it over. Taking all pertinent values and possible consequences into account, what would be best? Analyze the case until it is RESOLVEDD.

16. SHOULD I LEAVE OR MAKE UP?
Personal Appearance and Company Policy

You had been working as a travel agent for more than a year. You couldn't believe it when you first got the pink slip in your paycheck envelope. You had been fired! What amazed you even more was that the cause was your refusal to wear makeup on the job. Now you are trying to decide whether to sue your former employer.

You have been talking recently to representatives of the Americans for a Free Workplace (AFFW), a group similar to the American Civil Liberties Union. The AFFW had contacted you to encourage you to pursue a lawsuit for wrongful discharge.

To think, this had happened when all you had wanted was a nice job at a travel agency, to earn a little money, meet people, and work part-time so you'd have time to spend at home with your three-year-old daughter. At first the whole thing seemed silly, but as you thought about it, you realized there were a number of important rights and principles at stake.

You took the part-time (25 hours a week) job as a travel agent with Cheapo Travel Agency partly because it seemed to be a moderately sized corporation (250 employees at ten national locations) with a sense of humor. "Just look at their name," you had thought when noting the employment ad in the paper. During your interview it seemed like just the place you were looking for. The managers you talked to did have a sense of humor, had no disagreement at all with your working part-time, nor with juggling your schedule to fit the needs of your daughter. They especially liked your previous experience as a real estate salesperson and your manner of dealing with people. They hired you right on the spot.

There was an employee group, though not a union, that asked you to join despite the fact that you were only part-time and not really eligible for membership. This group did not negotiate contracts or require dues but did consult with management in the making of policies for the agency and its workers. It was the action of the employee group that led to your firing.

This group had agreed with management that the company's image needed to be improved, to have a more glamorous and "European" feel. Most of the improvements were matters of changing the names of vacation packages to sound more European, the decor of the offices, and other rather superficial measures. However, at the suggestion of the employee group's female officers, the company had adopted an appearance standard that included the rule that female employees who deal directly with the public must wear "at least a minimum amount of makeup." Male employees were required to wear suits and ties that reflected current European fashion standards.

You had refused to wear makeup, saying that you had never worn it in your life and were not about to start at 36 years of age. Upon stating your refusal, you had been asked to meet with a committee composed of management and representatives of the employee group. During the meeting, you explained that you had nothing against makeup or people who wore it, but didn't use it yourself and didn't wish to start using it. One of the managers, Mike Redstone, explained that the policy was meant simply to present a "Continental European look" to the customers, thus giving them a flavor of the style and elegance of France, where most women were known to wear makeup. He added that this was the reason the male employees would wear "French-style" suits and ties. Marge Doctrowe, the employee group's president, told you that the idea for the makeup rule came from the group's executive council, which had suggested the idea to management.

"It was our choice, you see, and you are a member of the group, so you shouldn't look at this as something the company forced on you," Marge concluded.

"Do you think I don't look good enough to sell European vacation plans? Don't I have a right to dress and look the way I want to look, so long as it isn't outrageous or harmful to business?" you asked.

Everyone in the group had responded that you are a highly professional worker and an attractive representative of the company. They all agreed, however, that the rule must apply to everyone. When you again declined to adopt the policy, Mike offered you a job confirming reservations and flights, a phone job behind the scenes, but at your normal salary and work schedule. Following your second refusal, the meeting was terminated.

A week later, the pink slip appeared in your pay envelope. You then filed a formal grievance. But the grievance review committee, composed primarily of the same people you had met with earlier, denied the appeal. One member, Bart Lincoln, had been adamant in his defense of your personal autonomy. He argued that requiring makeup seemed to be left over from the old days when "women were expected to be glamorous even on the job."

You suspected that Bart had contacted the AFFW's lawyers, who then contacted you to encourage you to file suit for wrongful discharge. The AFFW lawyer, Michelle Permenter, argued that you should file suit because this is an issue of women's choice and privacy, a matter not just of personal autonomy but of the rights and freedoms of all female workers. You are not sure you want to go this far, but recognize the larger issues beyond your own case.

Should you file the suit? Is this really a serious rights issue, or are you just being stubborn? Are you bound by the rules freely adopted by the employee group and presented by it to management? What are the central issues? How should you react? Analyze the case until it is RESOLVEDD.

17. AFFIRMATIVE ACTION AND COMPANY PROMOTION POLICY
A Company Tries to Foster Fairness

The statistics did seem to support the claim that the company had engaged in racial discrimination in its hiring practices over the course of its first twenty years. In those twenty years PlazTech had hired roughly 600 people, only 15 percent of whom were minorities. This did not square well with the racial make up of the community where PlazTech was located and from which it drew most of its employees. The local population is 42 percent black, Hispanic, Asian, and Native American. When this discrepancy was recognized, the company made a concerted effort to try to correct the imbalance by following its own voluntary affirmative action policy.

There had never been any overt policy of discrimination, nor intent to do so, according to the company; the statistics simply had never been compiled. Once they were, the executives expressed shock at the situation and the affirmative action policy was put in place. Since then, the composition of the workforce has reached 35 percent black, Hispanic, Asian, and Native American. As the director of human resources at PlazTech for the past four years, you were especially proud of your role in the company's response and recent hiring record.

But if you thought you could relax and enjoy the results, you were in for a surprise. During the yearly discussions of working conditions with the union, a question about managerial and executive-level positions became a hot topic. While the union representatives had lauded the company's voluntary affirmative action program, they also pointed out that the ranks of mid- and upper-level management remained 90 percent nonminority. They identified the in-house training program for entry-level management positions as being responsible for what appeared to be unintentional, but nonetheless discriminatory, promotion practices.

The in-house management training program had been in place for fifteen years and had been designed to allow workers from any area in the plant to get training and a possible promotion to an entry-level management position. The nine annual slots in the program had been based on voluntary application, seniority, and job performance evaluations. Over the years it had resulted in numerous promotions, which in turn had led to further promotions to mid- and upper-level management positions. About 45 percent of your management positions, from entry-level to upper management, had been filled over the years by graduates of the program. How could this be bad? As a member of the management group doing the review of working conditions, you were amazed at the union's statement and negative attitude about the program.

What followed opened your eyes. When the union presented its evidence, it argued that although seniority was almost a "sacred cow," and one they could not ignore, the way it was applied accounted for the discrimination in the training program. Of the 45 percent of your managers who came out of the in-house training program over a fifteen-year period, only 4 of 67 remaining on the job had been minorities. That was less than 6 percent! Since seniority was the first criterion considered, and the company had admitted it had discriminated in hiring for twenty years, these two practices had produced a bias against minority applicants to the management program.

"How could a qualified minority applicant, hired five years ago under the affirmative action program, have more seniority than someone hired eighteen years ago? Even with equal qualifications and prior experience, that minority applicant probably would not have been hired at PlazTech many years ago. How could minority workers get eighteen years of seniority if they had never been hired?" The question raised by the union spokesperson was a good one, and one you had not considered before. To use seniority as a criterion seemed to penalize minority workers and apply "unintentional discrimination" to promotions rather than hiring.

The union representative had concluded, "This isn't a level playing field. It gives the impression that the company thinks minorities are OK for the plant floor or clerical slots, but not the office suites. Intentional or not doesn't matter. Just look at the numbers."

The statistics were in fact clear and correct. The rest of the negotiating team, however, was not entirely sure that apparent discriminatory results are discrimination. After all, they said, how many minority applicants to the program had there been? Of the minority applicants, 50 percent had been accepted (10 of the 20 applicants in the last ten years; none had applied earlier), while only 33 percent of the nonminority applicants had been accepted (115 of 344). Surely that was not a sign of discrimination, one manager had said.

"But we'll never know how many minority workers just didn't apply because they knew they didn't have enough seniority or because they thought there was discrimination in the program. Only 20 actually applied, and that's a pretty small number," another committee member noted.

In the end, the committee decided it had to make a good faith proposal. The talks about the proposal were heated and lengthy. The other six members of the committee are now split as to whether the program was, in fact, discriminatory to begin with, and on how to correct the impression that it remains so.

The first plan offered had suggested eliminating seniority as a criterion and merely using job performance and merit to evaluate applicants. But this had been rejected as too passive by doing nothing to correct the imbalance created by the previous program. It might or might not result in a balancing of the ethnic mix. Eliminating seniority altogether seemed likely to meet with union resistance, as well. Something more active, while keeping seniority, was needed.

The current proposal under discussion would keep the number of slots in the management training program at nine. It would also use seniority, thereby hanging onto that "sacred cow" so many union workers respected. It would be active in attempting to increase the number of minority workers getting into the program and later into managerial positions. The proposal was to set aside six of the nine slots for the next five years (the length of the union contract) for minority candidates. The argument was that since only 33 percent of nonminority candidates had been accepted over the years, why not make 33 percent the number for the program? This had been controversial, but was finally left in the proposal.

Seniority, next, would work at two levels. Of the minority applicants, the top six in seniority who applied and had good work records would be in. Of the nonminority candidates, the top three in seniority who applied and had good work records would be admitted. Thus, had there been unfair discrimination in the past, resulting in less seniority for minorities in the present, the new guidelines would eliminate the problem. Minority candidates would be competing only with each other, nonminority candidates with each other.

Finally, minority applicants would be actively recruited for the program, and there would be a public relations campaign throughout the company to convince everyone that the program was fair.

There have been serious, fierce, and emotional discussions about the plan. One argument was about whether or not pitting minority against minority and nonminority against nonminority candidates gave the impression that minority candidates could not compete evenly with nonminority candidates. Another centered around the whole idea of a "set-aside" and whether, given recent court decisions, this amounted to an illegal quota. If it did, would the company face lawsuits and legal actions from nonminority candidates who were rejected, arguing that this was reverse discrimination? A third issue had been about whether or not having 66 percent of the slots reserved for workers who came from only 35 percent of the workforce was any different than having 90 percent of the managers come from 65 percent of the workforce. Is this discrimination in reverse? Questions about whether the minority candidates admitted would be viewed as simply "tokens," or as less qualified because they had had less time on the job, were also debated. Many other issues were raised as the talks continued.

It is now time to take a vote. The current proposal has its problems, you think, but so do any others. With the split on the committee, every vote one way or the other could make a difference. The committee is having one more session devoted to the affirmative action plan for the management training program, culminating with a vote. Both sides, and the union, have made good points, you think. It just does not seem the kind of issue that can ever be perfectly settled, and yet you must make some offer to the union. There is no way you can ignore this issue. But you also want to be fair to everyone, minority and nonminority, do not want even the impression of discrimination to continue, but do want to avoid reverse discrimination charges or lawsuits. There is much to be RESOLVEDD in your mind before the last session when you will have to state and support your position and then vote accordingly.

18. A DAMAGING AD OR
AN EFFECTIVE MESSAGE?
Do You Use a Positive Role Model to Sell
a "Negative" Product?

Your ad agency has been employed by many different companies to sell their products over the years, but none has caused as much controversy internally as this new campaign. As the partner in charge of this new account, you have the final say on what will be sent to the client, or whether your company decides to stay on the account. When you originally took on the account, it had all seemed fairly straightforward. There was no way you expected events to unfold as they have.

Beast Malt Liquor, a subsidiary of a large brewery and alcoholic beverage conglomerate, hired your agency to design a new, "hip" ad campaign to be aired on networks and on billboards in various minority neighborhoods. They said they wanted their message aimed at young inner-city blacks, considered to be their most important customers. This market population has consistently purchased Beast Malt Liquor for years, its consumption is continuing to grow, and there is great room for further growth.

The representative from Beast gave very explicit instructions to your agency as to the thrust of the campaign. You were to aim the ads at young inner-city blacks and especially at upwardly mobile professionals in the black community. The ads had to be tailored to two different income groups, those who had already "made it" and those were hoping to do so but were still locked into lower-income jobs. Beast's representative said they knew this was a tough goal, but that your company was chosen for its innovative techniques. The appeal should give a modern, "hip," "upscale" look to the malt liquor as a way of "upgrading the image" of malt liquor. The representative had said, "Try to make us look sophisticated. We want to be the malt liquor that the wine and cheese crowd would accept. But don't forget our loyal lower-income customers, either."

This had indeed been a challenging task. The creative department had worked long and hard on the theme for the campaign, as well as the first set of commercials and billboards that would be shown to Beast's account executives. The initial product seemed to have everything the client wanted. The first thirty-second film showed a black man dressed in a shirt and tie against the background of a rather bleak inner-city neighborhood. He is, as one of your writers put it, "sitting on the front porch with one of his old homies, sipping Beast Malt Liquor and passing on some good advice." The well-dressed man is telling his pal, who looks barely out of his teens at best, the story of how he got out of the projects and became the first member of his family to go to college. He tells his young friend that college was "cool" and that the education he got now lets him do good things for old neighborhood. The dialogue plays on the fact that the man sees himself as a role model for his "brothers and sisters who want to break out of the hood just like I did." He hopes they can see how good life can be and will follow his lead by going to college.

Initially you thought, "A stroke of genius!" It had the upscale image, an appeal to upwardly mobile black consumers, yet included the old lower-income market segment in the image. Then, too, it appealed to the older age group while including the younger consumers that Beast wanted to capture. And the message was very "upbeat and positive," as one writer put it. What could be wrong? You soon found out.

When the ad was test-marketed in five or six selected cities, there was a good deal of positive feedback, but also a great many negative reactions. Some of the negative criticisms were aimed at the very idea of marketing a high–alcohol content malt liquor to the youth market. This was, as one of your creative people said, "to be expected whenever you market alcohol products of any sort using young actors." You believe that this is probably true. If this were the only criticism, your company could probably write it off as a generic anti-alcohol comment. It isn't the only, nor even the main criticism of the ad, however.

Many of the critics in the test markets said the whole commercial was in poor taste. The ad depicts a positive role model on a mission to show that education is good and can put your life on the right track. Nothing wrong there, the critics said, until you realize that the ad loses all its credibility by the role model's "guzzling a malt liquor" as he delivers it. In addition, many of the critics point to the fact that the messages in the ad—the education message and the malt liquor message—are aimed at a teenager. One comment said it looked as if the "home boy" was doing the safe thing by sitting on his porch and drinking malt liquor instead of "being out on the street gang-banging." Doesn't this look as if the ad is saying that sitting on a porch drinking liquor is a reasonable alternative to other dangerous activities? This was certainly a mixed message, to be sure.

A second set of criticisms questioned the misleading nature of the ad. They felt that it did no better than earlier commercials that related drinking to romantic, social, and financial success. "This is just the same old story—drink our stuff and the babes and money will come to you" was the way one woman put it. Drinkers show class and succeed. Do nondrinkers lack class and fail? A number of comments made this same point. Was the viewer supposed to see that the way to bond with other people or to act as a mentor was through liquor?

Other comments were even more serious. There was one that criticized what looked to be a paternalistic and racist attitude in the commercial. The targeting of urban blacks and other minorities is clearly wrong, given that statistics show this group suffers more than any other from alcohol-related diseases and poor health care. To trade on such a group seemed racist to many critics. Others noted that a liquor company trying to tell people how to live their lives seemed very paternalistic, as if the makers of liquor had "gathered the wisdom of the ages while brewing booze." How patronizing!

You were stunned by the number and ferocity of the criticisms. Could you have so misread the ad when you saw it? Or were these criticisms just the latest statement of the overly sensitive "victim mentality"? Some of the people you had working on the account agreed with the critics and thought maybe the firm should back off the account. They said they personally had never thought about the effects of such advertising, but the critics had opened their eyes. Your creative department was equally shocked. They believed that they were merely trying to show the values and concerns of inner-city consumers. The background images that concerned some critics were not intentionally included, but just showed up on the film. Finally, they assured you that everyone in the film was at least 25 years old and that there were no underlying "hidden" messages. In short, they thought the criticisms were unjust.

After recovering from your initial shock, you began to analyze the situation. You could send the client the ad, along with the marketing studies. They might reject it or accept it. The problem is that if they accept it and the critics do represent the reaction of the public to the ads, the client suffers, your company suffers, and you personally may be put in a position of having to defend ads that have already been called racist and exploitative. There might even be lawsuits filed by citizen groups, especially within the black community. Could your firm and the client be branded as racists? These are all consequences everyone would like to avoid. But is it part of your job to protect the client against such negative reactions?

But if you withhold the ad from the client and they find out, you could suffer a loss of the account and the financial effects of that. This could be a multimillion-dollar account. Besides, you have a very good idea that the client would like the ads, so should you worry about the consequences? Isn't your job to give the client what they want? Could your creative department come up with a whole new approach as quickly as necessary? There are deadlines coming up soon—too soon, in fact, to even reshoot or severely edit the present ads before having to let the client into the discussion. Maybe you should consider just living with the consequences.

As you talked this over with your staff, one member did raise the question of what happens if the critics are indeed correct. That is, what if the ads are exploitative, will convince young people to drink, do portray drinking as much too glamorous, and are racist, at least to many people? Is this possibly going to affect your company's reputation negatively? Are the images and message of the ads harmful, misleading, and an example of using any approach that will sell the product? If so, do you personally want to be associated with them? Does your company? Does this matter, though, if the client is satisfied? Isn't the real moral choice the client's and not yours?

What does seem clear, though, is that some of your own people are convinced that taking the account is a very bad idea. A couple have even said they would not work on the account in the future regardless of whether you decide the company should continue with it. They say they would have to resign unless transferred to other accounts. You don't want to lose these valued employees. But aren't they maybe overreacting a bit? Shouldn't they realize that there are always people ready to object to any liquor sales? If the product is legal and the ads done according to all network guidelines, which this one is, isn't it ethical to take the account?

There seem to be many issues that need to be RESOLVEDD here, both for you personally and as the account executive. What should you do about this already expensive ad proposal, and why?

19. IS THIS DOCTOR SICK?
AIDS Testing for Doctors, Honesty, and Personal Loyalty

You could not believe it when your brother, Carl, told you that he had just tested HIV-positive. You knew, of course, that Carl was gay. But you thought that since he was a doctor, there would be little chance he would become infected with the AIDS virus. Carl had tried to ease your fears with the information that ongoing studies of HIV-infected people indicated that, with the new drugs on the market now, only about 1 in 3 would actually contract full-blown AIDS. You had read, though, that the studies were far from complete, and that some experts maintain that most HIV-infected persons would get AIDS.

This was a long-term worry. However, there is a more immediate problem. You work in Carl's office as the office manager. Twelve people, including two other doctors, four nurses, two receptionists, and two X-ray technicians, also work there. The problem is that Carl has asked you not to tell anyone at the office of his test results. "We especially can't let the patients find out," he said.

"But Carl, the AMA (American Medical Association) has required HIV-infected doctors to disclose their condition," you protested.

"Not quite. What the AMA says is that it is unethical for a guy like me not to inform his patients of his condition. Well, ethics cuts two ways here. The AMA is just reacting to AIDS fears and anti-gay sentiments in the country. Other conditions, even those that are highly infectious, do not require disclosure. What does that tell you? Then there's my privacy. This information is between me and my doctor. My medical history is my private business just as much as my sexual orientation," Carl answers.

"That's true, but AIDS is all-consuming and still essentially fatal. What about 'Do no harm'? Isn't that one of the primary ethical obligations of a physician?"

"First," he replied, "I haven't got AIDS. Second, there's a chance I'll never develop it. Third, I'm an internist, not a surgeon. Even if I were, the statistics indicate that the chances of a patient's getting infected during surgery are about .0065 in a million. Not exactly a high risk, even in surgery. Imagine how low the risk is for non-surgical contacts," Carl said, rather angrily. "Besides, I'm asking you, as my brother, to keep this confidential. Believe me, when I feel it's a significant danger, I'll tell every patient we have."

"That makes it a bit tough on me, Carl. I am the office manager, remember. Don't I have a duty to tell the rest of the staff? At least they should know."

"And if they blurt it out to a patient? Do you know how many ridiculous lawsuits we'd get from patients who have a cold and are convinced it's AIDS? Not to mention former patients who haven't seen me in years, and who come down with something, even test HIV-positive for reasons totally unconnected with us? I've told you because I trust you. Let's just keep this in the family."

For all the reasons you had mentioned, you are deeply concerned about your brother's request. Then again, Carl is right about the minuscule risks involved. The AMA's position is probably overly conservative and may well be formulated just to promote the public image of the profession. Moreover, the AMA has no legal control over a doctor. Many doctors do not belong to the AMA, which is a voluntary professional organization. Finally, there are no federal or state laws requiring it. In fact, in many states there are laws prohibiting a person from disclosing someone's HIV status to a third party, though your state is not one of these. But even if it were, you still couldn't shake the feeling that this is a fact that patients have a right to know and make up their own minds about.

In reviewing some literature on HIV and AIDS, you find that Carl's estimates of the chances of getting infected from a doctor are correct, and maybe even too high. The chances may be as little as .00065 in a million for surgical patients. Only between .3 and 3 patients in a thousand whose blood actually mingles with the blood of a surgeon will contact AIDS. The odds must be even more astronomical for non-invasive procedures. Carl does perform some minor outpatient surgery in the office, but rarely anything more than removing stitches and lancing boils.

So, you wonder, if the chances of Carl's infecting a patient are so low, shouldn't I honor his request? He is my brother, and he did tell me about this as his brother, not doctor to office manager. Family loyalty is a precious commodity. But so is patient trust. You talk to dozens of patients a week who trust you, Carl, and the whole practice to do your very best for them. Don't you owe them something? If only this AIDS epidemic were not such a political football. There is too much misunderstanding and hysteria involved, so maybe Carl is right. But this is not merely a political decision, for there are lives involved.

You wonder if your worries will ever be RESOLVEDD and the basis of your decision clarified. But you must decide, and then live with the results.

20. WORTH THE EFFORT?
Handling Sexual Harassment

Violet Spear had done her homework. But then, she felt she had to in order to know whether or not she should file a grievance against her coworker, Theo Lucasey. Violet did not want to jeopardize her job as a junior marketing executive by appearing to be a "bad sport," "overly sensitive woman," or "hysterical female." Theo had called her all of these in the last few months when she complained to him about his conduct toward her. As a member of your company's grievance committee, you must review Violet's charges and decide whether or not Theo is guilty of sexual harassment.

You and the committee first looked to the legal guidelines on sexual harassment as part of your procedure. Under Title VII of the 1964 Civil Rights Act, sexual harassment is defined as follows:

Unwelcome sexual advances, requests for sexual favors, and other verbal or physical conduct of a sexual nature constitute sexual harassment when (1) submission to such conduct is made either explicitly or implicitly a term or condition of an individual's employment, (2) submission to or rejection of such conduct by an individual is used as the basis for employment decisions affecting such individual, or (3) such conduct has the purpose or effect of unreasonably interfering with an individual's work performance or creating an intimidating, hostile, or offensive working environment.*

While the definition was clear to you and the committee, there were complications in the case of Violet and Theo that made the decision tricky.

Violet had been successful in her marketing position. She attributed this success partly to the fact that her clients trust her professionalism, as well as her knowledge of her job. Part of what Violet sees as important to her professional image is her wardrobe: she dresses in very conservative business suits that are feminine yet reassuring to her conservative male clients. Prior to Theo's remarks, no one had ever referred to her wardrobe as anything but tasteful or stylish.

Theo was transferred from a regional branch about six months earlier and almost immediately began to make comments to Violet whenever they worked together. At first it had just been things like "Very nice suit," but soon he began to add a growl or a low barking noise to his comments. She had called him on this right away, but he accused her of being overly sensitive. The comments continued, and gradually became more suggestive. Again Violet told him to keep his comments to himself. He responded by accusing her of being a bad sport.

The situation reached its peak, she alleged, when once again Theo made a comment about her clothes, "That suit is so sexy I can't stand it. Why don't we go into my office where you can take it off so I can get some work done. You know what kind of work I mean, right?" Violet then replied angrily, "Why don't you just knock it off. Act like a grown man instead of a fourteen-year-old kid with a hormone problem. I simply will not tolerate these remarks anymore. One more and I'm going to have to file a complaint." She felt that she had made it very clear to Theo that she felt harassed and would file a formal grievance if he continued with his remarks.

But, and Theo does not disagree with Violet's report of the facts, he replied, "Don't be a hysterical female, dear. Those business suits of yours really turn me on. I've always had a thing for women who dress in those 'power suits.' I like power. Why not just stop wearing those clothes? Maybe then I'll be able to control myself." Theo argues that he was merely flirting and teasing a coworker. If he were Violet's boss, he says, this would be different and could be seen as harassment. However, he believes that there was nothing going on that could be called harassment, though perhaps he had teased a bit too hard.

Violet had walked away in disgust and began her research into sexual harassment. In the next week she looked up the harassment guidelines and talked to a number of women at her office about what had happened. When she asked what to

---

Guidelines on Discrimination on the Basis of Sex (Washington, DC: Equal Opportunity Commission, November 10, 1980).

do, she received replies that were not encouraging. One woman, she told the committee, said it couldn't be harassment because Theo wasn't her boss and had no power over her. Another said that she had no confidence that any of the male executives would take her complaints seriously. She even thought that some might make sure the complaint never reached the committee. A third said that unless one of the male executives actually witnessed the harassment, nothing would be done. In all, five different women expressed the sentiment that no male executive would take her seriously, and that they would probably believe Theo's comment about her being overly sensitive or hysterical.

"It's the way men are. Must be genetic. No government guidelines are going to reverse 41,000 years of habit," one had said.

Violet felt a little betrayed by the company and the comments, but the terms of the guidelines seemed to cover Theo's actions: the environment had become oppressive. Yet she had gotten no encouragement from other women at the company. She had also come across some statistics that stated that 67 percent of the women who complained of harassment lost their jobs within one year, either by being fired or by leaving voluntarily. The same source stated that only 9 percent of the complaints ever resulted in an end to the harassment.

Despite the lack of support by her coworkers, the bad news, and the opposition, Violet had gone ahead and carried through the step-by-step procedure for sexual harassment claims at your firm. The result was much as predicted: The male executives she approached tried to smooth over the whole thing and had no interest in any formal action. One suggested that he meet with her and Theo to mediate. Another suggested she consider requesting a transfer. Such responses made her more and more angry as she moved up the ladder. Now she had filed a grievance and was presenting her case to the grievance committee.

Violet testified that she is afraid of being labeled a complainer or a troublemaker. She also admitted that she had even wondered if Theo's comments might be correct: maybe if she just stopped wearing those suits he'd leave her alone. She didn't want to compromise her career; she had worked too hard and had done too well to give it up for antics of a jerk like Theo. Her clients responded well to her professional style of dress and had never insulted her like Theo. Would they be bothered by a switch in her wardrobe? Yet if she didn't complain, work would continue to be oppressive, and there was no telling how many other women Theo would insult.

During his interview with the committee Theo continued to argue that he had not intended to harass Violet. He thought that she was truly being oversensitive and that a little teasing or flirting should not be considered a serious offense. He is aware that he can be suspended or even terminated if the committee finds against him. In fact, if the committee agrees with Violet, she could file a legal suit against him as well. He commented that these consequences are far in excess of what might be considered fair. If he had power over Violet or if he had intended to harass her, he might be guilty of harassment. But he pointed out that one cannot harass someone unintentionally.

When you put yourself in Violet's position, you can understand her annoyance. However, when you think of yourself in Theo's position, you can see how he fears being treated too harshly. Some committee members agree that Theo's actions are immature and that Violet has every right to be annoyed; but they do not think that he should be punished by suspension or loss of a job for such comments. They believe that even if he is wrong about Violet's being overly sensitive, he did not really intend to create a hostile environment and therefore should not be punished for something he did not intend. Other members of the committee are firmly on Violet's side, saying that harassment is in the eyes of the beholder, not the harasser. Violet's repeated requests that Theo stop constituted fair warning and should have made it clear that his actions were harassment, whether he saw them as such or not. Therefore he should be punished according to the company's guidelines, which provide for either termination or suspension without pay for a period to be determined by the committee, along with a record to be included permanently in his personnel file. They do not think that opening Theo to further legal action by Violet is a consideration upon which they should base their votes. Those committee members who disagree say that Violet has not been harmed, merely annoyed, and should not be set up to bring even more serious legal actions against Theo.

Your vote is obviously going to be crucial, given the split on the committee. The issues above do raise significant questions. Can you be fair to both Theo and Violet? You consider justice an important consideration and are worried that either decision can easily be construed to be unfair, whether to Violet or to Theo. Moreover, the company's guidelines do leave a lot up to the committee. Is there an appropriate length of suspension? If so, does Theo deserve one? Or does he deserve more severe punishment? How will Violet feel about the company and her job if nothing is done? Will she pursue legal action? Could ignoring Theo's actions make the female employees even more cynical and certain that the company will not take them seriously? Why have a sexual harassment procedure if the company isn't willing to enforce it when a complaint is made? Could the company be sued by Theo if you rule for Violet or by Violet if nothing is done? All of these are important considerations that you must get RESOLVEDD personally and then communicate to the committee.

21. IS NOTHING PRIVATE?
Using Computers to Obtain Advertising Information

After leaving your boss's office at the advertising agency, you were feeling both complimented and concerned. He had offered you a new assignment based on your expertise as both an advertising agent and the most skilled computer user in the office. But the assignment seemed to push the limits of privacy. Of course, there was nothing illegal in the new assignment, and if you accepted, you would need to complete it.

The agency you work for had recently taken on a new and lucrative account with a company called FatAway, Inc. This company specialized in a new, very expensive dieting plan, complete with its own food supplements, diet aids, and medical advisory board for its users. As far as you know, the products being offered were safe and worked for many people. Your problem lies not in the product, but in the advertising plan your company had been asked to initiate.

FatAway's president, Monique Masters, had conceived of a plan to gain national attention for her company. As the ad agency handling her account, she expected your company to follow through on her "brilliant idea." The idea occurred to her as she was reading a newspaper article called "How Fat Are Americans?" This article had mentioned statistics that ranked states by how much the average citizen exceeded the recommended weight for their height. She thought about these statistics, checked with people who knew something about databases and access to them, and concocted her advertising plan.

Access to public information in databases of the departments of motor vehicles across the country would help her get what she wanted: to identify the "ten fattest people in each state." FatAway would then contact the individuals and make them an offer to participate in the new advertising strategy. Those who agreed would be named in a national ad in newspapers such as *USA Today*. The new celebrities would each be given a free membership in FatAway's program and paid a negotiated amount for each pound they lost. Some would be given opportunities to appear in future ads and company literature. They might have the opportunity to become spokespersons for the product and be paid a salary. All this would be contingent on people's accepting the offer and actually losing weight.

"This could make us the best-known dieting company in the U.S.," Monique had gushed to your boss. "And you folks can find the information, design the ads, market the campaign, and reap a huge profit."

Your boss fully bought Monique's reasoning. Given your abilities, especially with the computer, he had called you in and offered to make you the executive account manager in charge of the whole campaign. To begin, you would need to access fifty motor vehicle databases. If they could not be easily accessed by computer, you could perhaps find other ways of accessing them or, as a last resort, purchase them from the individual states. The boss explained that most secretaries of state sell such lists for modest sums to all sorts of marketing firms, and that such information is obviously not considered confidential or private. In fact, he thought that many states' databases were open to access from anyone who subscribed to particular database services. Your company, as an ad agency, subscribed to almost every major service of this sort. Thus, he said, you should be able to access whatever information the states made available legally.

His next comment started you thinking about the ramifications of this information search. He added that you could find out the height and weight of all the people in each state who held driver's licenses. It would then be a time-consuming but simple matter to look for people who were grossly overweight for their height. Then just narrow down the list to ten per state and "we're in business, nothing illegal, nothing shady."

Well, you thought, I can probably handle all the computer work and design the national ads for the newspapers, but do I want to do it? While all the information was public, in a sense, wouldn't this be an invasion of people's privacy? That is, when they gave the information to the departments of motor vehicles, they had no idea that it would be used this way, and many departments never indicated it would. Isn't that a violation of some unspoken agreement? Even if you say it's the states that are violating the trust, is it ethical to reap the benefits of that violation? Then there is the question of publicly embarrassing up to 500 people by printing their names in national publications and making it clear that they are grossly overweight and should do something about it. This seems insensitive at best.

The fact that the people are being asked to consent does not clearly show that they are not being embarrassed. Some are likely to give consent without giving the whole matter full consideration. Other, poorer people, might be unfairly coerced by the "negotiated amount for each pound lost." They might later find that their consent was given prematurely with too little thought and brought unexpected negative consequences.

Upon returning to your office, you did some research concerning computer ethics. One document you checked was the "ACM Code of Ethics and Professional Conduct," the ethics code adopted by the Executive Council of the Association for Computing Machinery in 1992. Among the twenty-four imperatives listed were the following, which seem to pertain to FatAway's marketing plan:

> 1.2 *Avoid harm to others.* This provision includes cautions against undesirable loss of information and also against unintended harm that might follow one's actions. It requires the computing professional to carefully weigh the impact of any actions on "all those affected by decisions made during design and implementation."

> 1.7 *Respect the privacy of others.* This provision recognizes the vast potential for information gathering that exists today and warns professionals to restrict gathering of personal information to "only the necessary amount."

> 1.8 *Honor confidentiality.* The Code states, "The ethical concern is to respect all obligations of confidentiality to employers, clients, and users unless discharged from such obligations by requirements of the law or other principles of this code."

> 3.5 *Articulate and support policies that protect the dignity of users and others affected by a computing system.* Here the unintentional or intentional use of computers to demean individuals or groups is forbidden.

After reading this, you had serious reservations. When you explained your concerns to your boss, he listened carefully and then answered. First, you are not a computer professional in the sense of being a systems engineer, programmer, or any other kind of expert. Therefore, the code doesn't apply to you. Next he repeated the claim that states often sold their lists legally, so they must be public information. If that was true, you were not violating privacy and confidentiality. Then he added that since neither the states nor the individuals on the list were your clients, you could not possibly be violating their trust by using the information you were to obtain. He finally did admit that there could be some embarrassment for the people on the list, but that this should be unimportant if they are clearly informed of what they are asked to do. Furthermore, the offer will probably do the volunteers more good than harm. They will be motivated to try a product that is safe, effective, and makes them healthier.

It seems to you that the spirit of the code's guidelines apply to anyone who works with computers. Privacy, harm, and confidentiality are not the concerns just of computing professionals, but of all workers and people. Yet there is nothing illegal in Monique's plan. As an advertising professional, it is clear that her idea would generate tremendous publicity. But would it be a triumph or a disaster? Ultimately you have to ask yourself what duties you owe to whom.

These issues must be RESOLVEDD to enable you to decide. Your boss expects you to "do your duty," as he said. But what exactly is your duty? And the real question now is what to do in the circumstances.

22. BRINGING HOME THE WAR ON DRUGS
Can You Inform on Fellow Employees?

As a resident of St. Clinton, a prosperous city of about 30,000 people located nearly an hour's drive from a metropolitan area, you are one of many civic-minded citizens who are involved in all sorts of volunteer work that contributes to maintaining the high quality of life in the area. You and your fellow citizens are proud of your public schools, of the many and diverse activities available for people of all ages, and of your extensive volunteer services directed to helping the needy. For years you had been proud that the epidemic of illegal drug use that had swept the nation and the business world had largely bypassed your little city.

But just as change is the hallmark of the information age, it is not always change for the better that comes knocking on our doors. A seven-part investigative report last month by the local newspaper, the *Holy Herald,* has shaken the confidence and pride of the town. You and others have been troubled by the extensive reports revealing that drugs are widely used by children in all the schools, and that they are readily available in the community.

Just as new problems beget new solutions, the *Herald* has in the past week formulated a seemingly innovative and promising way for ordinary citizens to fight the drug trade. The paper's call to action was accompanied by a coupon with spaces for the names of drug users and drug dealers and also to report suspicious activity and license plate numbers of cars involved. Citizens were asked to fill out the forms anonymously and turn them in to the newspaper. The editor would forward the completed anonymous forms to the police to spark investigations, which should make the drug culture more than unwelcome in St. Clinton.

Although a letter to the editor in a subsequent edition of the paper complained bitterly that such tactics would call forth a kind of witch-hunt, many citizens liked the initiative. You have talked to several who argue that the police are powerless against organized crime and that only widespread citizen action can root out the drug menace. Moreover, the accusations will spark investigations, not recrimination of innocent citizens. Only those who are proven through legal means to be users and sellers will be pursued. You, however, are not so sure that this approach is a good idea.

Your objections and those of other opponents are based on your understanding of democracy and individual rights and freedom, as well as awareness of similar tactics used by totalitarian regimes such as those of Hitler, Stalin, and Mao Tse-tung. The civic atmosphere created by citizens who become informants may be like an epidemic, and you suspect that in the end there may be damage to the reputations of innocent people who may have a suspicious appearance such as a long beard or a "spaced-out" personal manner. There are good reasons why ordinary citizens should not seek to become police informants and why police work should be left to the police.

Police investigations are carefully regulated by the legislative and judicial branches of government in order to protect the civil rights of innocent citizens who come under suspicion. Society has made a major value preference in formulating rules to implement the principle that it is worse for government to harm one innocent citizen than to set free a guilty one. If citizens are encouraged to inform on suspicious people and activities, some citizens who are innocent will surely feel the sting of a personal investigation. They in turn will become suspicious of possible informants, thus perpetuating the spread of suspicion, distrust, and strife.

It is, however, not the newspaper that has raised a problem for you but rather the response of your supervisor at Colossal Health, where you work. She is so enamored of the newspaper's campaign that she called a meeting of you and ten other administrative employees on Monday and told you she expected filled out copies on her desk by the end of the week. She plans to give them to the newspaper herself, thus providing a second shield of protective anonymity for those who cooperate and turn in leading information.

"This is an idea whose time has come," she said definitively. "We now have an opportunity to show the nation that caring citizens can make all the difference. And besides, just think what this will do for the image of the St. Clinton division of Colossal Health!" Of course, she neglected to point out that she was infringing on the employees' right to privacy. But you know from former experience that she meant what she said, that she would deplore an attempt by her subordinates to dissuade her on the matter, and that she was entirely capable of harassing any who did not comply.

The question at issue is what you should do in the circumstances. You have many choices here, and many reasons to favor each. You will need to sort them out and analyze the options if you are to avoid some serious pitfalls and thorny complications in getting it all RESOLVEDD.

23. PROFIT AND PORNOGRAPHY
A Family Values Pornography

Baron Theaters Incorporated owns three movie theaters that have gone through some difficult times recently. When the corporation was founded nine years ago by your father, Amos Baron, it was a family business that operated a single theater in the downtown of a mid-sized city in the Midwest. Initially, your parents, you, and your two adult brothers ran the theater and showed the usual mixture of first-run family-oriented films. Two years later, the family decided to begin to show some of the more adult action-oriented R-rated films that were popular. The choice was partly an economic one, but was also motivated by your father's desire to appeal to the widest audience possible. His decision proved to be a good one. Business soared, and within a year the family company owned two more theaters located away from the downtown area but still within the city limits. All three were doing well. But it was not to last.

The downtown area of the city was beginning to lose business to outlying malls, and fewer and fewer people went downtown to see films on the weekends. The downtown Baron theater began to lose money. Since the two outlying theaters were making a small profit, the family kept the downtown theater open. However, attendance at the downtown theater declined to almost nothing, and income from the other theaters failed to cover the losses.

Just when the downtown theater was about to close, your oldest brother, Charles, suggested running a weekend festival of XXX-rated films. He had discovered that the town's obscenity laws did not ban such films. Although your parents initially objected, they changed their minds and told Charles to go ahead. Your father said, "We aren't prudes, some people like such films, and it is the twenty-first century. Why not?"

With some good pre-festival advertising and some fancy promotions of his films as "couples" movies, Charles' idea was a monetary success. In one weekend the downtown theater earned as much as the two outlying theaters and more than it had ever earned in a single weekend through its whole existence. Good old supply and demand, Charles had said to himself as he tallied up the revenues for the XXX-rated weekend. This was too good to do just once, so Charles planned another XXX-rated weekend for the next month.

In the next three weeks the downtown theater did just slightly more business than it had been doing before the festival. When Charles talked to some customers who were leaving, they told him they had only come downtown to his theater because they thought it always showed XXX-rated movies. Charles discussed this with your father and got permission to make the theater permanently XXX-rated.

For six months everything went very well. In fact, it was then the downtown theater that supported the other two theaters, which had started to lose money for a variety of reasons. The revenue from the downtown theater enabled you to keep the other two theaters open and to show a variety of films, including some first-rate foreign films your father had always wanted to show.

The crisis came as a result of opposition from local religious and other groups offended by some of the XXX-rated films. The groups orchestrated support for their claim that the downtown needed revitalizing and that the XXX-rated films were not only immoral but attracted the wrong kind of people into the downtown area, thus deterring legitimate businesses from locating there.

Your family tried to ignore the protests, but the conflict intensified. The groups wrote letters to the editor of the local paper, pointing out how the films exploited and degraded women, violated common standards of decency, were direct violations of God's laws, and promoted attitudes of violence toward women. Some letters in response pointed out that these arguments lacked real data or facts to back up their claims. Finally, the protest groups picketed.

Although business remained brisk throughout it all, your parents suffered from the pressure. They agreed to stop showing the XXX-rated films if the groups could guarantee help in scheduling acceptable films and supporting the theater so Baron Inc. could survive as a business. The groups agreed.

For two months after switching to the new films, the downtown theater did well enough, although not as well as in the times of the XXX-rated films. Although the good publicity generated by the various groups seemed to help, attendance downtown soon dwindled. Neither new strategies of advertising nor further appeals to the groups reversed the downturn. Now all three theaters were losing money.

"Well, Dad, we can always go back to showing the porn films. Not just downtown, either. Why not do it at all three theaters?" Charles suggested.

Your father had become increasingly sensitive to the arguments about exploiting women, violating peoples' religious beliefs, offending decency, living on the edge of what was ethically acceptable, risking more confrontations with the opposition groups, danger to the family reputation, and having to fight a court order threatened by one. Recent Supreme Court decisions had granted individual communities the right to enforce local standards, and some members of the protest groups were talking about toughening the obscenity laws in your town.

Baron Incorporated does have the resources to go into another business venture. But Charles argued persuasively that many perfectly decent people do like XXX-rated movies. He maintained that there is no obligation to allow the tastes and mores of some people to overrule those of others. After all, freedom means tolerance of diversity. Those who do not like such movies can easily stay away. Your opponents do not in fact speak for a majority of the local populace, and do not clearly have the influence or power to succeed in efforts to pass more restrictive standards. And no one has ever proven conclusively that XXX-rated films actually cause increased abuse of women or children.

Your parents have called a family meeting with notice of their intent to put the matter to a family vote. It is clear that all family members want to do the right thing, whatever that is or turns out to be. Your position is that of a swing voter. You feel sure Charles will want to continue showing XXX-rated films. Your parents seem genuinely on the fence about it all, and your other brother seems willing to give up on the porn films and withdraw from the business. That means your opinion and vote may decide the issue.

You share your father's concerns about the community, the family, and the morality of XXX films, but you also share his belief that a business has a right to earn a profit in any way that's legal. Now you must clarify and evaluate the arguments on both sides in order to present a convincing case to your family and get this matter RESOLVEDD.

24. EMPLOYMENT AT WILL, YES.
BUT IS IT FAIR?
Was Termination Justified?

You have always had some mixed feelings about working for Jordun Corporation, a small security company, because of their strict policy of employment-at-will. Employment-at-will is the doctrine that employees can be terminated at the discretion of the management, with or without cause. The company policy is based on the idea that the employer owns the jobs it creates, the workplace, tools, machines, and raw materials, and can do with this private property whatever is allowed by law. So employees are like guests of the company and have no right to a job or continued employment. The company informs all prospective employees of the policy and highlights it at a number of places in the company handbook. It is understood that to accept a job there requires knowing of the employment-at-will policy, so every employee is expected to understand it. The company takes it for granted that accepting a job at Jordun means employees accept the policy.

On the other hand, Jordun has always had a policy of due process for its employees. There is a grievance and appeals process in effect, although no one has had to use it since you began working there five years ago. Although you are uncomfortable with the official employment-at-will policy, the company's commitment to due process has given you a feeling of security and justice. And the fact that the policy had not been invoked indicated to you a general harmony among employees. No one had to accept a job there, no one had signed on without being informed of the policy, and no one that you knew had ever appealed to the grievance committee to contest an unjust termination. So you had few reservations when asked recently to serve on the grievance committee, a standing committee that would only meet if there was in fact a grievance.

This week, however, you have begun to have doubts. For the first time since the company instituted its appeals procedure, someone is using it to protest being fired. Karl K. Klondike had been terminated by the president of the company following a number of complaints by both fellow employees and management officials. Karl's termination stemmed from a series of incidents concerning some of his political and personal views.

The first complaint had been lodged after Karl pasted a large poster on his locker door advertising a lecture by the Grand Duke of the local "skinhead" group. The poster included racial slurs, causing two employees to complain to management. After his immediate supervisor talked to him, Karl removed the poster from the outside of the locker and taped it to the inside. The same two employees complained again, and the supervisor again talked to Karl. Even though he complained that he had a right to free expression, Karl took the poster out of his locker entirely.

While that could have been the end of it, Karl didn't give up easily. He parked his car in the company lot the next day, having plastered the bumpers and windows with stickers extolling the "skinhead" group's philosophy in graphic terms. There were offensive slogans and pictures ridiculing a number of ethnic groups and homosexuals. This time three other employees and one midlevel manager complained to the vice president of the company. The VP directly asked Karl to remove the stickers and to keep his offensive views out of the workplace. Again, Karl claimed that his right to free speech gave him the right to put anything he wanted on his own car. The VP responded that the parking lot was company property, and the company wanted to avoid offending people. The VP then told Karl that he was banned from using the company parking lot unless he removed his offensive stickers.

Karl, deciding to continue his fight for his rights, now began to park his car on the street directly in front of the entrance to the building where everyone could see it as they came to work every day. Since the street was public property, no one at the company could do anything about the car's being there. For a few days everyone just tried to ignore Karl's car and get on with their jobs. But then the final incident and complaint came in.

While he was on an assignment as a security guard at the local baseball stadium, Karl's car was spotted in the stadium employees' lot by one of the owners of the team. When he discovered that it was Karl's car, he told Karl to get it off the stadium lot or else. Karl complied, but made it known that he felt the owner was wrong and violating his civil rights. Although he worked through the ballgame that day, he spent a lot of time grumbling and asking other workers if they thought he had been treated unfairly. The owner then called and asked that Karl not be assigned to his stadium ever again.

This time the president of Jordun Security was informed of the situation. He talked with various employees and managers about Karl's views and the previous incidents before deciding to terminate Karl. He gave Karl one week's notice as required by the termination policy. During that week, Karl filed an appeal to your committee, claiming that he was being unfairly terminated. His main argument was that no one, not even the stadium owner, had ever complained about how he performed his job. He said that until he tried to express his personal beliefs, he had never gotten anything but good performance reviews. He also pointed out that he had never been late for work, had never missed an assignment, and had never even taken a sick day in almost two years of working for Jordun.

When Mr. Scott, the president, appeared before your committee, he did not dispute any of Karl's claims about his job performance. He did, however, point out that there had been a client complaint and a number of complaints from other workers and two managers. Although none of the complaints involved bad job performance, morale and the company's image had surely suffered. Therefore, he had invoked the employment-at-will doctrine in terminating Karl. And now that he had made his decision, it did not matter why Karl was being fired, Scott said. As president, he no longer wanted Karl working for Jordun Corporation. Just cause was not required.

Karl then addressed the committee, saying that employment-at-will was an unfair policy that had been abandoned by many companies over the years for that reason. Moreover, he was being fired for no reason except that he had chosen to exercise his right to free speech. He argued that when asked, he had complied with everyone's requests. He had moved his posters, had parked outside the company lot, and had moved his car from the stadium lot as well. Did employers have the right to fire someone for his political views even when there were no real problems with that person's job performance? Sure, he knew of the employment-at-will policy at Jordun, but had thought that it would never be invoked unfairly and in violation of an employee's civil rights. Finally, he asked whether such an unfair policy took precedence over the U.S. Constitution and its guaranteed right to free speech.

After hearing all the facts, you had to wonder about Karl's final question. It seemed to you that Karl had not violated any company policies. He had always performed his job satisfactorily. He had indeed complied with all the requests concerning his poster or stickers. And, you thought, it does appear that he was fired for his personal beliefs rather than a job-related error. Can the fact that Karl's beliefs appear racist and disgusting to management and many employees justify his firing?

There is, however, the employment-at-will clause in the company's policy handbook. Strictly speaking, any reason is enough reason for termination. Yet why have an appeals policy and a grievance committee if that is all there is to it? Doesn't having such a committee imply that some firings could be unfair? If not, then at least it must indicate that management has some concern about employee rights, or due process. Are these contradictory policies?

Does the company's right to do as it pleases with its private property outweigh Karl's right to free speech? He must have known his views would be offensive to someone, so was he trying to upset his coworkers? Does such a consideration even make a difference? Could it be fair to fire someone for non-work-related factors? Or were the complaints of other employees and one client enough to constitute just cause? In fact, they had complained of nothing but Karl's expression of his personal beliefs.

Whether or not this is a contradictory policy, there is the employment-at-will policy in the handbook. Karl knew about it when he brought his personal views to work. There is also the important question of whether the employment-at-will doctrine itself is ethical. If not, how can it justify Karl's termination? But isn't the company entitled to follow a stated and known policy?

All these questions are important to you as you decide whether to uphold Karl's termination. One vote might make a difference here, and you are glad that all votes will be cast by secret ballot. There is much to be RESOLVEDD before you cast your vote.

25. PADDING OR PROFIT
Are You Willing to Pad a Sales Price?

This was your first business trip. Now that you had worked as a sales trainee for six weeks, your supervisor felt it was time to send you along with one of the company's best salesmen to observe his handling of customers. Vince Collier was generally referred to in tones of respect and wonder at the office; he had been the company's number one sales rep for five years running. If you were ever going to learn the secrets of good sales techniques, it would be on this trip with Vince.

On Sunday evening you met Vince at the airport and boarded the plane bound for Cincinnati. On the flight Vince told you a little about his start in sales with the company, while you told him how this was your first sales job and you wanted to learn how to be successful.

"A real go-getter, eh? Well, I can see that I've got a willing student here. Don't worry, kid, I'll show you the ropes," Vince said.

On Monday morning you accompanied Vince on two different calls and observed him in action. He was very good, but he told you these first two calls were the easy ones since he had been dealing with these companies for years. The next was where your education would begin. After months of persistent calling, Herb Norton of Apex Corporation had agreed to let Vince explain your company's product line. He explained that he had been happy with his previous suppliers until recently. They had become more difficult to deal with, so he was looking around for new options.

"Herb's a hard sell, but I think we can get him to throw some business our way," Vince told you as you entered Apex's front door. It turned out to be no exaggeration.

Every time it looked like he was going to agree to make a purchase, he'd pull back. However, Vince was up to the task and kept plugging away until it looked like this was it. But there was one more hitch.

"Look, Vince, I'll be honest," Herb began. "I had a pretty good deal going with my old suppliers until they had a big turnover last month."

"Well, you'll get a good deal from us," Vince answered.

"That remains to be seen. Suppose I lay it out for you? Your prices are a little high, though I believe you when you say the quality is worth the extra cost. But how about this? Suppose I agree to pay you 1 percent more than you're asking?" Herb leaned back in his chair to watch your expressions. You noticed at once a change in the expression on Vince's face.

"What do you mean, Herb?" Vince asked.

Herb then asked Vince if you could be trusted, and Vince said you could. He explained that you were a real go-getter who was willing to do whatever it took to get a sale.

"Well, it would work like the deal I had with our previous suppliers. What I mean is, I'll authorize our company to pay the higher price, but you report the lower price to yours. We now have a 1 percent surplus to play around with. You take half of that, and I'll take the other half. I figure with our volume, we'll each make about

$5,000 a year free and clear. You can split yours with the kid any way you want. All you have to do is write up two order forms—one for my people with the higher price, one for yours with the lower. No one will know except us."

Vince said he'd like to think about the offer overnight and talk it over with you. After his last call tomorrow, he would call Herb with the answer.

That night Vince and you discussed Herb's offer. You told him you were absolutely against it. But Vince said you ought to consider all the angles. He told you that this sort of thing was not at all uncommon and that it would not hurt the company. You would be getting the right price for your materials, so the company would make its usual profit. And a little extra cash would come in handy for both of you.

When you objected that the deal was illegal, Vince countered that since no one could find out, there was nothing to worry about. And if questions arose, you could say it was Herb's scam and you didn't know he was doing it. If Herb got caught, you could deny having written up two order forms since they were typed and couldn't be traced back to either of you.

To all of your objections Vince had smooth and rehearsed answers. He was a powerful salesman, yet was unable to allay all of your doubts.

"Look, we get paid to bring in sales. I bring in $400,000 of business every year, and our company loses nothing. You said you'd do anything it took to be successful. Well, did you mean it? I've had similar arrangements in the past, and they worked out well for everyone." Vince explained that a 1 percent markup would not hurt Herb's company, especially since your product was worth at least that much more.

As you left to return to your room, you told Vince that you would sleep on it and let him know in the morning. But now, in the darkness of the night, questions keep running through your mind that Vince did not answer. It is the ethical ones that seem the most troubling and important.

Sure, the economics seemed right. But isn't honesty worth more than the money? You could just refuse to participate and let Vince and Herb do whatever they wanted. But aren't there ethical principles that require you to report Vince to the company if you think he is doing something wrong? Or is it best for you just to forget it, since Vince is so well respected and successful? It is obvious he has done this sort of thing before. Maybe such deals are the key to success in sales. Perhaps the company knows or suspects that Vince has been pulling things like this all along and really does not care as long as he brings in big contracts. Would you be seen as naive, a crybaby, jealous, disloyal, or not a team player if you reported Vince? And if you did so, what good would it do you and your career in the end? You must develop careful answers to all these questions before morning in order to have the problem RESOLVEDD as you promised.

26. LANGUAGE POLICE
IN THE WORKPLACE?
Dealing with a Bilingual Workforce

Being the owner of your own business has been everything you thought it was going to be, both the good and some of the bad. But you are now facing a serious morale problem and ethical conflict involving your workers on the loading dock. You employ nine workers in the loading dock area, including the supervisor. Seven of the workers and the supervisor are from Mexico, and the other worker is Puerto Rican.

All nine speak both Spanish and English, though not all speak fluent English. As a result most of the work-related conversation in the loading dock area is conducted in Spanish. This is the source of the problem you face.

Due to the location of the dock area, almost every worker entering the plant has to pass through it a number of times a day on their way in, out, to and from lunch, and to the locker room. It is not uncommon that workers overhear the Spanish conversations as they pass. The vast majority of these workers speak English, but no Spanish whatsoever. On a number of occasions in recent weeks, English-speaking workers have heard comments in Spanish that seemed to be directed at them only to be followed by laughter from the other Spanish-speaking workers. Whether or not it was because a joke had been made at the expense of the English-speaking workers was not clear to you, but these workers had begun to believe the Spanish-speakers were making fun of them.

Over the course of a few weeks, the situation had escalated to the point where the English-speaking workers had begun to loudly question the Spanish-speakers, asking "What are you saying? Can't you speak English?" Twice, when no English explanation followed, the English-speaking workers had yelled, "We're in America. Speak the language we speak, or go back to Mexico!" Finally, a near-fight had occurred, which prompted the English-speaking workers to come to you and complain about the situation.

After saying they were sick of being laughed at and ridiculed every time they passed through the dock area, they asked you to institute an English-only policy at the company. They argued that a number of nearby states had passed laws making English the official language for conducting most state business. They also pointed out that many local county and city governments in your state were considering adopting such policies. Since the morale of the English-speaking workers was being seriously undermined, a policy seemed to be the solution. Moreover, the English-speaking workers said that there had been problems with on-the-job communication because they could not understand the dock workers, who tended to begin every conversation in Spanish. They contended that time was lost and efficiency compromised because of the "bilingual shop" you had allowed to develop in the plant.

When you spoke to the dock supervisor, he tried to explain that it was difficult for some of his workers to switch to English, even when they were dealing with non-Spanish-speakers. They felt very uncomfortable with English, spoke Spanish at home and in their neighborhoods, and were afraid of being made fun of when they misspoke at work. He said that a number of such incidents had occurred, although, until the last few weeks, none had occurred for more than a year. But he did say that he understood how the English-speaking workers felt about the situation and would try to get his people to be more careful to avoid offending anyone. He acknowledged that his workers had made some jokes in Spanish, but also said that they were in no way serious or offensive. His workers were really just nervous, and the jokes had helped them cope with feeling out of place in an English-speaking country.

As a result of these talks, you brought the leaders of the two groups together to try to establish an understanding. However, very little compromise seemed likely. The spokesman for the English-speakers demanded an English-only policy. The dock supervisor responded by saying that such a policy would be insulting to his workers and himself. Additionally, he said he had thought the United States was a "diverse society" and could tolerate a little linguistic freedom. The morale of the English-speaking workers shouldn't suffer that much if his people avoided making any more jokes.

While this seemed initially reasonable to you, the English-speaking workers were not satisfied. They still contended that jokes and comments about them would go on. Their main argument, however, continued to be that in the United States, English was the language of business. If workers could not rely on other workers' speaking English, the result would be lower productivity, misunderstandings, and possibly more violent incidents. The English-only policy was the only remedy, they said. If you wouldn't institute such a policy, trouble would follow.

The Spanish-speaking workers repeated their contention that they had a right to speak their own language wherever they wished. The United States guarantees free speech, not free English speech only. To be insulted by being forced to speak a language someone else required them to speak was something they could not accept. Indeed, a number of them mentioned quitting if you adopted the English-only policy.

It seemed that whatever remedy you sought would offend one group or the other. The situation was difficult for you in other ways as well. The English-speaking workers tended to be more senior, having been hired ten to twelve years ago when you began the company. The Spanish-speaking workers had been hired more recently, having moved to your area of the country only in the last couple of years. Did you owe more to the workers you had employed for a longer time period? Shouldn't they have a right to feel they were not being ridiculed at work? Or did you owe something to the Spanish-speaking workers who had performed well but tended to have more problems finding jobs in your city, if statistics were any indication? It seemed the Spanish-speaking people would be harmed more if they felt they had to quit or were being driven out by the English-only policy. On the other hand, is there anything to the idea that English should be the "language of business," as the English-speakers contended? It is true that English-only policies had been gaining acceptance across the country.

It will not be easy for you to sort out all the issues that could be important. Certainly there did seem to be a right to speak freely in the United States, even in Spanish. Is there something wrong with compromising that at work? Even if it is legal, there are other considerations here. Would English-only at work be a form of ethnic discrimination? Are the morale and productivity of the English-speaking workers really being negatively affected by the Spanish spoken on the job? You understood how there might be problems from time to time. Maybe efficiency would improve with a single language policy. It all seems so confusing, especially given the emotional nature of many of the issues. Did an employer even have the right to demand that workers speak a particular language on the job? Is this a violation of their autonomy and privacy? How can this linguistic dispute be fairly and ethically RESOLVEDD? Will an English-only policy clear it all up?

27. AN OFFER TO SPY
Can You Help Set Up a Candid Camera?

You had been working for almost three months for a discount store when the manager called you in one morning. She wanted to recommend you for a job that would nearly double your salary for at least the next three months. Tired of the boring work of stocking shelves and the lower wages, you were very interested. Your boss then added that the job would be confidential and that everything about it, including the required interview, could not be discussed with anyone. You were surprised, but agreed. She then handed you the address of the local corporate offices for the franchise and told you to drive there at once for the interview.

When you arrived, the receptionist promptly led you into the executive office of the local franchise vice president. She was cordial and began by asking you about yourself and your ambitions. You explained that as a third-year university student, you liked the opportunities offered by big business and were planning to find a management trainee position after graduation. After you had talked awhile, she made you the offer. She explained that they needed a trusted employee to help management find the thieves who had been stealing electronic equipment from the stores for almost six months. The company had tried several strategies which had failed, including notifying the police, hiring a detective firm, and interviewing employees. Now they were going to install hidden cameras in the employee lunchrooms and lounges and on the loading docks of each store for 24-hour surveillance.

Noting that she had seen your interest in amateur radio and electronics listed on your resume, she thought you were the perfect choice. You were being asked to do the installation because you were a relatively new employee, were not a union member, could not have been involved in the past problems, which had started months before you were hired, and had experience with electronics. She stressed that there seems to be no other way to catch those who are stealing, and that you could be sure of the company's gratitude for your help. "No one could be better for the job," she concluded.

However, you have doubts. You are concerned about likely violations of privacy resulting from the hidden cameras. It seems clear to you that such hidden cameras are highly objectionable even though perfectly legal. What you are sure of is that you wouldn't want someone else to install cameras that spied on you at work. What troubles you most is going behind employees' backs and setting up equipment that allows people you don't know to spy on those employees while they are eating, on break, relaxing, and unaware of being watched.

Now you must decide whether or not to take this job which you want and need. So you thanked the vice president and told her you would think about it and would give her your answer. Thinking it over, you consider the logic of the vice president's plan, the legality of using hidden cameras, and the fact that you aren't putting them in the locker room or washroom where privacy is surely expected. But your initial doubts and concerns remain. Before you give your answer, there are many questions to be RESOLVEDD.

28. BLOW THE WHISTLE
OR BREATHE INSULATION?
Health and Safety on the Job

In your late twenties, and glad to have the job you do, as supervisor of files for Manly Construction Company, you are exposed to asbestos every day at work. Manly's file office is located in two former vaults in the basement of an old, converted bank building. You recently discovered that the vault was lined with asbestos-impregnated wallboard, and that the overhead pipes are insulated with asbestos. You had worked there for a year without knowing any of this.

As part of the yearly inspection of all businesses, a county inspector cited Manly for various minor building violations last week. The most serious was the asbestos contamination in the vault. The county gave Manly seventeen days to clean up the fallen asbestos fibers in the vaults. It also fined Manly $1400 for the violations. However, it did not require the company to remove or seal off the asbestos in the wallboard or on the pipes, although it strongly recommended doing so.

The company said that it had complied with the citation by cleaning up the fallen fibers. Beyond that, nothing was planned. A memo from the president's office stated that employees would be required to perform their normal job duties, including entering the vaults when necessary. The memo went on to note that no employees would be required to move any boxes or perform any activities that could damage the asbestos or release fibers into the air. It also stated that the county citation did not require the areas to be restricted.

You and the other clerks have been talking about the citation and the hazards of asbestos. One employee, 68-year-old Rocky Pedowski, vehemently supported management's memo. In fact, he said that you were all "nuts" to be worried about this asbestos scare at all.

"You youngsters are all worrying about nothing. If you don't bother the asbestos, it won't bother you. Most of us old guys were educated in schools that used asbestos insulation. Every hot water pipe was covered with the stuff. I don't see any evidence of an epidemic of lung cancer or asbestosis in my old schoolmates," Rocky argued, rather sarcastically.

"But what about all those lawsuits against companies like Johns-Manville? All those people with cancer who worked there?" you ask.

"Hey listen, those people worked in very confined areas where the air was filled with asbestos so thick you could cut it with a knife. It's no wonder they got problems. We've wasted millions in this country on asbestos cleanup when the safest thing is just to leave it alone or cover it with a good-quality paint . . . you know, like in the vaults," was Rocky's response.

You have seen TV home repair shows that pointed out that it is sometimes better and cheaper just to let the asbestos sit. The real problems occur when asbestos is disturbed and particles are released into the air.

"Look, the report said it was dangerous to let us into the vaults. That's the bottom line. Why are they forcing us to go in? I say we refuse," Kiesha Black exclaimed. "And Rocky reminds me of those people who say that if it was OK for their fathers to beat them, it's OK for everyone. I just don't buy it."

"You know how much asbestos removal costs? I would guess about $15,000 for those two vaults downstairs. The company isn't going to do it unless the county makes us," was Rocky's last remark as he left the lunchroom.

It turned out that Rocky was right. The company refused to do more than the citation demanded, so the asbestos was not removed from the vault area. The president circulated a further memo that merely restated the earlier one in slightly stronger terms.

A series of complaints by employees and discussions with management followed, but in the end the president refused to discuss the case any further. At the meetings, you heard the president refer repeatedly to the fact that a reinspection by the county had verified compliance and that the county was satisfied. Beyond that, he said, the company had no obligations.

You must either continue to work in the vault or quit your job. Of course, if someone exposed the incident to the public, other consequences might follow.

There is little doubt that the environment poses a threat to your health in the long term. It is well known that even one asbestos fiber can cause lung cancer, though this may take twenty years or more. Even if the asbestos is not directly disturbed, there are almost certainly a few fibers floating around. It seems likely that the State Department of Health or the federal Environmental Protection Agency would require abatement or relocation of your work environment. But there is no way to find out without a formal invitation to them or an accusation that would have to be revealed to Manly management.

Perhaps making a major statement to customers or the general public would pressure the company to remove the asbestos. But such whistle-blowing would surely threaten your job and clearly go against the orders of management. You would surely become a target of management, who would find a way to terminate your employment.

On the other hand, the risk to your health and that of the half-dozen employees you work with is significant over a period of five or ten years, given the levels of asbestos in the air before cleanup and EPA documents about health risks. Much of the literature you found indicates that the levels of asbestos in the air will return to the pre-cleanup levels in a few months.

In the end, the question is how to weigh the risk to health against the risk to your jobs and also to the company. The company might well lose some forthcoming contracts in the local area if the whole issue became public and local unions protested publicly against Manly.

Whatever you do or do not do, you must analyze the case until it is RESOLVEDD.

29. REPAIR QUOTAS
When Your Job Conflicts with the Customers' Best Interests

As the repairs manager at a franchised but independently owned auto repair shop, you have been given a monthly volume quota by the owner of the shop. For each 30-day period that you meet the quota, you are rewarded with a bonus that amounts to 20 percent of your monthly salary of $2,500. This is an important opportunity for you now that you have two daughters and a mortgage. In addition, you tend to view the quota as a test of your skill, giving you a chance to exceed your base salary on a regular basis. If you fail to meet the quota for three consecutive months, however, the owner has made it clear that he would consider hiring a new manager and either letting you go or demoting you to a lesser position with a smaller salary and no bonuses.

For the first four months of your job at the shop, you had no problem meeting the quota. Since it was summer and vacation season, many people brought in their cars for maintenance and repairs prior to leaving on their vacations. Now, in mid-fall, however, business has started to taper off, and you have barely made your quota for the last two months.

As business continues to decline, it becomes clear that you will have to sell the customers on repairs and parts that are desirable but not urgent. This troubles you, as candor and honesty have always been among your highest values. You are also concerned that losing your job or taking a cut in salary may force you to look for a new job in a very tight job market.

Recently, even the mechanics have pressured you to "give the customers the old hard sell" so there would be more work. The mechanics want to put in some overtime before Christmas, and have even been "coaching" you on how to encourage customers to spring for additional repairs "as a safety precaution." The mechanics also have mentioned that their livelihoods depend on your drumming up some business. You still feel squeamish about trying to pressure customers, and so far you haven't tried very hard to sell optional repairs as if they were more needed and more urgent than they are.

When you talk to the owner about your doubts, he says not to worry. "With a little practice, you will become a pro!"

"After all," he explains, "the repairs are, in reality, preventive maintenance. They'll save the customers money in the long run by helping them avoid costly breakdowns with heavy towing fees." He reminds you that his quota policy is nonnegotiable, and that failing to meet it will necessitate evaluating your future at his shop.

Your talks with other employees have convinced you that this policy is the creation of this shop owner. It is not part of the general policy of the corporation that sells the franchise. In addition, you are aware that the company retains considerable control over its franchises, although each is a privately owned shop. From what you gather, a call to the nearest franchise representative might get the company involved and lead to the elimination of the quotas, or even the cancellation of the franchise. However, you are unsure of the company position on such issues, and hesitate to risk your boss's becoming aware of your meddling. If he found out about your effort to restrain his approach to employees and customers, you might lose your job, whether you meet the quotas or not.

Wouldn't it be safest just to go along with your boss's desires? Why not just look at it the way he suggested, as a way of getting the customers to buy preventive maintenance? Is it, after all, unethical to sell safety?

On the other hand, warning your customers of the possibility of a breakdown and their chance to prevent it now can be a kind of scare tactic. After all, breakdowns are always possible. The mere fact that a part is, for example, visibly worn is not good justification for telling a customer that a breakdown is possible when you know full well that such parts often go for another 50,000 miles without trouble. Is there any way to distinguish a warning that is motivated largely by your desire to sell from one motivated by an impartial, objective, and responsible finding that prudence and safety require you to inform the customer of a possible accident?

This is clearly a case in which the devil is in the details. That is, examination and interpretation of the likely impact of each of your main options and the principles at stake in each will reveal the relative positive and negative value of your options. Once you have RESOLVEDD the case, you must be proud of your decision.

30. PIECE WORK OR PEACE?
Coworkers Demand Another Worker's Removal

You have been listening to the union steward for the assembly area, Jasmine Booth, for a few quiet minutes about the trouble that is brewing. Four weeks ago the company, an electrical supplies manufacturer, hired a number of college students for the summer.

One of them, Paul Monroe, was assigned to Jasmine's area, a diverse shop that completes seven different kinds of assemblies. As shop superintendent, you remembered Paul from his interview with you. He seemed like a good summer worker, and you had liked him. Who knew he'd be the center of a troublesome complaint?

Paul began his job by working at a threading machine. His task was to center a metal cap and washer on the screw threads of an electrical conduit pipe, an insulating pipe through which wires are run. Then he was to hold the cap in place while pushing a pedal with his foot that started the threader turning, thus tightening the cap. It was a job that required practice and concentration. Paul never came close to making the piece rate of 175 per hour. He just didn't have the manual dexterity to thread the caps quickly. During his first week at work, Paul never completed more than 75 pieces per hour. In the next two weeks, he worked his way up to about 125. Meanwhile, a number of the women who worked nearby took a liking to him and tried to help him improve at his job. However, he just did not develop the skill needed to earn a bonus. But the women, all in their fifties, encouraged him and treated him as if he were a family friend.

Paul seemed to be a well-liked member of your department until you moved him to a new job during his fourth week. This job required little dexterity but a good deal of muscle. He was to put a metal cover onto the body of a fuse box and pound the cover on a metal block to snap it into place. Paul, a weight lifter, was able to knock the cover into place with one hit. The four women who were doing the same job had to hit the cover three or four times to snap it into place. By the end of his first day, Paul was finishing more than 250 fuse boxes an hour, 100 more than the hourly rate set by management.

This was the source of the trouble. Piece rates were set by management in conjunction with the union. Every six months or so, a manager from the main office would come to observe a job, tally the number of pieces completed by three selected workers in an hour, then average their rates, which would then become the hourly standard. If too many people earned bonuses, or if one person worked significantly faster than anyone else, management would review the job and raise the standard rate to the number done by the fastest worker. The rate for fuse boxes was 150 an hour. Paul's extraordinary productivity had caught the attention of a number of union workers. Two of them complained to you that Paul was wrecking the rate. They were afraid that some manager would think that it was possible for everyone to do 250 boxes an hour, and then raise the rate.

These two women had always exceeded 175 when they were put on this job, thereby making a bonus that amounted to around $40 a week. If the rate went up to 250, they would no longer earn their bonuses. They had demanded that Jasmine advise Paul to slow down his rate. They claimed that as their union steward it was her job to look out for the union members. The women pointed out that Paul was not in the union since he was just summer help.

Jasmine had told the women that she did not think it was fair to prevent Paul from earning a bonus. No one had worried when Paul couldn't make a bonus before. They responded coldly that they did not care, since he would be gone in another month, and they would be stuck with the higher rate. She had reassured the women by suggesting that they wait a few days to see if Paul might not slow down some on his own, fatigued by his fast pace.

After hearing Jasmine out, you decided to take a look at the situation for yourself and casually walked around the shop observing Paul. You noticed, over the next day or so, that none of the women would talk to Paul or sit next to him at lunch. Even Martha Lahti, who seemed previously to look out for Paul, stayed away. Paul looked confused and hurt by the situation.

That afternoon, you mentioned the problem to the union vice president, who agreed with the women. The VP simply said that Paul was not your concern, but that the raising of the piece rate was union business. It was unreasonable for you expect women to work as quickly at that job as a 19-year-old, 210-pound male. He then told you to either slow Paul down or ask upper management to transfer him out of your area, since there were no other positions in your shop for Paul. Jasmine had clearly explained the situation to the VP, and he had certainly reached his decision quickly. He even blamed Paul for a drop in morale, citing the fact that many of the women seemed to be avoiding him and were obviously angry with him.

As you reviewed the situation, a number of questions came to mind. Isn't Paul producing more for the company? Isn't that what everyone was supposed to be doing to increase profits? Weren't you all working for the same thing? Didn't Paul deserve to earn as much as he could honestly manage from his own hard work? After all, he wasn't doing anything wrong. In fact, he was doing too much right. Surely there is some way of addressing this issue that would be fair to Paul, the company, and the union workers. Then again, you are management, so the question of whom you owe more to, the company and its profits or the union workers who help produce that profit, is important. Many of these union workers are people you have worked with for years. Yet you feel the union is being very unfair to Paul and may be acting out of pure self-interest. How far they will go to get Paul removed is not clear. Could they begin a work slowdown? How will your working relations with the union workers be affected by your decision? Can you look yourself in the mirror and feel good about removing Paul? Does this matter? You will need to consider very carefully the options and the values at stake in order to see that the situation is justly RESOLVEDD.

31. PERSONAL BELIEFS, PUBLIC POLICY
Can a Union Force a Member to Support
Its Political Causes?

You had been serving as the president of the local union for almost five years, after twenty years on the loading dock, when Guido Contralli's appeal came to you. Guido was not a full member of the union, but rather paid "compulsory agency fees" that allowed him to work at Cash Standard Motors (CSM), a manufacturer of small engines. CSM operated according to an agreement with the union that sanctioned nonunion workers in certain areas of the plant as long as those workers contributed agency fees to the union.

The union position was that Guido and the other nonunion workers benefit from negotiations conducted by the union, receiving higher pay, more benefits, and better working conditions as a result. Therefore, the union reasoned, he and the others owe something to the union in return. Since CSM is not a closed shop, Guido had not been forced to join the union. The agency fees amounted to two-thirds of regular union dues, which are deducted from workers' paychecks in twelve monthly payments. For years you had thought that this was fair, as did those workers who paid the two-thirds fees, since the union had secured for them all the benefits enjoyed by regular union members. The health coverage alone would have cost nonunion members twice as much as normal union dues, so everyone seemed happy with the arrangement, at least until recently.

The problems began when the union, considered liberal in its political leanings, decided to put its influence and financial support behind candidates and organizations campaigning for abortion rights for women. The union subsidized a number of pro-abortion political candidates in the last election, as well as donating a significant amount of money to Planned Parenthood, a group known for its support of abortion rights. In addition, a number of other union officials had spoken out publicly in favor of a woman's right to choose abortion up to the end of the second trimester, the legal cutoff point established by the U.S. Supreme Court's *Roe v. Wade* decision. Guido Contralli had responded last month by canceling payroll's authority to take his monthly deductions for union agency fees. You had talked to him at that time.

It isn't that Guido is opposed to unions or that he does not believe the union has a right to speak out on political or moral issues. His problem is that, as a political conservative and a devout Catholic, he believes that abortion is immoral and ought to be made illegal. As far as he is concerned, abortion is the unjustified taking of a human life for what usually amount to less than compelling reasons. He also agrees with the Catholic church's official anti-abortion position, which holds that having an abortion is a sin. As a result, he has refused to allow any of the money he pays to the union to be used to back causes and actions that he personally believes are immoral and unethical. Originally, Guido had offered to pay the agency fees to a local charity that secures adoptive parents for unwanted babies. The union refused this offer, but did suggest that he reduce his agency fees by an amount proportionate to the percentage of its budget that goes to support pro-choice causes. Guido had refused, saying that any money he paid to the union gave at least tacit support to its liberal stance on abortion.

Last week, CSM's personnel director came to you saying that, with the agreement of the union, they intended to fire Guido on the grounds that the union-management agreement required all nonunion members to pay the appropriate agency fees. It would violate company policy and the union contract to allow him to keep his job. Management and the union should agree, he said, that Guido's continued employment would amount to freeloading on the union. It would cost the company, the union, and union workers money which they had no obligation to provide. They would be supporting the costs of negotiating for him without appropriate compensation. You realized that this was exactly what you and other union leaders had used as an argument when negotiating with management for the present arrangements years before. How could you disagree now?

Guido, on the other hand, believes that this violates Title VII of the 1964 Civil Rights Act, which prohibits firing employees for their deeply held religious beliefs. CSM denies that he is being fired for his beliefs. They argue, rather, that he is being fired for not paying his agency fees, a clear violation of the contract. CSM wants you, as union president, to back them up. Union membership is split on the issue, so no clear majority exists. Even the other union officers are having trouble deciding here.

Some believe that Guido has a point, others that it would be a very bad precedent to set if Guido were allowed to flaunt the union regulations.

You would like not to have to pursue the matter in court. However, you have discovered a recent decision concerning a related case (*Employment Division v. Smith*, U.S. Supreme Court, 1990) that is especially pertinent. In that case, the Court ruled that the First Amendment's clause guaranteeing the free exercise of religion does not apply to labor issues. In light of this decision, an attorney you consulted advised you that Guido's case has little chance of success. Moreover, the legal fees alone would be more than he could handle. He has no realistic chance of finding work elsewhere in Burlington, and will probably have to relocate to find a job offering comparable work and pay.

All of this is what bothers you. Legally Guido seems doomed, but is it right for your union and you to force him to support causes he rejects? Ethically, this seems to violate his autonomy, religious beliefs, and personal integrity, even though he did sign on to the agreement when he needed the union and the benefits it brought him. Isn't he violating that contract and the principle of fidelity? With all this in his mind, you have to decide what to do. What options are available? Would forcing him to choose between his job and paying for causes he denies be an unfair act on your part? You are his union president, too. Would this be denying him the right to exercise his own religion? What does he, in fact, owe to the union, and how important is this obligation? Just what is your obligation to Guido and the rest of the union members in this case? Will you agree to his termination or not? Analyze the issue until it is RESOLVEDD.

32. ATV DEALER ENCOURAGES USE BY KIDS
Do You Sell a Dangerous Product to a Willing Customer?

All-terrain vehicles are rather squatty, big-wheeled, knobby-tired machines often seen in commercials roaring through the woods at high speeds, slashing across shallow streams, and climbing rugged hills. Such vehicles may have three or four wheels, and engines ranging from 50 to 500 cubic centimeters in size. They look like fun, don't they? According to some private consumer groups, they look like too much fun for kids to resist. The problem, such groups say, is that although these vehicles are built for adults who know how to use them correctly, dealers have been targeting their sales to children.

In a recent national survey reported by the Ralph Nodder–founded U.S. Public Interest Research Group (PIRG), almost half of the ATV dealers questioned said that ATVs designed for adults should not be used by children under the age of 16. However, about 75 percent of the dealers responding also agreed that children 10 years of age would have very little trouble mastering the operation of an ATV. A spokesperson for the PIRG asserted that ATV dealers are continuing to mislead consumers about the dangers of ATVs even after the adoption of an agreement between the dealers and the U.S. government.

The agreement, signed by Honda, Suzuki, Kawasaki, Yamaha, and Polaris, all makers of ATVs, in January 1988, bans the sales of three-wheeled vehicles in the United States. The agreement states that only vehicles smaller than 90cc can be sold to children between the ages of 12 and 16; it limits the sales of larger four-wheeled

ATVs to buyers 16 years of age and older. It is the responsibility of the manufacturers to notify the dealers and enforce the provisions of the agreement.

Of the dealers surveyed, 46 percent said that they would sell large four-wheel-drive ATVs knowing that children as young as 10 might be using them. This, however, would be a violation of the agreement. Furthermore, the telephone survey revealed that 99 percent of the dealers did not inform customers that the larger, adult-sized vehicles were inappropriate for use by a 10-year-old child. In fact, fifty of the dealers admitted that they would sell machines with engines between 90 and 149cc knowing that they were intended for use by 10-year-olds. Indeed, eleven dealers said they would sell the larger, 150cc, adult vehicles for use by the young children. A spokesperson for a California PIRG stated that some dealers downplay the need for any special training in the handling of the larger machines. This also violates a part of the agreement, which calls for the manufacturers to supply free training and to add incentives for ATV purchasers and their families to take advantage of it.

The statistics compiled by the Consumer Product Safety Commission demonstrate that there is significant risk associated with use of ATVs, especially for children. In 1988, almost 40 percent of the deaths and injuries reported for ATVs involved children under the age of 16. There were 1,346 ATV deaths reported from 1982 to June 1989, and 36 for all of 1989. Of these, 20 involved four-wheel machines. Before 1985, a commission memo states, 156 people were reported killed in ATV accidents (11 four-wheel deaths), while in 1988, 112 deaths were reported for four-wheel vehicles, and 103 on three-wheel vehicles. Such statistics seem to indicate that these are vehicles to be taken seriously, even by adults, and are not the kind of toy intended for young children who may be less able to understand their dangers or know how to minimize them.

You have read two newspaper articles concerning such studies since your new job began at Marty's Cycle and ATV. In fact, you have talked them over with Todd and Larry, the other two college students who work part-time at the store. Their attitude is, "Don't worry about it, we've never had a 10-year-old come in to buy a cycle anyway." You have tended to agree, and have not thought much about these problems.

On Tuesday morning, your fifth day on the job, a man came in to look over your selection of ATVs. You introduced yourself and told him you'd be happy to answer any questions he had about the 125cc model that interested him. After a few questions about speed, acceleration, and how easy the ATV was to operate, he said, "I'm sold! My kid's gonna love this thing. He's been asking about one for three weeks since he saw a commercial on TV, with the guys jumpin' the hills and the river. His eleventh birthday will be a big one, all right."

"He's eleven?" you ask.

"Not till next Friday. But what the heck, I might as well buy it today, right? He'll be able to handle it. He's a strong kid."

You hesitate, a puzzled look on your face. Marty, who's been listening to your sales technique, steps over and says, "Right you are, sir! This baby's so easy to handle that a real baby could run it with no special training."

"Great! Well, wrap her up. I'll pay with my American Express."

"Ring it up," Marty says, pointing at you as he walks into the back room.

It is a $3,000 sale, on which you will receive a 5 percent commission. This is your second sale and your fifth day on a job that will provide your tuition for the fall. The money is exciting to you, and so is the sweet smell of success.

What should you do? Examine your options and the implications of each in light of your own knowledge and responsibility in the case. You must make a decision, once you have analyzed the case until it is RESOLVEDD.

33. COFFEE, TEA, OR THE SALE?
**A Clash Between Japanese and American
Treatment of Women**

You have had a reputation for efficiency, brilliance, and the ability to sell computers and business systems to the most reluctant corporate clients. As a result, you are the senior sales representative and vice president of Business Office Systems. You also have the reputation of being a pioneer for women's rights in the corporate world. You have fought discrimination for more than twenty years on your way to the top. Now you may have to overlook some of your feminist principles while negotiating your first sale to a Japanese company.

You have done your research. You have studied the Japanese way of doing business, reading late into the night about the differences between the Japanese and American corporate cultures. You know that during negotiations, Japanese body language differs from American body language, and that you must not misread the signals. Timing, etiquette, and cultural details differ. But you are set to do business in the Japanese way. The sale of a multimillion-dollar computer system to Oyakawa International Bank rides on your ability to convince the four Japanese executives at today's meeting.

You also know, to your dismay, that women in executive positions in Japanese firms are not treated like their male counterparts. This bothers you, especially since one of the executives you will be dealing with is a woman. While doing your research, you read a newspaper article that outlined the way in which women in Japanese businesses are treated. According to the article, Japanese men expect that women will not put in the time and work necessary to succeed in the tough world of Japanese business. Moreover, female executives often serve as waitresses during business meetings! Yet none of this is taken as sexist, and a Japanese woman executive is quoted as saying "It would be unthinkable to protest this treatment, especially when I'm on a career track." The fact is that only 1 percent of executives in Japan are women, although women make up 40 percent of the workforce. The double standard in Japanese business is widely accepted, including dress codes at some companies that require all female employees, from filing clerks to vice presidents, to wear the same blue suits.

As the meeting began with the four executives of Oyakawa International, you hoped that it would pass quickly, with no cultural conflicts. But it was not long before this began to look like a false hope. The Oyakawa negotiating team included two men and the woman, all of roughly the same rank. The third man, however, had higher rank than the others, and considerably more experience. However, the other two men had considerably less experience than their female counterpart. About thirty minutes into the meeting, the senior officer said something in Japanese to Ms. Akiyama. She nodded, left, and returned about five minutes later with coffee and donuts for everyone present.

Despite your background reading and research, you were mildly shocked to see this in practice, but tried not to let on. The negotiations proceeded smoothly for another forty minutes. You felt sure that Oyakawa Bank was going to buy the whole systems package your chosen account representatives had prepared. Caroline Knight and her assistant, Delia Star, were your best reps. They had negotiated almost all of BOS's biggest contracts and had put together an exceptional package for Oyakawa. There were no other people at your firm that you would trust with such a lucrative account, even if some of your other reps were familiar with the Oyakawa account.

So what followed next at the meeting was a real shocker for you. At this point, the senior officer again addressed his associates in Japanese. They all nodded again and again, Ms. Akiyama included. They were smiling and nodding at you the whole time the senior officer spoke to them. You watched Ms. Akiyama closely and she was smiling very enthusiastically at you, so you thought she was indicating that you were about to be awarded the contract.

Before you could begin to feel good about the deal, the senior officer of Oyakawa said to you, "We are very pleased with your proposal, and would like to finalize this deal. Would you be so kind as to grant us just one request, however?"

"Of course, if I, rather we, can!" was your immediate reply. But the request floored you.

"Wonderful. We are very pleased to be having you handle our account, but would very much prefer if you could have your best men take over now. We appreciate the work you and your helpers have done so far, but we would feel much more comfortable with male account reps. You understand, don't you?"

This whole plan was yours, Caroline's, and Delia's creation. It also seemed clear that what the senior officer meant was that he did not expect to close the deal with you, a woman, or have women handle his firm's account after the deal was closed. You thought that he probably did not realize what a breach of American corporate culture had just occurred. He probably had no idea how insulting you found his request. As you were about to say something in response, the senior officer added, "And could you please have your assistants there bring us more of your excellent coffee? It has been a long day with too much talking, don't you think?"

This was it! Not only had he presumed that you would not object to his request and dismissal of you and your staff, not only had he been constantly sexist in his treatment of his female colleague, but now he expected your account reps to cater to his wishes for coffee as well. The insult might have been easier for you to take but for the problems it created for Caroline and Delia, as well as your firm. Your first instinct was to tell him off and give him a lecture on feminism in business, but you caught yourself.

"Stop and take a deep breath. This is a multimillion-dollar sale," you think. How can you handle this in such a way as to protect your own dignity but not insult your clients? Is that possible? Must you just meekly give in for the sake of the sale? Different cultures are one thing—you were ready for some adjustments—but demeaning treatment is another. This violates every belief you have about equality for women in the workplace.

It strikes you that this sexism is not much different than requesting someone of the "right" race as an account rep. Beyond all this is the fact that both Caroline and Delia deserve the account and all the income from commissions it would generate for them. Then, too, you actually have no one else who's ready to handle the account. Can you tell your clients that? But why should you have to anyway? This is

America, and Caroline and Delia are the best people Oyakawa could have handling the account. Even if they wanted to step down and you agreed, there would be no one able to take over, and the account would have to be dropped. You could try to explain this, but have a feeling it would do no good. The senior officer clearly prefers a male account executive.

Isn't the customer always right? Or is this a case of unfair discrimination that you cannot honor? Would you be replacing them if they were, say, black and your client objected to them for that reason? And, after all, don't you owe more than this to Caroline and Delia? What might they think of you and the firm they thought they could count on for fair treatment? But don't you also have a duty to your firm to bring in business? If replacing female account reps with male reps will do it, shouldn't you try? Although this is a remote possibility, could Caroline or Delia sue you for discriminatory treatment if you take them off the account after all their work? These are just some of the thoughts running through your head as you analyze this problem until it is RESOLVEDD. With a multimillion-dollar account on the line, can you afford to offend your prospective client?

34. OFFICE GOSSIP
Do You Act on Rumor or Respect Privacy?

It had never seemed to you that gossip among company employees presented any ethical issues. You always thought that gossip was simply unreliable, potentially hurtful, and best avoided. But now, as the manager of a sales group for industrial biocides and its small office staff, you are faced with a sticky ethical problem created by gossip among your staff.

One of your best salespeople, Lilly Kropov, a married woman, seems to be romantically involved with a married man, Keith Laski, who is a buyer for one of your largest accounts. You have just discovered that the five members of your office staff and your ten salespeople have talked about little else now for more than a month. Indeed, the stories have grown juicier and juicier, including references to sightings of the couple together overseas on business trips and a sexual encounter in Lilly's office after hours. The latter was detected by an unsuspecting janitor who happened to hear noises from the office before he turned on the lights one evening . However, you have no idea how the couple could have arranged to meet overseas on a business trip, although you do regular business with companies in Southeast Asia, as does Laski's company.

Your problem stems from the fact that three of your salespeople and all but one of the office staff are well known to be thoroughly disgusted by the affair. They have been expressing disgust to each other, talking openly about it, and apparently spreading the rumors. This caused you considerable embarrassment when you learned that your boss had discovered the whole thing before you did! In a meeting with him late last week, he surprised and embarrassed you by ordering you to talk to your people, silence them, and stop these rumors now before they spread to higher echelons of the company. He made it clear that if you need to fire someone to purge the company of this cancer, he will stand behind you.

You were at first puzzled as to why your boss was so adamant about what seemed at first to be a private and personal matter unrelated to work. But the dimensions of the whole thing have become increasingly clear. Your company is proud of its record in the local community, encouraging family values, community involvement of its employees, and religious affiliations. Lilly has two children in grade school, a husband on the local school board, and attends the same church as some of the company's top executives. She and her family are highly visible and respected members of the community.

For someone with Lilly's prominence and success to be so strongly reviled by her coworkers is a significant matter. This point became even clearer to you earlier this week when Lilly stormed into your office with some pretty strong demands. It seems that some other coworkers in the company had left some suggestive, anonymous messages and limericks in her office. She brought three of them in to you and demanded that you take steps to put an end to them at once. When you asked Lilly what prompted them, you received a hostile response to the effect that it is no business of yours or of whoever left her the dirty notes. Her life is her own business, and you need to respect separation of work and personal life. You have the power and influence to stop the notes, and you need to take action now!

At this point it seemed clear that you needed to have a meeting with the rest of your staff. But that merely exacerbated the problem. When you met this morning with all those available, which included everyone but Lilly and two other salespeople who happened to be out of town, the intransigence of the problem emerged. More than half of those present expressed open hostility and resentment toward Lilly, insisting venomously that we should terminate her work with the company. Your explanation of why you need to end all this talk and these childish and dangerous anonymous notes was met with the retort that you should fire Lilly now before it all blows up.

You responded to those present by telling them that they have no business being so judgmental of the lives of others. They in turn said that Lilly was ruining the lives of her husband and children, destroying a beautiful family, and that this is in fact a community issue and a matter for the company to address directly. The failure to do so will only bring disrepute to you and the company, which has no obligation to continue to employ people who are immoral and untrustworthy. The implication is that when higher management finds out you have let this fester, your career will be damaged.

The other workers reacted by saying that since Lilly was carrying on with a buyer, it seemed to them that she was the one who needed to be disciplined. How can you allow her to continue in this way? Won't someone get the idea that doing well in the company depends upon having an affair with a buyer? You have to admit that this raises another significant issue, namely that of company morale. Will other employees, hearing the gossip or finding out that it's true, feel they are at a disadvantage? Won't this hurt Lilly's reputation as a professional in her field? If so, should you allow her to claim that her private life is private and let it go at that? It certainly seems that her private life has gotten very public and is affecting the internal and possibly external atmosphere surrounding your company. Maybe it should be Lilly who is "corrected," not those who started the rumors.

Your subsequent meeting with Lilly is what crystallized your problem. After you told her all that you had been told and had said regarding the problem, she seethed with anger, alleging slander designed to destroy her. Yet when you asked her to tell you the facts so that you could help her out, she refused, repeating with great emotion that it was a bunch of lies which she would fight to the bitter end. However, never did she specifically deny that she was having an affair. Her vow to fight probably meant that she intended to sue you, the company, her coworkers, and perhaps others if the gossip did not stop or if you attempted to fire her. In any case, she specified that she would talk to no one about this now but her lawyer, and certainly not to anyone else in the company.

As you think it all over, several important ideas keep bothering you. What if she is right and many of the stories and allegations about her are untrue, even if the overall fact of her having an affair with Laski is true? What if, on the other hand, she is having an affair with someone other than Laski? Is it right for you to fire her on allegations of immoral conduct? If what is being said is true, don't the other workers have a right to free expression of their opinions? Maybe the anonymous notes are going too far, yet aren't other expressions of disgust and disapproval simply exercising free speech? Then again, if the rumors are true, isn't it bad business to let employees carry on with customers? This can come to no good end for your company, can it? Although you do not clearly violate any laws by firing her, she certainly can sue, and could win a large settlement if she could prove that you are releasing her on the basis of unsubstantiated gossip. On the other hand, on what ethical grounds does the company owe her a job if in fact she has been engaging in behavior that so clearly contradicts the values, goals, and image of the company? Finally, can she be fired because her actions are harming company morale and because she is involved in a situation that can easily affect her work? What, then, should you do to see the problem RESOLVEDD?

35. IS THIS THE JOB YOU HAVE BEEN WAITING FOR?
Can You Tolerate Environmentally Unsound Practices?

Although Just Green Corporation has made you an offer you thought you'd never refuse, you are no longer so sure. Having just graduated from college with a B.A. in general business, you were at first pleased by the prospect of a position in their largest field office overseeing day-to-day aspects of their operation. JGC specialized in timber products and had three field offices located in different timber-producing regions. You would be working in the Washington State office. JGC was also a part of a much larger conglomerate that owned companies that produced, literally, everything from soup to nuts with everything else in between. It was the connection with the conglomerate that was causing your indecision.

After your interview with JGC, you had gone home to study the various pieces of informational literature the personnel manager had given you. When looking over one prospectus, you noticed the name of the conglomerate that owned JGC. Immediately you felt a little uneasy. The name was familiar to you, but not for positive reasons. You thought at first that maybe you had it wrong. However, your uneasy feelings were confirmed by a little searching on the Net. The conglomerate was implicated in a number of lawsuits and mentioned in the newsletters of several environmental groups as a very "non-green" company. There were at least five major lawsuits going on in which environmental groups were suing one or the other of the conglomerate's subsidiaries for environmentally damaging practices. As near as you could tell, though, JGC was not one of the subsidiaries being sued.

What bothered you about such suits was your own concern for the environment. While you do not consider yourself an environmental fanatic or activist, you do worry about many of the dire predictions scientists have made in the past few years. In particular, the destruction of the remaining old growth timber in the United States and wholesale cutting of rainforests in South America were on your mind. It seemed to you that it was just common sense to say that people could not just keep cutting down forests, even if they were replanted, without either eventually using up all the timber that remained or causing the destruction of a natural habitat for many animals and plants. You are aware of the extensive documentation which shows that old growth forests are profoundly different from replanted second and third growth forests, despite what many timber industry spokespeople say.

On the other hand, you are also aware that there are reputable scientists who disagree with the dire predictions of ecological disasters. There is some conflicting opinion among experts about whether or not cutting the rainforests is a cause of the hole in the ozone layer, global warming if it truly is happening, or a whole host of other items listed by the environmental groups. The evidence is very difficult to weigh and understand given its highly technical nature, as well as the fact that the disasters being forecast are speculation, not proven facts.

Perhaps you could feel a little better about working for this conglomerate if you simply chose to believe that the doomsayers were wrong and everything would be OK. However, you can't quite convince yourself that it is safe to ignore so much scientific evidence. Maybe, you had thought, if you examined JGC carefully, it would turn out that they were a responsible "green" company just as their name suggests.

That was when you realized that you had a difficult decision to make. The literature the personnel director supplied looked very reassuring, of course. It contained many statements designed to give the reader the impression that JGC was following all the latest environmentally conscious practices used in the logging industry. Yet when you read more of the environmentalists' literature on the Net, it seemed that JGC was guilty of exaggerating their commitment to sound environmental precautions. In fact, one rather radical Web site implicated JGC in clear-cutting, the complete deforestation of an area that leads to erosion and destruction of the soil and all animal habitats in the clear-cut area. There was a picture of a clear-cut area that looked as if someone had firebombed the side of a mountain. The picture was not of any area logged by JGC. But if JGC followed the same process anywhere, it meant damage equal to that of the area pictured.

When you called the personnel manager at JGC and expressed your concerns, he assured you that JGC did no clear-cutting anymore, though it had in the past. He told you that JGC had eliminated the practice, following the guidelines of all governmental agencies and knowledgeable environmentalists. When you pressed for names of individuals in these agencies or of the specific environmentalists, he had effectively dodged the question and simply kept repeating the company's claims as if he were reading out of the same literature he had given you. You were less than certain JGC was a good, green corporate citizen. However, you were far from convinced that they were as bad as many other logging companies.

Their connection to the large conglomerate still bothered you. The conglomerate was often in the news, usually as the object of protests, lawsuits, and government actions against it for some unethical or illegal activity. Not all of the activity was connected to environmental issues. Some were questionable investment practices, violations of agreements with foreign governments, unethical hiring practices, and other such activities. The environmentalist groups also listed four of its subsidiaries in the top ten offenders against the earth. Again, JGC was not one of the companies listed. You couldn't shake the worry, however, that if JGC was owned by a conglomerate with this reputation for being unethical and nongreen and for breaking the law, it would be engaging in similar activities itself.

Try as you might, you couldn't uncover any hard evidence that JGC was guilty of any illegal actions nor of causing massive environmental damage. There were a few small incidents and legal warnings that followed them in which JGC had caused minor damage to the environment. These included using a bleaching agent that was slightly stronger than allowed by law at one of the paper mills JGC owned, and of taking about 2 percent more old growth timber than the law allowed in the last fiscal year. These seemed almost unavoidable transgressions to you, though. After all, a company the size of JGC was bound to run afoul of some law sooner or later, especially environmental restrictions.

Now you had to decide. Can you accept the job with JGC or not? What do you owe to yourself? The money they offered was exceptionally good. You would be moving into middle management immediately upon graduating with a B.A., which would make you the only member of your class to do so, at least as far as you could tell. But are JGC and its parent corporation responsible companies? If JGC is, it seems clear that its parent company is not. Are you going to be contributing to destructive and harmful practices if you become JGC's branch manager? Do you owe anything to future generations and the earth itself? And, even if you do, is it clear that working for JGC violates such duties? Who are you harming if you merely oversee JGC's office? Could you get into a position to rectify any questionable practices, or would you get dragged into becoming a participant? What kind of pressure might come from the conglomerate?

While these are all important questions, time is running out on JGC's offer. The personnel director said he needed your answer in two days. Can your concerns be RESOLVEDD before then?

36. AN ETHICAL SURVEY
Should You Follow the Law Even If It Harms Someone?

Citizen's Gas Company hired you and Felicia Alden, independent surveyors located in a nearby county, to map the property line between two farms. The reason for the survey, they said, was that they had to be sure who owned the land they needed to lay a new pipeline. The problem was that Mr. Mander, who owned one of the farms, had refused to give permission to lay the line on his property. Mrs. Kildare, a widow, said they could lay the line anywhere on her property, which adjoined Mr. Mander's.

This was good news for the Gas Company, as there was only a small slice of land that was geologically suitable for the pipeline. It seemed that the slice of land ran almost right along the boundary between the two farms. It would cost the company a great deal of money to have to lay the pipe elsewhere, because most of the county was situated on solid bedrock that began only a few feet under the fertile topsoil. Except for this small strip of land, under which was almost pure clay, there was no inexpensive place to put the pipe. Mr. Mander warned them that they'd better be sure where his property ended and Kildare's began, or else. Felicia and you had been hired to do just that.

Following your obtaining the appropriate maps and legal descriptions, the two of you headed out to the farms. As expected, when talking to Mr. Mander, he was very unpleasant, if not downright threatening. Neither of you cared a bit for him.

Mrs. Kildare, however, was as sweet as she could be, offered you lunch, and said to take as much time as you wanted on her property, then stop by for coffee and cake. During your visit to her house, you noticed that she seemed to be struggling to make ends meet; the furniture was old and worn, as were the rugs and her clothes. She even remarked that if it weren't for her land, she'd be almost completely broke.

You both went to work plotting the boundary lines between the Mander and Kildare farms. After about an hour you began to recheck all your findings against the maps and legal descriptions. There was a major problem. The legal descriptions and maps didn't match the fence line or the boundaries that Mrs. Kildare said marked her property. In fact, her property line was about twenty feet onto Mr. Mander's farm. There was an old fence there, but no matter how you rechecked all the figures, it was clear that Mr. Mander owned all the land the Gas Company was interested in. Moreover, Mrs. Kildare was going to lose a sizable chunk of real estate once the Gas Company filed the survey.

Felicia and you skipped the return visit with Mrs. Kildare and a week later turned in your report to the Gas Company. You received your check, but went away feeling bad for Mrs. Kildare. But what could you do? The legal boundaries were set. You were feeling guilty for not telling her, but didn't have the heart to do it.

Six months later you had completed a job near Mrs. Kildare's farm and decided to stop in to express your concern over what the survey had shown. When she saw you at the door, Mrs. Kildare welcomed you as an old friend. Before you could say anything, she told you that the Gas Company had purchased the rights to lay the pipeline on her property and for a very generous sum. She said the money was making a big difference to her.

Upon making a visit to the boundary area, you noticed that Citizen's Gas had installed the gas line as originally planned, for there were warning signs indicating the presence of an underground pipeline. Then you noticed that the old fence on Mr. Mander's property was exactly where it had been six months earlier. The markers ran right along the Kildare side of the fence, but you know they are well inside the Mander property. Citizen's Gas had apparently ignored your survey report and gone ahead with its original plans as if Mrs. Kildare owned the property. Apparently, it had not filed the survey with the county. Citizen's Gas was evidently disregarding both the truth and the law.

Knowing that you both have some professional responsibility as certified public surveyors, you and Alden wrote a letter to Citizen's Gas advising it of the apparent problem. You received no acknowledgment of your letter and saw no evidence that it had any effect. When Felicia called the Gas Company, she was put on hold for twenty minutes before being cut off. It seemed you were being completely ignored.

Now what? What should you do?

On the one hand, you have accurate and reliable knowledge of an ongoing violation of the law. You both have a professional ethical obligation not to be parties to fraud. To fail to pursue the problem might be a violation of professional ethics or the law.

On the other hand, to take further action would harm all the wrong people. It would ultimately deprive poor Mrs. Kildare of much needed cash, give extra, unneeded support to the unpleasant Mr. Mander, and likely cost Citizen's Gas a pretty penny. Finally, it would ensure that you would not receive any further business from Citizen's, and might well damage your reputations.

Is there any way out of this difficult situation? Analyze the case until you have RESOLVEDD the important issues, all things considered.

37. DRUG TESTS AS PREVENTIVE MAINTENANCE
A Company Considers Drug/Alcohol Testing

DeltaMatic (DM) is a company specializing in children's toys. It has had no known drug- or alcohol-related accidents of any consequence in its ten-year existence, but can management rely on this to continue? One of DM's executives, Molly Beagle, has just returned from a workshop that included a presentation on the positive effects of correctly administered drug and alcohol screenings of employees. She was excited about the idea and pushing to have DM consider it.

The presentation began with some chilling statistics concerning lost time, injuries, and health care costs of drug and alcohol abuse to American corporations. The total costs estimated topped $80 billion, once all the factors were considered. The presenter then argued that even the federal government had mandatory drug and alcohol screenings, as did many private corporations such as Mobil Oil and Exxon, so it did not violate workers' rights to require random screenings for substance abuse. It was this that DM's upper management was being asked to consider.

DM employs approximately 600 full- and part-time workers over its three shifts. The plant has many hazardous areas because of its use of lead for die casting, hot shrink-wrapping machines for packaging, and a machine shop for making the die casts for its toys and metal pieces for board games. The foundry has a lead smelting pot that contains boiling lead, the shrink-wrapping machines reach temperatures well over 300 degrees, and the machine shop has all the potential hazards of any machine shop. In addition, the production line can be dangerous for careless workers, as can the operation of forklifts, especially if the operators are incompetent or impaired. Thus, Molly has argued that it cannot be safe to let workers with drug or alcohol problems operate any of these machines nor work in any of these areas. The potential for harm to themselves or others is simply too high. That no one has ever been injured as a result of another worker's being drunk or stoned on the job is simply good luck, and good luck the company should not expect to continue.

With the statistics on the number of drug abusers and alcoholics in America, Molly argues, a company like DM must protect itself from financial loss, injury-related time off, and expensive health care coverage because of workers who are substance abusers. Even though there have been no identifiable substance-abuse-related accidents, there is no telling how many workers arrive late or leave early, take sick days, and claim illnesses because of substance abuse at DM. Just because there have been no *known* accidents due to drugs or alcohol, the company cannot be sure that seemingly unrelated injuries were not actually caused by workers who abused substances. For these and other reasons, such as the illegality of drugs, she is urging DM to implement a drug and alcohol screening program.

The program would be implemented in as "kind and gentle" a way for workers as possible. The proposal includes the following provisions: (1) The tests will be mandatory for all new job applicants; no one who refuses to take the test or fails it will be hired. (2) For all current employees, there will be a 90-day grace period from the time the program is enacted until their first random screening, which every employee will take once every year. (3) Should any current employee fail the test at any time, the policy will be to give a warning, followed by mandatory follow-up monthly tests over a six-month period, concurrent with required enrollment in a confidential assistance program to help overcome the problem. (4) Every employee will be entitled to "three strikes," with the second violation resulting in a return to the program and screening, following a two-week unpaid suspension, while the third offense will result in termination. Due process and appeals guidelines will be put in place to protect workers from false positives and other abuses. Further details will be worked out once the program is in place and specifics studied.

The workers, who are unionized, have heard of the proposal and are insistent that such a program *not* be instituted. The union representatives maintain that this violates the privacy workers are entitled to by the constitutional right of privacy and protection from "unreasonable search and seizure." The tests involve turning over bodily fluids (urine or blood), which the union feels is unreasonable and violates worker privacy. "If employees cannot refuse their employer bodily fluids, then what privacy is left?" the union rep has asked.

Whether workers smoke at home, spend time at a bar, perform dangerous sports like sky-diving, or engage in other unhealthy practices may all present ways for the company to save money. There is no predicting what will be called "work-related" and lead to intrusions into workers' lives after the new drug policy is enacted. This, the union says, violates worker autonomy and makes DM the arbiter of how one can live one's private life.

Furthermore, the union argues that good job performance does not require one to be drug-free. It is well known that many habitual drug-users do in fact live productive lives and work successfully and safely. On the other hand, workers who are in the midst of bereavement or divorces or other life crises often experience a decline in the quality and safety of their work. Will they be investigated and counseled and perhaps fired if their life crises persist?

DM's management replies that with the right guidelines there is no violation of privacy, that the company has no plans to go any further into workers' private lives, and that the company has a right to ensure safety in the workplace for all workers by screening out those who are potential risks due to alcohol or drugs. Finally, the cost-benefit analysis for companies with such programs proves that health care costs and lost-time accidents and illnesses drop. General productivity of the workforce is also better. All these factors are job-related, directly or indirectly, and therefore something an employer can monitor. It is in both the company's and the workers' best interests that DM start its testing program.

The union still holds that there is a world of difference between investigations of private lives and employer evaluations of work performance. Evaluations are specified in advance, their content is regulated, and their purpose is singular. Drug and alcohol tests evaluate a part of workers' private lives with no reference to actual work performance. Use of a drug or alcohol test as the sole criterion for firing ignores job performance entirely. That is irrelevant to the work contract, the proper role of management, and fairness to the workers.

As a member of the panel established by DM's management and the union, you are about to meet with both groups to hear their sides of the issue. It is a difficult issue, pitting the company's interests against the privacy of its own workers. But it may also be in the workers' interests to surrender their privacy in the name of safety and costs. On the other hand, privacy and autonomy are precious to most Americans and are not surrendered easily nor without hard feelings. In the long run, whose interests should take precedence? This and the other questions must get RESOLVEDD before you vote. What will your decision be?

38. BUYING STOCK AND SELLING ONE'S SOUL
Should You Avoid a Potential Conflict of Interest?

As a newly hired finance officer for an established brokerage firm with an excellent reputation for both success and honesty, you had, for your first six months with the firm, been riding a wave of enthusiasm. And your new assignment in the company has presented you with an exciting opportunity, even if it is a chance to profit from the misfortunes of others. But now you are realizing that the choice involves ethical as well as financial risk, and you must weigh the values at stake and the possible consequences of your options.

Your supervisor is the well-known and highly successful senior account executive, Carol Sakawi. Carol had assigned you to a number of new accounts during your first four months at the firm, and you had picked up a clear sense of the attitude of senior management toward the credit status of various corporate clients. The company seemed to take, in most cases, a moderate approach to credit risk, reducing the credit of clients only when such reductions were clearly demonstrated. Furthermore, you found that Carol, like other senior account executives in this particular firm, usually took the recommendations of her subordinates regarding changes in the credit status of clients. So you were finding the firm to be a congenial environment in which to work and also, in one particular case, financially promising.

You were assigned to the important account of the Lone Star Bank Holding Corporation just two weeks ago. Carol had told you of rumors that Lone Star was in financial straits and assigned you to investigate them immediately, together with Harvey Washington, another young finance analyst assigned temporarily from another department. You and Harvey decided together that he would talk directly with the Lone Star executives and you would investigate the supposed sources of the rumors. By the end of the first week on this assignment, a complex of events had taken place which had your head spinning.

By the end of the second day, the rumors had led you nowhere except to documentation of the fact that several top executives of Lone Star had, during the past month, sold off large blocks of their stock in the company. Given the information about the company available to the public, there was no good explanation for why this had happened. Indeed, one might suspect insider trading on the part of these executives. So you began to wonder if something big and bad was about to happen.

Harvey, however, found absolutely nothing of significance—not even a suggestive clue. From his perspective, everything seemed to be normal and financially sound. It was Tuesday evening, shortly after you had both agreed on further avenues to explore tomorrow, when the bombshells hit. And both came to you, of all places, on the evening news! First there was a news story that the local newspaper had reported earlier in the day that Lone Star was going to declare tomorrow a $12.1 million loss for the quarter. Then there was news that the Securities Commissioner of your state had suspended trading of Lone Star stock. You were stunned, and called Harvey at once.

The significance of all this was that you had clearly failed to provide your brokerage with any advance warning of the impending crisis. This might reflect poorly on Carol and the two of you. It would be especially bad if Lone Star had made any major leveraged stock or bond purchases that day. You could hardly wait to find out.

Once online and into the brokerage's computer, it was clear what had happened. Lone Star had actually leveraged the purchase of a huge block of its own stock before noon that day. So the Lone Star management was apparently acting to prop up the price of company shares by borrowing money from your brokerage! By hiding the real information from you and Harvey, Lone Star had smoothly and successfully used brokerage money to take a major first step in defending itself against collapse. You and Harvey, a couple of rookies, had been played for fools! What next?

Wednesday was a whirlwind of discoveries, consultations, and decisions. Carol stayed calm and tolerant under the circumstances, Harvey seemed nervous, and the Lone Star executives were understandably reticent. One tidbit of information which you discovered late in the day was particularly interesting.

Lone Star was scheduled to auction off, the next day, a block of stock with a book value of $7 per share. You knew it would sell for far less than that. And you also thought that Lone Star would, before long, come out of the financial crisis once it spun off two miserable small banks it had acquired last year from a hostile takeover in West Virginia. You knew the auction was possibly a rare, even if risky, opportunity. And the Securities Commissioner had already decided to allow this particular auction to take place. So you prepared to spend $4,000 on as much stock as you could get.

On Thursday, at noon, you found out that you were the owner of 20,000 shares of Lone Star stock! You had succeeded in picking it up for 20 cents per share by some careful bidding online during a midmorning break. That stock could make you rich someday, or possibly become worthless. But the risk was, in your view, surely worthwhile.

It was in the middle of the next week that Carol called you in for another talk. This time she seemed to have a different tone than before. And as she told you of her knowledge of your purchase of Lone Star stock, it dawned on you that there were implications of which you had not been aware. Carol raised the daunting question of a possible conflict of interest. She pointed out that you were now a stockholder in the troubled company to which your brokerage routinely lends money through stock margins and other types of loans. You are trying to profit from speculation on a future reversal of the company's misfortune.

You explained in your defense that the stock auction was public in every sense and advertised in newspapers all over town. The stories of the company's problems were also public knowledge, and you had not used any privileged information.

When Carol asked if you thought you could continue to work on the account, you said "Of course." Your job is to recommend to your brokerage the best policy for granting stock margins and other forms of loans to the bank holding company. Such matters are irrelevant to decisions about personal stock holdings in Lone Star. Naturally you know that under certain possible future circumstances, your conduct could become highly suspect. If, for example, the holding company's stock and credit ratings drop further, as they well might, and you continue to recommend that its credit at your brokerage remain the same, it may appear as though you are trying to prop up the holding company in bad times in order to facilitate its recovery. If your superiors then discovered that Carol knew what you did about the case and allowed you to continue, you and Carol might well both lose your jobs.

Carol, in her characteristically kind way, has asked you to advise her on the realities, the risks, and the best course of action for you and for her given the circumstances. Of course, you know that the decision is, in the end, hers. But you also feel convinced that she really does want your honest and considered opinion on what to do. So you promise to think it over carefully and give her a full report next Monday.

The problem you now face is how seriously to take the potential conflict of interest. It is very clearly at this point only a potential conflict. But is that acceptable to you, and should it be acceptable to other managers? Many options are available to you at this point, and you will need to assess carefully the ethical and practical considerations in order to see the case RESOLVEDD.

39. TOYS MAY NOT BE US*
Marketing to Please the Customer

You understood Tom Daner's position when it came to the new toy helicopter that Crako Industries had created. Crako had asked Daner Associates, under contract to Crako, to design the advertising for TV. It was a violent toy, a Vietnam-style attack and rescue helicopter complete with detachable machine guns and battlefield stretchers. Daner was reluctant to give Crako's sales manager, Mike Teal, the blood-and-guts style commercial Crako had requested. Tom felt that since the ad was aimed at children, violence should be very limited, and ideally nonexistent. As the head of the creative department for Daner's company, you had been intimately involved in the discussions about and making of the commercials the creative department had produced. You also served as one of five members on Daner Associates' executive committee, now faced with deciding how to approach Mike Teal and which ad to show him.

Tom Daner had acquiesced to Teal's demand that a violent, "guns blazing," "macho," and "mean" ad be produced for Crako, to compete with the toy company's

---

*This scenario is based on the case study "Toy Wars" by Manuel Velasquez, widely reprinted, 1986.

rivals' ads marketing similar toys. The first ad showed the helicopter roaring out of the clouds, shooting at a jungle village below it. When Tom protested the violence, the people who worked for you in the creative department maintained that this was exactly what the client wanted. They felt certain Crako would be very pleased and didn't share Tom's worries about the effects of violence on young children, the target audience. Tom was not convinced they were right.

Daner had then asked that a milder ad of some sort be filmed. The creative department had produced a milder ad showing the helicopter being "flown" in a young boy's hand in the family room. Then the ad fantasized a large rock springing up in the room, stranding the boy atop it. At this point, the helicopter, now on its own, flies down and rescues the boy from the top of the high rock. The creative department was fairly satisfied with the ad, but considered it much too tame for what Crako would buy. This was confirmed when Mike Teal rejected it, even though Tom loved it. The film was trashed, just as the first violent ad had been. Tom then told you to produce yet another ad.

Your people took to the task well and quickly, created a jungle village set, including a river and bridge next to the village. The helicopter, once again, blasted away, with the bridge and village set used as background. The violence level was very high, with the helicopter's machine guns firing loud and long. Explosions and fires flared throughout the ad.

After seeing it, Tom once again protested the level of violence and asked for a softer ad. The changes included the helicopter now flying in to rescue people from the burning village rather than blowing it up. The newest film added exciting music, flashing lights, and expensive special effects. It was exciting, tense, and very realistic. You and your people thought it promoted life-saving but still gave Crako the excitement and tension it wanted.

But there was a problem here, too: Network censors would probably reject the ad because it used so much technical equipment, special effects, and music. The guidelines for network ads require that ads not give children unrealistic expectations and depict only things that kids could actually reproduce in their home by buying the toy. Clearly, any kids who might be able to do this with the helicopter, as presented in your ad, would need a movie company at their disposal to recreate the set, lights, and music. That the helicopter seemed to be self-propelled and under its own control in both ads complicated things even more.

When Tom spoke with Mike Teal about these special effects and the issue of violence banned by the network guidelines, Mike responded that the ads would go on local affiliate stations, not national networks, so the guidelines didn't really apply, technically. Besides, he said, even if they did, the local stations were much looser in their interpretation of the guidelines. Mike said the ad Crako wanted would be no problem.

Tom called a meeting of Daner's executive committee. At the meeting he rehashed the issues and his concern with contributing more violence to what kids already see on TV. As a family-owned company, he did not really want Daner Associates to produce commercials that he would not want his own children to see. That, and the idea of "pulling a technicality" concerning network guidelines, troubled him.

The account executive in charge of Crako replied, "Tom, this is a million-dollar account. It's one twenty-fifth of our annual income! Can you really say you would take a million-dollar loss here? Besides, the customer hired us to fill their needs and we agreed; we have a contract. I think we give them what they want; we owe them that." Another member seemed to agree, while one member stuck with Tom. You and another member remained silent.

Daner thought for a while and decided he would put it to a vote. He said, "We have two ads made right now: the very violent one and the rescue ad, which includes some violence but does not show the helicopter shooting and blasting a village. We have a number of options, so I'll ask for a vote from the committee and stick by it. Maybe I am being too sensitive, maybe not; you'll decide."

Tom then laid out the options to consider: (1) Give Crako the most violent ad you had produced. (2) Offer Crako both ads and let them pick. (3) Offer Crako the rescue ad only and take a loss if they refuse it, or feel good about it should they buy it. He was asking for the committee to choose one of the three options. You were pretty sure that both options 1 and 2 would result in Crako's having the violent ad on TV as soon as possible. They might take the rescue ad if it was all that was offered, but they might also leave Daner high and dry and take their business elsewhere. Whatever happened, there was the possibility that Daner would become known for its actions in the ad industry and among clients. It could be seen as a company with principles and gain a positive reputation. Or it could be seen as a company that would not meet customers' expectations and gain a negative reputation. How might the public and future customers perceive whichever ad made it on TV? You couldn't be sure.

You know how much work your creative people put into option 1, and that they would want you to go with it. They worked hard on the rescue ad, too, but were clearly not quite as happy with the final product. Do you owe them anything in terms of trusting their judgment? With the possible effects of each ad on children, as well as the contract you had with Crako, the situation concerning the censors, your own department's feelings, and the future reputation of Daner Associates in mind, how will you vote? Win, lose, or draw, you have to live with yourself after the decision is made. Yours may be the deciding vote, so it is important to have things RESOLVEDD before you vote. What is your choice?

40. TOO PERSONAL TO ASK?
Violations of Privacy in Hiring and Testing

For three years you had worked in the personnel office of Jefferson Security, a private security company that provided security guards for banks, malls, and other businesses. Your job was to interview prospective employees and administer the company's personality exam, a standard requirement in the security field. The candidates that you interviewed had all been carefully screened for criminal records and had placed well on the aptitude tests given to every promising applicant. Your job was to judge their character through a personal interview and administer the personality exam.

Until this week you had enjoyed the job and felt confident that between the interview and the test, you were giving objective evaluations of the candidates' honesty and trustworthiness. But now there was a problem, brought about by the institution of a new personality exam. Your supervisor had instructed you to use the new, "more accurate and in-depth" exam and to do away with the old, "rather cold and impersonal" one. You decided to review the new exam to see how much improvement had been made in the questions.

As you began reading the questions, your anticipation turned to disbelief. Some questions seemed overly personal, while others could not possibly be answered without reflecting poorly on anyone who replied honestly. Scanning the question booklet, you saw the following true-false questions:

Sexual things disgust me.

As a child there were times I hated my parents.

I feel like jumping off when I'm on a high place.

I have never done anything I was punished for.

I have never had black, tarry bowel movements.

There is nothing wrong with masturbating.

There is a big difference between a person who steals because he has to and a person who steals because he wants to.

I often insist on doing things my own way.

Low wages force employees to steal from their employers.

I have never taken anything home from places where I have worked in the past.

Some of the other questions required short essays, and included questions very much like the true-false ones. No honest person could complete this test without looking like a thief or a liar.

As you sat and considered what to do, you remembered reading about a lawsuit brought against a company that had used just such a test. A famous Yale law professor had taken the case to court. The article included an interview in which the professor had said that such tests were seriously flawed. The answers were supposed to help employers predict future dishonest actions, but when used as criteria for hiring they could cause a person to be denied a job without ever having done anything wrong. They were, she had said, potentially discriminatory, an unconstitutional invasion of privacy, and contained questions that were unrelated to the job or its requirements. Your new test seemed to have all those flaws and more.

You decided to talk to your supervisor. After listening to your reservations about the test, he tried to explain the theory behind the test. He said that a security job demands employees of the highest moral character, and that the test is designed to evaluate a person's character. Then he enumerated three factors involved in employee dishonesty: opportunity, attitude, and need. Opportunities will always be there, and needs may arise anytime in the future. But an employee who has the right attitude is unlikely to act dishonestly. If employees have the attitude that dishonesty or theft is OK, then any unimportant need may trigger them to break the law. Moreover, since other security companies began using the test, the number of complaints against their guards had declined dramatically.

It sounded good in theory, you thought. But what about all those problems mentioned by the law professor? What about the invasion of an applicant's privacy? Or the fact that almost any honest person has to look bad when answering these questions truthfully? Does any employer have a right to this kind of compromising information about anyone? It would be difficult to give your own mother such information, let alone some stranger in a personnel office. And how do questions about your bowel movements, sexuality, and masturbation help predict whether you will act dishonestly?

Noting that you are bothered about administering the test, the personnel director suggested that you take the day to think it over and return tomorrow. If you felt you could not administer the test to people, he would see about giving you another assignment or transferring you elsewhere. He assured you that none of this would be held against you, and that he was sure you would come to the right conclusion.

Should you administer the test or not? You wonder whether the company will hold it against you if you refuse to use the test. Besides, you genuinely enjoy doing the interviews and can't think of another job that you'd want in the company. But you are very troubled by the kinds of questions asked and the issue of privacy they raise. The problem must be RESOLVEDD by tomorrow, however, since there will be a waiting room full of applicants at 9:00 A.M.

41. PROFIT OR LOSS
OF THE ENVIRONMENT?
Installing Pollution Controls that are Not Legally Required

Your father and you had been discussing his latest idea for the family business, a small metal plating company. He had just finished reading a series of articles on the environmental problems caused by various processes used in the plating industry. Because of the caustic and toxic chemicals used in these processes, the rivers and lakes near many plating plants are dying. Those that are still viable are in serious danger of becoming polluted past the point of easy recovery. Your father, the founder and president of the company, was troubled by these articles.

Your father wanted you to set up a study of the feasibility of installing a series of purification and pollution control devices that would treat the liquid wastes leaving your plant. He gave you a number of articles that described such devices, but that did not include details about their related costs. He told you to ask Claudia Bertrand and Juan Higueras, two plant engineers, to help prepare the reports. Finally, Paulette Kaye, your accountant, was to calculate the costs involved.

The task consumed most of your time for the next month. You and Juan visited a number of facilities utilizing similar devices, but which were not in the plating industry. You obtained pollution figures from them, both before and after installation. Claudia studied the details of the devices and ways to apply them to the plating processes. It became clear that such procedures would be effective in reducing your output of pollutants.

One of Claudia's assistants, however, raised an interesting question. Why were you thinking about new pollution control equipment when the wastewater you produce is well under the legal EPA requirements? Claudia checked the figures and pointed out that you were meeting EPA guidelines for all of the pollutants your plant discharges. In the worst case, your plant discharged acid at the rate of 8 parts per million (ppm), compared with the EPA standard of 10 ppm. The other toxic wastes were even further below the EPA standards.

When you raised this question with your father, he handed you a number of reports and articles that cast doubt on the EPA standards. For acid, one report recommended no more than 4 ppm, saying that anything more is a significant hazard for fish and wildlife. Your father explained that he would like the entire plant to conform to the other levels recommended in the articles.

You took the articles to Claudia and Juan, recommending their standards. You also told Paulette to calculate the costs of reducing pollutants to the levels suggested in the articles.

After four weeks, your report was complete. The various purification devices seemed more efficient than even your father expected. All of the toxic wastes produced by your plant could be cut down to the levels recommended in the articles.

The problem, of course, was the cost. Almost 40 percent of your profit margin would be eaten up by the costs of installation in the first year. After that, running and maintaining the equipment would significantly increase your production costs. To cover them, price increases or a smaller profit margin would be inevitable.

In an industry as competitive as plating, it could be disastrous to raise prices as much as you would need. No other plating companies were using the new purification devices. Most were meeting EPA standards, just as your company was. So far as you know, however, not one is even close to the recommended levels outlined in the articles. So you would be competing with companies not hampered by the costs of purification devices.

When your father read the full report, he was pleased that the devices would greatly reduce your toxic wastes. He was troubled by the prospect of reduced profits, but said he would be more troubled by continuing to pollute at the current levels. He suggested that the company would receive some good public relations from making such an environmentally sound decision. And he thought the company could exploit that to its advantage.

As he looked over the figures Paulette had prepared, he commented that he was sure you could remain viable, and make about a 10 percent profit in prosperous years. During a recession, though, he admitted that you would have to hang on and swallow some losses once the purification devices were installed. All in all, he preferred to go ahead and install the devices. But he was willing to listen to any counterarguments you had. If you could convince him to leave well enough alone, he assured you that he would back you 100 percent. "After all, everything is legal as it is, so maybe you can convince me I'm being too demanding."

The decision is complicated. What is the price of a clear conscience? Do you have obligations that go beyond merely obeying the law? Should you do what will be most profitable for the company and its workers or not? There are clearly many questions that have to be RESOLVEDD.

42. ABRACADABRA!
Unauthorized Computer Files and Your Personal Values

You have heard of computer "snoops" who tap into various data banks to obtain helpful information. Much of this snooping, you know, does not violate any laws, despite its ethically dubious nature. You know that there is even an organization, with a code of ethics, called the Society of Computer Intelligence, formed by a concerned group of computer "spies." You have also heard rumors that, in the corporate world, French and Japanese firms are masters at obtaining information this way.

For more than a year you have worked as a data systems specialist at Griggs Toy Company, which has about 100 full-time employees. The company creates new toys and games, preferring to sell its ideas to the much larger, well-known companies, though it markets some of its own creations.

Although you are by far the most experienced and knowledgeable computer engineer in the company, until now you never dreamed of becoming a computer spy. It was last Monday morning that the CEO of the firm, Darren Griggs, approached you with the need to obtain more information about your competitors. He explained that the time had come to delve into various data banks containing information on rival toy companies. He explained that competition is getting very stiff and that recently foreign firms have been competing directly with American firms all over the world. Any edge would help in this competitive business.

Griggs pointed out that Japanese companies have been gathering computer intelligence for years and consider this a normal business practice. Since they think nothing special of it, he explained, neither should we. It is time to turn your expertise toward the gathering of information. Griggs pointed out that the company subscribes to a large computer network database that compiles information of all sorts on toy companies, and that the firm could benefit from your searching the database for information about the financial activity of your competition.

You hesitated at first, and Griggs reacted at once by stating that you would not be doing anything illegal. "We don't want you to illegally penetrate confidential information networks or bug corporate boardrooms. We just want you to tap into the network for information freely given to it by its subscribers. It's all legal."

You are still a little hesitant given that your parents, devout Christians, raised you to be honest and to do unto others as you would have them do unto you. But Griggs has convinced you it's all legal, others do it, and you would only be compiling freely given data.

Only last week at a party you had heard about the Web site of a hacker who had recently been caught and detained and would soon be charged with illegal activity. The hacker had apparently formulated a list of instructions on how to break into databases of networks supported by subscribers and supposedly secure. Perhaps out of spite, he had put the instructions on his Web site for all to see! It had been the talk of the party.

When Griggs left the room the next day at work, you promptly found the hacker's Web site and sure enough, there were the instructions. You copied them and then followed them to see what might happen. Amazingly, it worked on your first try, and you were inside the database of code numbers, including the code you use to access the network in the toy industry.

It was at that moment that Darren stopped by unexpectedly and looked over your shoulder, immediately seeing what was on the screen. "Whoa, how'd you get those numbers?" he asked. You explained what had happened, and Darren grinned and told you to access the confidential files of the rival companies, which contained all sorts of information that could give your company an advantage in planning corporate strategy for the coming year. "Now that's the magic of a good employee!" Darren exclaimed gleefully.

"What do you mean?" you asked. "How can that give us an edge?"

"Look, our confidential file contains our budget figures, including research and development. If we know how much our competitors are spending on R&D and just what kind, we can raise or lower our own budget, increase our R&D efforts, and maybe hit the market first with some new products. Who knows what else we'd learn that would give us a leg up on them?"

You don't know what to say, but are feeling some real hesitation, aware that now you are doing computer spying. These files are confidential, the network would never release such information, and you'd never want your rivals to have access to your confidential file. Yet isn't business a matter of outcompeting the other companies? Besides, you got the numbers by accident. In the same position, your competition would check your files. And you have no legal obligation to keep their files private. Since this doesn't violate the law, many businesspeople would consider it justifiable. You've been handed a lucky break that gives you an advantage over the competition. It's no different from finding a confidential memo on the street.

You know this is true, but still feel somehow compromised and dirty. What would your father and mother think? On the other hand, many traditional Christian values are clearly inconsistent with modern corporate culture. How would it affect you to turn down this order? Should you even worry about such questions? Or should you just follow the order, accept the practice as legal, and go ahead? These issues are not easily RESOLVEDD. But you must decide now, and live with the outcome.

43. A CHALLENGE TO ANTI-NEPOTISM POLICIES ABROAD
When in Rome Do You Do as the Romans Do?

You have been working for almost a year now as the manager in charge of a small but growing office of a multinational company in a South American country. The office has been in existence in this country for almost three years, and you are the second manager in its history. You were advised by your mentor in the corporation back home to take the position if offered because it has enormous potential for growth and could well become the central success of your career, eventually sending you right to the top of the company.

Your best salesman, Miguel Fontina, comes from a large, established, wealthy, and influential local family and was educated at the nation's leading university. Indeed, there is no doubt that some of his success in sales is due to his personal contacts with other businesspeople all over the country. With nearly half the business you do in the country being with firms outside the local metropolitan area in which you are located, Miguel's connections are important.

The problem you are having with Miguel is based on a conflict between the stated anti-nepotism policies of the company and the customs and values of the local population. The corporation permits the hiring of relatives of employees, but requires that no relatives be allowed to work as subordinates for their relatives. It also requires that no special business preferences such as lower loan rates, lower prices, or deferred payment plans be given to customers related to corporate employees. That is, the official minimums approved by the central management of the company abroad are not to be violated for any reason, including family connections.

The country you are located in, however, is famous for its family networks, its cronyism, and the peddling of influence. It is a society in which the people one knows are as important in business success as what one does or accomplishes. Before leaving for your assignment here, you were warned of the complications and dangers this can cause and were given company policies, as well as several books to read on the subject. You are fully aware that Miguel was hired as much for his family connections as for his promise as a salesman. And now the conflict is in your office, here on your desk, and on your mind!

It came to your attention early yesterday morning when you were reviewing a large new sales bill to a company with offices that are local and in other cities in the country. Two things were clear on paper, and a third was brought out by Miguel in person. First was the name of the customer: the Fontina Canning Company. You wondered immediately if this was Miguel's family. Second were the price and terms of payment for your product. They were both a little below the company's stated minimum, and also below the standards of your competitors. They were, moreover, low enough to virtually eliminate any profit that you might make from the sale.

It was only an hour later that Miguel came bouncing in cheerfully to your office to discuss the order. He explained that this order was a major coup for the company, as it would establish a new account with a major producer, replacing the account that Fontina Canning had with one of your prime competitors. It would open the door to considerable new business in the future and was well worth the initial sacrificial terms, which made it what is often called in business a "loss leader."

When you asked Miguel if the Fontina Canning Company was run by his relatives, he answered that it was his cousins who now controlled the firm, his uncle having retired just last year. When you reminded him of the corporation's anti-nepotism policies, he looked at you as if you were crazy. "I signed this contract for the benefit of this company, not the benefit of my cousins" was his reply.

Then you asked him if he was receiving a kickback for the deal. He became insulted and cited company policy that kickbacks are forbidden. He next gave you a lengthy lecture on the need to be flexible in business and how the corporation needed to have an image of flexibility if it was to succeed here in South America. He explained that as a local citizen, he had a duty to help you understand the particular cultural climate of the area, and that you both have a duty to promote long-term business success, not just high quarterly profits.

You said that you would think it over, but that you were less than delighted with the arrangements. You explained that some rules are essential for a successful business and that choosing to violate company policy is a major decision which he should not have made on his own. You knew that you had some serious thinking to do on the matter.

Review of your notes, company policy, and your understanding of your job, its challenge, and your future clarified a number of important points for you. First, the company clearly expected you to make the decision on your own. Your boss back home had briefed you on the issues, given you all the relevant background information you needed to make the decision, and made it clear that in South America, you would be the boss. It would clearly count against you to call him up and ask for consultation on this question. To do so would be to admit that you could not handle such a touchy situation, showing timidity and a lack of strong business leadership. Managers are not expected to go whining to their superiors every time there is a difficult decision to make. One should seek advice from above only if a decision exceeds one's authority. You had heard your boss lecture other subordinates on these points a number of times in the past.

Second, to violate company policy in such a case would be dangerous for many reasons. It would set a precedent locally and establish a reputation that would no doubt spread, thus bringing in other customers expecting similar treatment. If in the long run your many contracts lost too much money for the corporation, the reduced profits might all be left at your door. To let this go uncorrected could certainly earn you a reputation for being spineless.

On the other hand, major risks sometimes lead to great business success. Flexibility is clearly essential for a multinational company. Is Miguel right that this is a case for which the risks are well worth the likely future successes? Don't you owe it to the company to build future business?

Then, too, this was not an illegal practice, but was merely one that compromised internal company policy. Wouldn't the possible increase in business in the future justify this small compromise of internal policy? Aren't policies subject to the discretion of the manager in charge of the operation, so long as they do not subject the company to legal action? Besides, when in Rome, or South America, shouldn't an American company do as the Romans or South Americans do? Foremost in your mind now is whether or not following corporate policy is really acting faithfully to the company. Is it in any way unethical to realize the limitations of company policy in order to advance the business? In the end, what is most important in deciding your best course of action and getting the case RESOLVEDD?

44. FAIR PRICING?
Taking Advantage of Circumstances

"The Corner Hardware Store" was the name of the business you had owned and operated for the last ten years in a southern city. As a neighborhood business you did fairly well, never really making a huge profit, but enough to be comfortable. Of course, there had been a couple of years when the economy was bad and your customers had to cut back on home projects, thus leaving you with some minor losses. The business had picked up since then, and you were running in the black.

As in many parts of the country, your area has experienced very unusual weather this year. There have been a number of small floods and a major one. Just last week, a tornado did heavy damage to your neighborhood. The results are that you are making very brisk sales as people begin to fix the damage done to their homes. In fact, there are some building supplies that you now must reorder. Consequently, you have been spending increased time trying to locate new suppliers and working out shipment schedules.

Your sister, who is the bookkeeper for your store, has been trying to convince you that this "building boom" is a golden opportunity for the business. She has suggested that since the market for building supplies and tools has created great demand, you should take advantage of that fact and boost your prices to increase your total profit and compensate for your extra work locating suppliers.

"You need to let the market dictate the prices," she told you. "After all, this kind of a situation isn't going to last forever, is it? There are so many items you can sell for more because the customers just have to have them. You can double or triple your profits while the demand lasts."

"That sounds kind of unfair to the customers," you responded.

"Why? Isn't supply and demand the name of the game? Isn't capitalism all about making profit? The demand is much higher than the supply can satisfy right now. To me that means higher prices will not cut down on sales and will bring in some real money for a change" was her answer.

"But we are making money already. It's not like we're in the red. Besides, this sounds unethical to me. I'd be taking advantage of people's misfortunes to make a larger profit. Most of the people coming in lately are neighborhood people whose houses were damaged by the floods and tornado. I mean, they're really hurting. How can I reap windfall profits off of their hardship?"

She just looked at you and shook her head. "Where were all these customers those two years when we almost went under? Don't you think they know the situation? Most people understand that when supplies are short, prices rise. Look at what happened during the gas crisis of the 1970s, the Gulf War, and the last couple of years of tensions in the Middle East, even before the Iraq War. Gas prices went up when the supplies were cut down. People understand this. Why not make a little extra for us now? Besides, this certainly isn't illegal, so how can it be unethical? And remember, this little building boom isn't going to last forever."

You considered her arguments and had to admit they made some sense. There was no law against raising prices to suit the circumstances; merchants often charge "what the market will bear." Many resort towns and tourist-related businesses pump up their prices during the busiest parts of the season. You knew a couple of towns up north where the locals stopped eating at the town restaurants in the summer because the prices went up so much during the fishing and camping season. Those same local folks came back and patronized the restaurants from Labor Day to Memorial Day the next year. They understood the situation because many of them worked for businesses that followed the same practices. Everyone took it for granted that this was just good business. Maybe your sister was right.

Then again, this seems like a very different situation from "summer tourist season" price increases. Those tourists are there voluntarily and know ahead of time what kind of prices to expect. Your customers are having to rebuild their homes after a series of disasters over which they had no control. This raises a couple of serious questions in your mind. First, is it ethical to make a profit by charging more to people who are recovering from a disaster? They have no choice but to rebuild, and therefore are acting under a sort of duress to begin with. Is it fair to exploit them? But many are also getting insurance settlements to cover the rebuilding costs. Second, the price increases are unexpected and may cause hard feelings if the customers think you are taking advantage of them to increase your own profits. This might leave permanent resentment and cause them to shop elsewhere in the future, even if you lower the prices back to normal later on. In fact, lowering the prices after they have fixed their houses may just convince them that you do not care about them as people, but only as "cash cows" to milk for your own benefit. Given that this is a neighborhood business, alienating the community seems like a risky proposition. It seems that you owe your regular customers more than this.

When you discussed all of your thoughts with your sister and the other four regular employees, they all agreed that these were concerns to take seriously. But apart from trying to be as gentle as you could in raising prices, they all agreed it made sense under the circumstances to increase prices. One employee again pointed out all the extra work you had done trying to locate more materials and tools for your customers. "Shouldn't you be compensated for that?" he had asked. Your sister simply repeated her earlier points about supply and demand, the legality of a price raise, and that the customers had to understand that shortages meant higher prices. She ended by saying that any customers who felt alienated and then took their business elsewhere were customers you probably could not count on if a big hardware chain store ever opened up nearby. She urged you to "Make it while you can."

Both sides of this issue have merit. Capitalism has traditionally and still does function largely on supply and demand. Prices in the hardware business are set largely on that basis, and in light of the competition. If all this is true, what is wrong with your doing the same? On the other hand, you have the feeling of "kicking someone when they're down" in the current situation. Is it right to capitalize on storm and flood damage? Can you afford to alienate your customers? Or do you have a right to make a legal profit regardless of the circumstances? It is true that this building boom can only last a short time. Who knows what the future of your business will be? Shouldn't you do as well for yourself and your employees as circumstances allow?

It seems that you must act quickly if you are to maximize your profits. How should this issue be RESOLVEDD? It's all up to you, but others will be affected by your decision.

45. DOUBLE BAD LUCK
Firing at Will or Compassion?

There were times you hated having chosen a career in human resource management, and this is one of them. The decision you face is difficult, involving such intense ethical conflict that you wish you had stuck with Art History back in college. To terminate a worker is never a pleasure, but to decide whether to terminate Rowna Sanchez is especially unpleasant.

You are the manager of a franchise office for Quick Help, a staff-leasing company that provides workers for businesses. The company specializes in high-tech and highly skilled office workers, even providing a money-back guarantee for any client who is dissatisfied with Quick's workers. It is because of the high levels of performance required of all Quick employees that Rowna is being considered for termination. Her job performance has slipped badly in the past month, and her last assignment brought a costly complaint from a client. As a result of several of Rowna's errors, the client had lost business. Quick reimbursed the client, and the total bill to Quick was nearly $4,000.

Your supervisor, a vice president in a major city some distance away, noticed the debit on your balance sheets, called you, expressed surprise and dismay at your apparent poor judgment in hiring Rowna, and ordered you to terminate her now. The supervisor did not even want to hear the full nature of the problem. Rowna's problem was well known to you, understandable, forgivable, and, yes, medical in nature.

It has now been more than three months since Rowna was attacked by an armed robber who broke into her apartment, overpowered her, tied her up, robbed and then raped her in front of her six-year-old daughter, and left the two of them tied up on the floor. They were discovered two hours later by a neighbor. She was hysterical and incoherent at the time. With the help of her neighbor and friends, she recovered from her physical injuries and some of the emotional trauma over the next two months before returning to work at Quick. But the remaining psychological damage was longer-lasting.

After returning to work a month ago, Rowna had displayed a number of lapses of attention, abruptly left the workplace two or three times daily, and was discovered crying in the lunchroom on two separate occasions. The employer had complained of the slowness of her work, and also of her errors. It was clear that recovery lay somewhere in the future.

A dutiful employee yourself, you initially decided that you would follow apparent orders from the vice president, and so you notified Rowna this morning that she was finished at Quick for now. You were careful to tell her that she could reapply in the future when her problems were under control and her work performance had improved. You could release her in this manner because she is a temporary worker, under no contract, employed by you at will, and covered by no insurance, laws, or policies that prevent you from releasing her for lapse of work performance regardless of the cause.

The problem in all this stemmed from Rowna's reaction. She became tearful and begged you not to release her, explaining that this was the only job she could get in these hard times. If she lost it, she would also lose custody of her daughter to her divorced husband. She explained that she did not qualify for unemployment insurance or for general assistance. She went on to explain that she did not qualify for disability insurance because of a letter her psychiatrist had written to you indicating that she is currently fully capable of working! She begged you to give her another chance and assign her to any menial work, even cleaning houses.

The problem is that Quick specializes in business clerical positions and hires out no menial workers. Your suggestion that she is free to apply for such jobs at some other, appropriate agency was at first met by despair.

It was after you had met with her for a half-hour that Rowna brought forth the argument that the company owes her a position. She argued that firing her for being raped is akin to firing someone for a disability. She suggested that if she were a man who had been mugged, no one would consider firing her. If she were not a Mexican native, she would be back at work. It is, she said, an attitude of "blame the victim" that has overtaken you and the vice president. She went on to insist that Quick's lack of any medical insurance for its workers was simply economic opportunism. Employers hire Quick employees in order to keep their expenses low and pocket the difference. It is the workers who suffer, and now she is caught in the vise of some nasty bad luck. If you are even a hair's breadth better than old Ebenezer Scrooge, you would find a way to give her a break, even hiring her yourself to clean your own house and these very offices! After all, she concluded, she was not asking for a handout, but only for a chance to work.

The problem you face is whether or not to try to help her, to give her another chance, to defend her before the vice president and send her out to work again. To get this problem RESOLVEDD, you will need to develop well-supported answers to questions such as the following: Is the vice president in the wrong for wanting her released? Does the company owe her more help than indicated by its minimal contractual obligations? Is this a case where what is right is also risky or expensive?